Land Law in Nigeria

second edition

Malthouse Law Books

Abdulrazaq, M T, *Revenue Law and Practice in Nigeria*
Adah, C E, *The Nigerian Law of Evidence*
Asuzu, C., *Fair Hearing in Nigeria*
Bambale, Y Y, *Crimes and Punishments under Islamic Law*
Bambale, Y. Y., *An Outline of Islamic Jurisprudence*
Bambale, Y. Y., *Islamic Law Relating to Property and Commercial Transactions*
Beredugo, A.J., *Nigerian legal system: an introductory text*
Emiri, F, & Deinduomo, G., *Law, Oil and Development Challenges in Nigeria*
Emiri, F. & Deinduomo, G., *Law and Petroleum Industry in Nigeria*
Emiri, F., *The Law of Restitution in Nigeria*
Emiri, F., *Law and Medical Ethics in Nigeria*
Fogam, P, *Law of Contract*
Emiri, F., *Equity and Trusts Law in Nigeria*
Goldface-Irokalibe, I.J., *The Law of Banking in Nigeria*
Igweike, K, *Nigerian Commercial Law: Agency*
Igweike, K, *Nigerian Commercial Law: Contract*
Igweike, K, *Nigerian Commercial Law: Hire Purchase*
Ikoni, U.D., *An Introduction to Nigerian Environmental Law*
Ladan, M.T., *Introduction to Jurisprudence: classical and Islamic*
Maidoh, D.C., Oho, F. *et al., Judicial Administration and Other Legal Issues in Nigeria*
Mowoe, Kehinde, *Constitutional Law in Nigeria*
Okoh, Sheriff E. E. *Succession under Islamic Law*
Olong, Adefi *M., Administrative Law in Nigeria: an introduction*
Olong, Adefi M., *The Nigerian Legal System: an introduction*
Omorogbe, Yinka, *Oil and Gas Law in Nigeria*
Omotesho, Aboaba, *The Law of Tort in Nigeria: Selected Themes*
Sagay, I, *Law of Succession and Inheritance*
Sagay, I, *Nigerian Family Law: Principles, Cases, Statutes and Commentaries*
Utuama, A A, *Nigerian Law of Real Property*
Utuama, A A, *The Law of Trusts and their Uses in Nigeria*
Utuama, A. A., *Planning Law in Nigeria*
Uvieghara E E, *Labour Law in Nigeria*
Uvieghara E E, *Sale of Goods (& Hire Purchase) Law in Nigeria*
Yakubu J A, *Administration of Justice in Nigeria*
Yakubu J A, *Harmonisation of Laws in Africa*
Yakubu J A, *International Contracts: Evolution and Theory*
Yakubu J A, *Law of contract in Nigeria*
Yakubu J A, *Limits to the Application of Foreign Laws*
Yakubu J A, *Press Law in Nigeria*
Yalaju, J.G., *Media law in Nigeria*

Land Law in Nigeria

second edition

Adefi M.D. Olong, PhD
Lecturer in Law
Kogi State University, Anyigba, Nigeria

malthouse MP

Malthouse Press Limited

Lagos, Benin, Ibadan, Jos, Port-Harcourt, Zaria

Manufactured and Published by

Malthouse Press Limited
43 Onitana Street, Off Stadium Hotel Road,
Surulere, Lagos, Lagos State
E-mail: malthouse_press@yahoo.com
malthouselagos@gmail.com
Tel: 0802 600 3203

First Published 2011
ISBN 978-978-8422-64-4

Dedication

To:

His Excellency Rt. Hon. Dr Gabriel Torwua Suswam
The Executive Governor of Benue State

Preface

Overtime it became necessary to update a literature on Nigerian Land Law especially with the growing quest for reforms as canvassed in the classrooms, the courts, and government circles. This text remains a testimony to such aspirations.

It is a nineteen-chapter text that deals with various issues pertaining to land law in Nigeria. It closes with an enouncing of the grey areas in the Land Use Act that needed reforms.

Adefi M. Olong
Faculty of Law
Kogi State University
Anyigba, Nigeria
June 2011

Cases cited

Sanusi v. Daniels (1956) 5 CNLR,p. 288; 175
Sampson Ameh v. Innocent Ameh(2011)8WLR,85CA; 77
Southern Centre of Theosophy Inc v. State of South Australia (1982) AC 706 ,p. 716 E; 12, 13
Seidu Olowu v. Muler Brothers (of L'pool) Ltd. (1922) 3 NLR 110 ,p. 111; 167
Sabbach & Anor v. The Bank of West Africa (1962) All NLR,p. 1153; 168
Saow Okayor & Sons Ltd. v. Nigeria Housing Dev. Sons Industrial (1972) All NLR, p. 400; 170
Sale V. Nigeria Cotton Board (1985) 2 NWLR (Pt. 5); 195
Shonkan v. Smith(1960) NMLR 195; 225
Sosan v. HFD Eng. COP Ltd (2004) 3 NWLR (Pt. 80); 219
Titiloye v. Olubo (1991) NWLR (Pt.2005); 217
Unity Bank v. Bouari (2008) NSCPR 33 a,p.1297; 18, 45, 68, 76
UBN Plc v. Ayodare & Sons Nig. (2007) 13 NWLR (Pt. 1052); 121
Uke v. Albert Iro (2001) 17 WRN; 52, 60
Ukwa & Ors v. Awa Local Govt. & Ors (1966) NML; 78, 87
Usung v. Nyong (2010) 2 NWLR; 161
Ukaegbu v. Nwololo (2009) 1-2 MJSC,p.199; 37, 38, 53, 155
Umaru v. Pam (2010) 2 NWLR,p. 406; 42, 48, 53
Union Bank of Nigeria Plc v. Astra Builders (2010)5NWLR; 121, 219
Vaudeville Electric Co v. Muoiset (1920) 2 Ch. P.74; 17
Vincent v. Vincent (2008) 18 WRN p. 181; 56, 65, 71
Wright v. Gibbons (1999) 78 CLR,p. 313
Wibberley (Alan) Building Ltd. v. Insky (1999) 1 WLR,p 894; 10, 11
Wamabod Estate Ltd. v. C.O. Kotun (1997) 10 ICCHCJ 1331,,p. 2332; 190
Yusuf v. Adisa (2005) 21 NSCQR, p. 562; 191
Yusuf v. Adejoke (2007) 4 SCNJ, p.93-94; 39, 47
Yusuf v. Obasanjo (2004) All FWLR (Pt. 213); 188

Statutes

Contents

Chapter 1

Land *per se*

Any precise definition of land?

Land is looked upon as the nucleus of man's livelihood and survival as it provides the physical base for all human activities. It is the essential base of all social and commercial interaction. A recurring urge of human nature being a desire to have a stake in a particular society and roots in a particular place which in many cultures is manifested in a yearning to own immovable property, land or a house or both.[1]

It is apt therefore to define the word "land". A standard dictionary definition of land shows that land is the solid dry part of the surface of the earth as distinct from the bodies of waters.[2] It could be accepted to include not only the ground and the subsoil, and improvements of objects such as buildings, trees standing on the ground but bodies of waters like streams, seas and rivers.

A common understanding of land that can be of a universal acceptability still hovers ambivalently between a purely material conception of the physical stuff of land and a more cerebral image of land as comprising a coordinated set of abstract entitlements.[3] There is no

---

[1] See Chappella, D., *Land Law*, 6th edn. (London: Pearson Longman, 2004) at pp.3-5. See also Gray K. & Gray S.F., *Elements of Land Law*, 3rd ed. (London: Butterworths, 2000) at p.1-2, Gray *et al. Land Law*, 3rd ed. (UK: Lexis Nexis UK, 2003) at pp.2-3, See further, Abugu U., *Principles of the Land Use Act, 1978* (Kaduna: Joyce Publishers, 2008) at p.1-2, Egute M.A., *Essentials of Nigerian Land Law* (Makurdi: Onaivi Publishing Company, 2002) at pp.1-2, Egwummou, J.N., *Principles and Practice of Land Law* (Enugu: Onye Ventures, 2007) at pp.104-105 and Osamolu *et al. Real Property Law and Conveyancing Practice in Nigeria* (Lagos: Lawlords Publications, 2008) at pp.1-2-

[2] See Hornsby, A.S., *Oxfords Advanced Learner's Dictionary of Current English*, 3rd edition (London: Oxford University Press, 1984) at p. 472. See also Bird, R *Osborn's Concise Law Dictionary*, 7th edition (London: Sweet & Maxwell, 1983) at p.195, where land is defined as any ground, soil or earth whatsoever. See also, Niki Tobi, *Cases and Materials on Nigerian Land Law* (Lagos: Maorochi Books, 1992) at p.8.

[3] See Gray & Gray, *op. cit.*, at p.2.

Nigerian statute which gives a definition of land.[4] A look at a few of such relevant statutory provisions will however throw some light on what is the meaning of land. Section 18 of the Interpretation Act[5] posits that:

> Land includes any building or any other thing attached to the earth or permanently fastened to anything so attached but does not include minerals.

The Property and Conveyancing Law[6] which applies in the states of former Western Nigeria provides that: land includes land of any tenure and mines and minerals, whether or not severed from the surface, buildings or parts of buildings...and other corporal hereditaments, also a manor, an advoluson and a rent and other incorporeal hereditament and easement, right, privilege or benefit in, over or derived from land. The Registered Land Act[7] which applies only to Lagos defines land as:

> Including all things growing on the land and buildings and other things permanently affixed thereto and where land is covered with water, the land itself but does not include water or any mine, minerals, mineral oil or mineral gas.

Appraisal and critique of definitions of Land

As varied as definitions are to the term "land", they are without critique as it surrounds the Nigerian terrain; Smith sees the definition of 'land' as contained in the Interpretation Act as restrictive, the more reason why the method adopted in defining land by its discernable

---

[4] See Nelson D. "Real Property Management in Nigeria" *International Journal of Law and Contemporary Studies*, Volume 2 Number 1 & 2 2008 at p. 81.

[5] Cap 123 Laws of the Federation of Nigeria, 2004. In the statute contained within the corpus of 1925 English legislation 'land' is described as including: land of any tenure, and mines and minerals, whether or not held apart from the surface, buildings or parts of buildings (whether the division is horizontal, vertical or made in any other way) and other corporeal hereditaments; also a manor, an advoluson, and a rent and other incorporeal hereditaments, and an easement right, privileges or benefit in, over or derived from land. this cumbersome definition is explored with variations, in many other interpretation, in sections like the Land Registration Act 1972, S.17 and the Trustee of Land and Appointment of Trustees Act 1996, S.23(2). See also, *Comm for Railways et al* v. *Valuer-General* (1974) & *Bernstein* v. *Skyvews Commercial Estates Ltd* v. *Kato Kagatu Co ltd* (1998) Cf Gray & Gray op. cit., at pp.4-5.

[6] Cap.100, Laws of Western Region of Nigeria.

[7] (1965) At the United Nations Conference in 1948 on Political Economy on Rural and Urban Land Use, 'land' was defined as (a) a space or room and surface upon which life takes place, (b) as nature or natural endowment including access to sunlight, rainfall, wind and other climate condition and including soil and natural vegetation (c) as consumption good, especially when used as a site for dwelling parts, of and it is property with legal connotations as the rights of ownership of individuals and responsibilities of ownership and sovereignty of government. Whilst Sheldick V, defined land in its legal context to indicate not only the land surface but also the minerals found in and above the flora and fauna that subsists upon it, the water supplies it carries and the atmospheric advantages it enjoys. Cf. *Land Tenure in Basuto land* (1954) at p.2.

features is to be preferred.[8] The definition of land under the Property and Conveyancing Law of Western Nigeria is wider in scope, the more reason why Nwabueze whilst endorsing it added that:

> It seems to be agreed even among laymen that land does not just mean the ground and its subsoil, but includes also all structures and objects, like buildings and trees standing on it... But the legal concept of land goes further than this and includes even abstract incorporeal rights like right of way and other easement as well as profits enjoyed by one person over the ground and building as belonging to another.[9]

Olawoye, on his part, argued that land includes the surface of the earth, the subsoil and the air space above it, as well as all things that are permanently attached to the soil. It also includes streams and ponds. On the other hand, things placed on land, whether made of the product of the soil or not do not constitute land.[10] The Nigerian Interpretation Act[11] deliberately excluded mineral oils perhaps because a clear provision has been made in Section 3(1) of the Minerals Act which states that the entire property in and control of all minerals and mineral oils in, under and upon any land in Nigeria and of all rivers, streams and water course throughout Nigeria is and shall be vested in the Federal Government of Nigeria, same in so far as such rights may in any case have been limited by an express grant made before the commencement of the Act.

In accordance with the provision of the Act, no person can prospect, mine or move minerals, from land in Nigeria without a valid lease or licence from the Federal Government. Ordinarily, minerals should form part of the land, but for purposes of control and management of such minerals, the Interpretation Act excluded them from the definition of land. Individuals, may, however, remove salt, iron ore, soda, potash, et cetera from land 'outside' a mining area where it is customary so to do.[12]

In analysing the definition of land proffered by the Registered Land Act,[13] Nelson wrote that by including all things growing on the land, the definition gives the impression that emblements at included in land whereas at common land, they are excluded. This needs clarification; and it is intended that emblements are included.[14]

---

[8] See Smith I.O. *Practical Approach to Law of Real Property in Nigeria* (Lagos: ECOWATCH Publications Ltd, 1999) at pp.6-8.

[9] See Nwabueze B.O., *Nigerian Land Law* (Enugu: Nwanife Publishers Ltd, 1972) at p.3.

[10] Olawoye, C.O., *Title to land in Nigeria* (Evans Brothers Ltd, 1974) at p.9.

[11] Cap I.23 LFN, 2004.

[12] See Egwummou, *op. cit.*, at p.82.

[13] Egwute, *op. cit.*, at p.1.

[14] Ibid., at pp.1-2.

The legal conception of land under Customary Law in Nigeria has not been without controversy,[15] Obi maintains that a remarkable aspect of African Customary Law is the fact that land does not include things growing on, or attached to the soil and neither economic trees nor houses form a part of the land on which they stand.[16] Lloyd, on his part claims that in Yoruba Customary Law, a distinction is drawn between land (the soil) and improvements thereon.[17]

Whither the doctrine *Cuius est solum eius est usque ad coelum et ad inferos* and *Quic quid plantatur solo, solo cedit*?

Land in its artificial aspect could be man-made structures, dams, houses and other equipment artificially affixed or attached to the land. In its intangible aspect, land is the rights, privileges, benefits that can be obtained from or over land, helping to achieve the extra dimension required. On the whole, land is usually encapsulated in the above maxims, however, certain restrains and limitations have been placed upon these maxims.[18]

To Elias,[19] the doctrine of *quic quid platatur solo solo cedit* is a principle not only of English but of Nigerian Property Land. In his words:

> The Roman law doctrine of *quicquid plantatur solo, solo cedit* is a principle of English as of Nigerian Property Law. Like many other empirical rule of social regulation of a specific legal institution, the concept of the accession of a building or other structure to the land built upon it is reasonable, convenient and universal.[20]

Empirically, if Olong builds a house on Adefi's land, the house becomes the property of Adefi with the land without any obligation on

---

[15] The Land Use Act 1978 defines 'improvements or 'unexhausted improvements' as anything of any quality permanently attached to the land, directly resulting from the expenditure of capital or labour by an occupier or any person action on his behalf, and increasing the productive capacity, the weekly or the amenity thereof and includes the buildings, plantation of long-lived crops or tress fencing, walls, road and irrigation or reclamation works, but does not include the result of ordinary cultivation other than growing produce. But Coker states categorically that in any application of the term, 'land' includes buildings thereon. Cf. Coker, *Family Property Among the Yorubas* at p.65. Ollennu, *Customary Land Law in Ghana*, 1962 at p. 2 also supports the above view with regard to the customary law of Ghana.

[16] Ibid

[17] Ibid

[18] See Chappelle, *op. cit.*, at p. 24.

[19] Elias T.O., *op. cit.*

[20] Ibid.

his part to compensate Olong. This principle is well stated and tested empirically.[21] In *Francis* v. *Ibitoye*,[22] the plaintiff paid the sum of £26 as a deposit towards a proposed contract sale of land between the plaintiff and defendant's vendor. The contract of sale was after a consent judgement, abandoned. The plaintiff nevertheless built a house worth £120 on the defendant's land at Ebute Metta without the latter's knowledge, lease or license. The plaintiff then sued the defendant in this action for a sum of £146 representing as to £26 the deposit paid on account and as to £120 the cost of his erection of the house. It was held that:

a) the plaintiff could recover £26 as a consideration that had totally failed because the contract of sale of land was never carried out;
b) that the principle of *quicquid plantatur solo, solo cedit* applies to bar the plaintiff's claim to the cost of the building on the defendant's land without the latter's authority or ratification, because the defendant could not be made to pay compensation on what belonged to him.

From the decision in *Francis* v. *Ibitoye*[23] the question is whether the plaintiff would have been enticed to demolish the building and recover a lost – the building materials unto himself.[24]

The answer can hardly be in the affirmative for fear of trespass to land, because the adjudged owner of the land remains owner of every thing irrespective of what ever subsequently happens.[25]

The Supreme Court in *Ezeani & Ors* v. *Njidike*[26] stated that since the respondent agreed that the articles were not tenent features, the "demand that the respondent should remove and pack out all your belongings" is not apt the purpose to conferring a license to remove what belongs to someone else. Accordingly, the £407.75 damages awarded in respect of the removal by the appellant of the component parts of the house after they have been detached therefrom were not set aside in the implied principle that, the house erected by the respondent on the appellant's land without initial authorization belonged to the land in which it was built. In that case, the defendants were natives of Umuovi, a village in the

---

[21] Idrisu J., *Understanding Nigerian Land Law* 2nd edn (Zaria: Ahmadu Bello University Press Ltd, 2008) at p.2.

[22] (1963) NLR 11. See also *UAC* v. *Apaw* (1936) WACA 114, where the court held that by region of the principle, expressed in the legal maxim *quid quid plantataur solo solo cedit* the building becomes annexed to and form part of the building.

[23] *Supra*

[24] Idrisu, *op. cit.*, at p.3.

[25] Ibid.

[26] (1965) NWLR at 95.

then Eastern Nigeria which had obtained a declaration of title to a piece of land against the people of Orankwu village. The plaintiff a native of Orankwu was among those who had already built a house on the land in question. Agreement reached between him and Umuovi village was that, he was allowed to continue in occupation of his house for five years from the date of the agreement on payment of £1, yearly as rent. On the expiration of the period of five years, he was to move to another piece of land.

A person who in disregard of protests and warning, yet proceeds to build on a disputed land runs the risk, if it turns out that the land is not his, loose all the money he has invested in the building and in addition be ordered to pay damages for trespass. An injunction will be issued where appropriate, to restrain him, his servants or agents from entering the land or otherwise interfering with the possession of the real owner.[27] In *Chukwuma* v. *Ifeloye*,[28] the plaintiff claimed that she applied to the Federal Capital Development Authority (F.C.D.A.) and was granted a certificate of occupancy in respect of the piece of land known as Plot 496, Area A2 Wuse 1 District, Abuja, but the defendant trespassed on the land and erected a building thereon. Following a report to the FCDA, a stop work order was issued on the defendant. She further claimed that the defendant entered the negotiations with her but the terms were not favourable. She therefore instituted an action in the High Court of Justice, Abuja Judicial Division, claiming the sum of three million naira as general damages for trespass and perpetual injunction restraining the defendant from further trespass. The defendant claimed that he bought the land from a certain person and when he discovered the plaintiff's title to the land, he entered into negotiation with her which she resiled from when certain conditions required by her were not met. He raised the defences of laches, acquiescence, standby, long possession, estoppel by conduct and negligence and prayed the trial court to dismiss or strike out the case. The trial court dismissed the plaintiff's case. Aggrieved, she appealed to the Court of Appeal, where the appeal was dismissed. Yet aggrieved, she appealed to the Supreme Court where the Supreme Court

[27] See Idrisu, *op. cit.*, at p. 4. Alexander J. observed in *Oso* v. *Olayioye* (1966) NMLR 329 that the defendant must have been aware of the risk he was taking in completing the building on the land in dispute. In the circumstances, the equity of the case is entirely on the side of the first plaintiff who took all possible steps to protect his title to, and possession of his property and to warn the defendant of his rights. In spite of that knowledge, the defendant completed the building for which the foundation was being laid at the time of the earliest warning. He has brought upon himself any loss he may incur as a result of the application of the principle of *quic quid plantatur solo solo cedit.*

[28] (2009) All FWLR (pt.460) at 633-634.

allowed the appeal. The Supreme Court per Oguntade JSC (as he then was) held that:

> As soon as the plaintiff (now appellant) knew of the trespass on her land, she caused F.C.D.A. which allocated the land to her to serve a 'stop work' order on the defendant (now respondent). The parties opened negotiations which did not succeed. She then promptly sued. There was no evidence that the plaintiff at any stage caused F.C.D.A. to remove or vacate the 'stop work' order on the defendant. It is therefore unarguable that she tricked the defendant into investing further money into the project so that she could afterwards come to claim the land with the improvements made on the land by the defendant.[29]

In *Kyaawan Bernard* v. *Ali Ajivah*,[30] the appellant wrongly built a house on the respondent's plot. He bought plot No.7054 which he bought from a vendor. He did not develop that plot but rather decided to build on plot No.7044 which was not his own despite a timely warning to desist from such act. The maxim *quic quid plantathur solo olo cedit* was held to apply. For this reason, the appellant was not entitled to any compensation for the value of erection on the respondent's plot No.7044.

---

29 *Supra* at pp.634-635, where the Supreme Court continued that: if the reasoning of the two courts below be right, it would in my view create a very anomalous situation in the law governing trespass to land. It would lead to a position where the owner of land on which another has committed trespass would not be free to talk to the trespasser at all, lest he be taken to have compromised the trespass even when there has been no agreement reached with the trespasser. The important thing in my view is that the trespasser be not mislead into carrying out further developments on the land after the discovery of the trespassory nature of his entry on the land. My view in this appeal would have been different if there was evidence that the plaintiff/appellant had been aware of the trespassory entry upon her land earlier than the time she caused a 'stop work' order to be vacated before she ultimately sued in court. Merely negotiating with the defendant/appellant is not enough evidence to support the conclusion that she had waived the trespass committed on her land. It would have been a different situation if she had following the negotiation, caused the 'stop work' order to be vacated. See also *Adelusola* v. *Akande* (2004) 5 SCNJ 235, *Alli* v. *Alesinloye* (2000), *Ilona* v. *Idakwo* (2003) FWLR (pt.171) *Kayode* v. *Odutola* (2001) *Nsirim* v. *Nsirim* (2002) FWLR (pt.96) and *Ogunko* v. *Shelle* (2004) 6 NWLR (pt.868) 17.

30 (1997) 4 NWLR (pt.499) 365. In *Adebiyi* v. *Ogunbiyi* (1965) NWLR 395, the defendant claimed to have purchased a certain piece of land of which the plaintiff had for many years been the lawful owner and occupier; commenced the construction of a storey building whereupon he was immediately warned by the plaintiff. But he disregarded the warning and continued his building project even after the plaintiff had filed an action in court claiming damages for trespass and an injunction to restrain the defendant or his agent from entering the land. the plaintiff was granted both remedies claimed and the court observed that having unreasonably ignored the plaintiff's warning, the defendant must bear the consequences of his conduct. In *Adama Ibrahim* v. *Alhaji Bappa Yola* (1986) 4 CA (pt.1), the Court in emphasizing the *qud quid plantatur solo solo cedit* principle asserted that "Having sown the wind, she can only reap the whirlwind. She has lost not only the house, but whatever expenses by way of improvements that went into it." See also, *Amori* v. *Iyanda* (2008) All FWLR.

Land therefore means the surface of the earth, things below the surface of the earth, things attached to the earth, things rooted to the earth, things embedded in the earth; also things fastened on things embedded or permanent enjoyment of the things embedded except things declared not to be land.[31]

Understanding the Common Law concept of land

The world of the common lawyer has always been a curious blend of the physical and the abstract, a commixture of the earthily pragmatic and the deeply conceptual. Having broken away from the Romanist legal tradition, the common lawyer devised a distinctive regime of property rules which notwithstanding extensive statutory reform during the 20th Century is still piecemeal and full of internal ambivalence. This alternative to the dominium of civilian jurisprudence remains a collocation of organic adaptations, the common lawyer's crudely empirical outlook being encapsulated in a general reluctance to embrace any grand or overarching model of the phenomenon of ownership. In consequence, the common lawyer's understanding of land still oscillates between a purely material conception of the physical stuff of land and a more cerebral image of land as comprising a co-ordinated set of abstract rights[31a].

The common lawyer's primary concern is with the observable phenomenon of *de facto* possessory control as exercised over physically identifiable terrain or premises.[32] What actually happens on the ground – whether right or wrongly – has always constituted a powerful determinant of entitlement in English land law. The normative tug of sheer physical fact should never be underestimated. Yet, at another level, the common law perception of property embodies an obsession with the rational manipulation of abstract concepts and with the careful outworking of axiomatic truths. Nowhere is this fascination with the naked force of reason more apparent than in the law of land, with its remorseless taxonomy of estates and interests,[33] its sub-classifications of legal and equitable rights,[34] and with its multiple applications of

---

[31] Idrisu *op. cit.*, at p.5. In *Dantsoho* v. *Mohammed* (2003) FWLR (pt.150) at 1717, the court noted that title to the land being in the plaintiff everything that accedes to the land belonged to the plaintiff following the principle of *quid quid plantatur solo solo cedit.*

[31a] Gray & Gray, *op. cit.*, at p5

[32] Ibid.

[33] Ibid.

[34] Ibid.

propositional dogma.[35] In the hands of the common lawyer, land law became a field of highly artificial concepts, each defined with meticulous – almost mathematical – precision.[36]

The outcome of this creative tension between the physical and the abstract has been the elaboration of a pragmatic, but highly operational, law of land.[37] A rigorous preoccupation with earthy reality, coupled with the constant subjection of the inner workings of property to logical ordering, has for centuries rendered it unnecessary for the common law to construct any large or systematic theory of ownership.[38] The conceptual purity of a regime of individual ordered estates and interests in land seemed to provide a perfectly functional substitute for more holistic ideas of *dominium*.[39] It was, however, the characteristic interplay of empirical and conceptual concerns[40] which has made modern land law what it is, although the interaction was also served to infuse land law with a structural ambiguity which goes to the root of even the definition of such basic terms as 'land' itself.[41]

To Gray, the underlying tension between the material and the conceptual has imparted a multi-dimensional complexity to the understanding of the term 'land' in English law. The first three dimensions of land as a physical reality are perfectly consistent with the rough and ready empiricism which characterizes so much of our land law. To these crudely factual dimensions the common law as to add a fourth, more cerebral, dimension of *time*.[42] In this way, the common law gave a chronological significance to raw pragmatic notions of possession and, in the process, introduced the transformative concept of time-related 'estates' in the land. The fifth and sixth dimensions of land emerged when the common law was required to accommodate the interpenetrating impact of a competing system of conscience-driven rules of equity,[43] with the consequent recognition that 'estates' in land could be

---

35 Ibid.

36 That logic and casuistry in their severest form are to be found in the common law of property has amply confirmed by Sir Owen Dixon of the High Court of Australia. This greatest of common lawyers was able to observe, for instance, that central features of property law bear to this day 'many traces of the scholasticism of the times in which its principles were developed.'

37 For an account of certain fundamental features of the land law regime as it has evolved over the centuries, see P.B.H. Birks, 'Before We Begin: Five Keys to Land Law', in S. Bright and J.K. Dewar (ed.), *op. cit.*, p.457.

38 See Gray, *op. cit.*

39 Ibid.

40 Ibid.

41 See, for example the fusion of the material and the abstract which is evident in various statutory definitions.

42 Ibid.

43Ibid.

held either at *law* or in *equity*.[44] These multiple dimensions inherent within the concept of 'land' must now be explored in greater detail.

The first two dimensions of land lend themselves easily, and most usefully, to graphic representation in the form of maps and plans which depict the boundaries and other salient topographical features of specific areas of 'land'.[45]

One attempt at a definition of 'land' might focus, quite reasonably, upon the way in which the surface area of England and Wales has been meticulously mapped by the Ordinance Survey, a task which began in 1791 and continues to the present day. The mapping tools may have changed from theodolite and chain to digital imaging by satellite, but the product remains the same – a remarkably detailed two-dimensional representation of the defining contours, features and limits of the 'land' comprised in England and Wales.[46] Such maps are essential to the activities of conveyancers, surveyors and ramblers alike, but their usefulness in determining the boundaries of estate ownership is inevitably somewhat restricted. For instance, the Ordinance Survey can mark the position of a hedge or wall only by a solid line drawn along the centre of the topographical feature in question, but such marking provides no conclusive indication whether that feature is itself owned by one or other adjacent occupier (or is indeed shared by both).

The Ordinance Survey does not (and cannot) fix private boundaries.[47] Where a conveyance of land is accompanied by a plan of the area conveyed (usually derived from the Ordinance Survey map), the purpose of the plan is normally specified as being that of general identification only. In such cases, the exact boundary requires to be established by inference from existing or historic topographical features such as walls, hedges and fences or from other evidence.[48] In the rules which govern registered conveyancing, the impression of maps and plans is explicitly acknowledged in the so-called 'general boundaries rule'.[49] This rule

---

[44] Ibid.

[45] See A. Pottage, *The Measure of Land*, (1994) 57 MLR 361.

[46] The 'land' comprised within England and Wales clearly includes territory beyond the low water mark at the coastline. It is arguable that the sea bed underlying an encircling three-mile belt of territorial waters constitutes part of England and Wales (see generally G. Marston, *The Marginal Seabed* (Clarendon 1981), pp. 286-198). Moreover, in an act of territorial expansion, virtually unknown since England invaded France in the 15th century, the Channel Tunnel Act 1987 provides that, even outside the three-mile limit, the space of the tunnel and its immediately surrounding subsoil extending to the mid-point of the English Channel are 'incorporated into England' and form part of the country of Kent (Channel Tunnel Act 1987, s.10(1)).

[47] *Wibberley (Alan) Building Ltd* v. *Insley* (1999) 1 WLR 894 at 901H per Lord Hope of Graighead ('The purpose of the survey is topographical, not taxative').

[48] *Wibberley (Alan) Building Ltd* v. *Insley* (1999) 1 WLR 894 at 896A-B, 897B-C per Lord Hoffmann.

[49] See Land Registration Rules 1925, r 278(1)-(2).

recognizes that the filed plan or General Map relevant to any registered title is normally 'deemed to indicate the general boundaries only' and that the exact line of the boundary 'will be left undetermined'.

The more precise declination of boundaries is thus left to be ascertained from other evidence, supplemented by a number of rebuttable common law presumptions, of which the 'hedge and ditch' and '*ad medium filum*' presumptions are perhaps best known. The venerable 'hedge and ditch' presumption provides that, where a hedge and ditch are found along a boundary two parcels of land, the boundary is presumed to lie along the edge of the ditch on the far side from the hedge.[50] According to the '*ad medium filum*' rule, a conveyance of land abutting upon a highway presumptively includes the soil of the adjoining highway to its midway point,[51] a similar 'ad medium' presumption applying to the subjacent soil of any adjoining non-tidal river or waterway.[52] So conscious are the courts that boundary disputes are 'a particularly painful form of litigation', that a modern premium has been placed on ensuring that 'the law on boundaries should be as clear as possible.'[53]

In the vast majority of instances, neighbours are content to accept that absolute precision in the location of mutual boundaries is unattainable[54] and that a 'certain amount of vagueness' or 'latitude' inevitably attends the definition of the exact line.[55] Nevertheless conflict over land boundaries tends to be a fertile source of litigation, usually triggered by (and providing a focus for) other forms of unneighbourly discord or

---

50 See *Vowles* v. *Miller* (1810) 3 Taunt 137 at 138, 128 ER 54 at 55 per Lawrence J. (The presumption envisages that the ditch maker will normally cut to the extremity of his own soil, thereafter depositing the excavated earth upon his own land and, typically, planting a hedge on top of it.) The 'hedge and ditch' presumption even overrides the boundary as located on an Ordinance Survey map, where the two parcels have never been in common ownership and there is no evidence that the ditch was dug before the boundary was drawn (see *Wibberley (Alan) Building Ltd* v. *Insley* (1999) 1 WLR 894 at 900H-901A; [2000] Conv 61 (J. Cross and G. Broadbent)). See also *Hall* v. *Dorling* (1996) 74 P & R 400 at 406.

51 *Berridge* v. *Ward* (1861) 10 CB (NS) 400 at 415, 142 ER 507 at 513; *Pryor* v. *Petre (1894) 2 Ch 11 at 18; Commissioners for Land Tax for the City of London* v. *Central London Railway Co* (1913) AC 364 at 384; Collet v. Culpin (1996) CLY 5020; *Bellevue Crescent Pty Ltd* v. *Marland Holdings Pty Ltd* (1998) 43 NSWLR 364 at 373A-B. See also *Pardoe* v. *Pennington* (1998) 75 P & CR 264 at 270-271.

52 See *Micklethwait* v. *Newlay Bridge Co* (1886) 33 Ch D 133 at 145, 152, 155.

53 *Wibberley (Alan) Building Ltd* v. *Insley* (1999) 1 WLR 894 at 895G per Lord Hoffmann ('Feelings run high and disproportionate amounts of money are spent. Claims to small and valueless pieces of land are pressed with the zeal of Fortinbras's army'). See also *Clarke* v. *O'Keefe* (2000) 80 P & CR 126 per Peter Gibson LJ ('There are few disputes that raise passions more than boundary disputes').

54 Land surveying 'is not an exact science' (See *National Trustees, Executors and Agency Co of Australia Ltd* v. *Hassett* (1907) VLR 404 at 412; *Boyton* v. *Clancy* (1998) 9 BPR 16585 at 16589).

55 *Wibberley (Alan) Building Ltd* v. *Insley* (1999) 1 WLR 894 at 901E-F per Lord Hope of Craighead.

unhappiness.[56] It remains notorious that boundary disputes provide the easiest means of burning money.[57]

The delineation of an area of 'land' is sometimes affected, albeit in relatively rare cases, by the physical processes of *alluvion* (which causes an addition or accretion to title) and *diluvion* (which brings about a subtraction from title).[58]

The common law recognizes, as a matter both of fairness and of convenience, that where land is bounded by water, the forces of nature are likely to cause changes in the boundary between the land and the water. Consistently with a perception of property in land as largely constituted by empirical reality,[59] the common law on this occasion follows Roman law[60] in acknowledging that the 'long-term ownership of property' is 'inherently subject to gradual processes of change'.[61] So long as these geophysical changes are indeed gradual and imperceptible,[62] the law considers the title to land as applicable to the land as it may be changed from time to time,[63] even if there still remains a means of identifying the original boundaries of the property.[64] Accordingly land is

---

[56] For an extreme instance, see *Times*, 7 July 2000 ('Man shot dead after garden hedge dispute'). The aggressive use of fast-growing leylandii trees as a weapon of boundary warfare had led to so many disputes that the government is currently considering the imposition of height restrictions on such features (see *Times*, 7 August 2000 ('Leylandii will be cut down to size')). See e.g. *Jones* v *Stones* (1999) 1 WLR 1739 at 1741H; *Burns* v. *Morton* (2000) 1 WLR 347 at 349H-350A.

[57] See eg *Segaram* v. *Grant* (1997) 73 P & CR D35 (where a disagreement between neighbours over six inches of land had already cost J12,000 even before the matter reached the Court of Appeal) and *Targett and Targett* v. *Ferguson and driver* (1996) 72 P & CR 106 (where the equity in the relevant home was clearly insufficient to meet the eventual order for costs). See also *Jones* v. *Stones* (1999) 1 WLR 1739 (where the casus belli concerned, inter alia, six flower pots on a dividing wall); *RImmer* v. *Pearson* (2000) 79 P & CR D21 (22 day county court trial over three-inch boundary strip).

[58] Compare the case where catastrophic sea erosion cuts into cliffs and ultimately causes cliff-top buildings to collapse on to the foreshore, thereby altering the configuration of land (*Holbeck Hall Hotel Ltd* v *Scarborough BC* (2000) 2 WLR 1396 (hotel 65 metres above sea level)). Climate change and higher tides are beginning to weaken sea defences in certain parts of England (see *Times*, 5 November 1999 ('Three homes to vanish in futile battle with sea')).

[59] Ante, p.5; post, p.111.

[60] See Inst.2.1.20; *Attorney-General of Southern Nigeria* v. *John Holt & Co (Liverpool) Ltd* (1915) AC 599 at 613-614.

[61] *Southern Centre of Theosophy Inc* v. *State of South Australia* (1982) AC 706 at 716E per Lord Wilberforce, who attributed the doctrine of accretion to 'the nature of land ownership'.

[62] The requirement that the relevant change be gradual and imperceptible is widely accepted (See *Bl Comm*, Vol II, p.292; *Attorney-General* v. *McCarthy* (1911) 2 IR 260 at 276, 293 per Lalles CB; *Southern Centre of Theosophy Inc* v. *State of South Australia* (1982) AC 706 at 716C; Clarke v. City of Edmonton (1929) 4 DLR 1010 at 1015; *Port Franks Properties Ltd* v. *The Queen* (1980) 99 DLR (3d) 28 at 36; *Lawrence* v. *Kempsey Shire Council* (1995) 6 bPR 14111 at 14115).

[63] Any change caused by the deliberate action of the claimant falls outside the doctrine of accretion (*Brighton and Hove General Gas Co* v. *State of South Australia* (1982) AC 706 at 720A).

[64] *Hazlett* v. *Presnell* (1982) 149 CLR 107 at 116. The Prima facie effects of alluvion and diluvion can be displaced by clear evidence of a contrary intention, but the mere fact that a grant of land was accompanied by a map delineating the boundary is not conclusive against the operation of either

transferred prima facie subject to and with the benefit of such additions and subtractions as may take place over the course of time.

If an addition is made to land by wind-blown or water-borne deposit,[65] the landowner's territory is regarded as having been extended by alluvion into the area which was previously water.[66] This doctrine of accretion applies the equality of lakes and rivers,[67] and in the case of rivers may well reposition the boundary between two parcels of land by relocating the medium filum of the river bed.[68] The doctrine of accretion has no application to substantial and recognizable changes in the boundary between land and water which take place suddenly.[69] However, in the case of wind-blown deposit, the mere fact that the leading-edge of a sand dune may move forward two or three feet in a perceptible jump over a 24 hour period in conditions of strong winds does not disqualify such an advance as an allowable accretion to the land, if in the long term the movement is imperceptible.[70]

Again, if part of a landowner's land is removed by diluvion or gradual erosion caused by water-based advance or attrition, the landowner is simply treated as losing a portion of his 'land'.[71] In the lottery of life, the landowner 'may lose as well as gain from changes in the water boundary or level'.[72] However, no subtraction from title occurs in the case of rapid, easily perceived and violent shifts of land.[73] Such emergence of 'large

---

principle (see *Southern Centre of Theosophy Inc* v. *State of South Australia* (1982) AC 706 at 716F-G; *Attorney-General* v. *McCarthy* (1911) 2 IR 260 at 284).

[65] The distinction between these forms of deposit, even if possible, is irrelevant (*Southern Centre of Theosophy Inc* v. *State of South Australia* (1982) AC 706 at 719H-720A, 720D).

[66] *R* v. *Lord Yarborough* (1828) 5 Bing 163, 130 ER 1023, 107 ER 668 at 673; *Gifford* v. *Lord Dunstan* v. *Hell's Gate Enterprises Ltd* (1986) 22 DLR (4th) 568 at 584; *Sunlea Investments Pty Ltd* v. *State of New South Wales* (1998) 9 BPR 16707 at 16709. The title extended by accretion also confers a right to any mineral situated below the newly claimed land (*Re Eliason and Registrar, Northern Alberta Land Registration District* (1981) 115 DLR (3d) 360 at 364).

[67] *Southern Centre of Theosophy Inc* v. *State of South Australia* (1982) AC 706 at 715F; *State of Hawaii by Kobayashi* v. *Simring*, 566 P 2d 725 at 734 (1977). See (1983) 99 LQR 412 (P. Jackson).

[68] See *Stirling* v. *Bartleth* (1993) SLT 763 at 768K, 769D-G.

[69] See *Nebraska* v. *Iowa*, 143 US 359 at 361, 370, 36 L ed 186 at 188, 190 (1892); *Stirling b. Bartlett* (1993) SLT 763 at 767I-J, 769

[70] See *Nebraska* v. *Iowa*, 143 US 359 at 361, 370 L ed 186 at 188, 190 (1892); *Stirling* v. *Bartlett* 1993 SLT 763 at 767I-J, 769C. The Supreme Court Hawaii has held, for instance, that extensions of land created by catastrophic lava flows should inure, not for the windfall fain of a limited segment of the population of an overcrowded island, but for the public as a whole. The added land is held by the government in public trust.

[71] *Southern Centre of Theosophy Inc* v. *State of South Australia* (1982) AC 706 at 722F, 723B. It is sufficient that the transfer of sand or soil cannot be seen to happen before the eyes of the observer (see *Stirling* v. *Bartlett* 1993 SLT 763 at 768D).

[72] *Southern Centre of Theosophy Inc* v. *State of South Australia* (1982) AC 706 at 721D per Lord Wilberforce.

[73] *Southern Centre of Theosophy Inc* v. *State of South Australia* (1982) AC 706 at 721E per Lord Wilberforce

changes'[74] is regarded not as 'diluvion', but as 'avulsion', and does not affect pre-existing legal boundaries.[75]

Quic quid plantatur solo solo cedit and the rule of Customary land law in Nigeria

It is important at this point to examine the relationship between the maxim *quicquid plantatur solo solo cedit* and the rule of customary law in land matters in Nigeria. There is no doubt that according to the principle Nigeria inherited from the English, common law, land includes everything up to the sky and down to the centre of the earthy.

It is worth noting here that the legal conception of land under customary law has been a matter of controversy raging among legal writers generally. According to James, originally, land under customary law meant the soil and soil only. Thus, a building erected by a person, even by a trespasser, on the land of another, did not become attached to the land, but remained the property of the builder. Obi, asserts that a remarkable aspect of Africa customary law is the fact that land does not include things growing on or attached to the soil, and neither economic trees nor houses form part of the land on which they stand. Whilst, Lloyd, contends that in Yoruba customary law, a distinction is drawn between land, the soil and improvements thereon. On the other hand, Coker, states categorically that in any application of the term 'land', it includes buildings thereon. To Ollenu, as regards the customary law of Ghana, land includes "the surface of the earth, the sub-soil and the air space above it as well as all things permanently attached to the soil".

As far as the Nigerian Customary land tenure is concerned, land originally meant the soil and the soil only. That is, land under customary law did not mean or include whatever is attached to it. Thus, if for instance, a man uses his energy to farm or to erect a structure on a family land, it would certainly be unjust in the eyes of the community to declare such improvement on the land as belonging to the entire family simply on the basis that the piece of land in question belongs to the family.

There is a general consensus among Nigerian Lawyers, jurists and writers who have expressed that all known Nigerian customs make some

---

[74] Thus a river which suddenly changes course, by cutting through the neck of a band, causes no change in land boundary (*Nebraska* v. *Iowa,* 143 US 359 at 370, 36 L ed 186 at 190 (1892) Per Brewer J.).

[75] See *State of Hawaii by Kobayashi* v. *Zimring,* 566 P 2d 725 at 734 (1977); *Stirling* v. *Bartlett* (1993) SLT 763 at 767J, 768J.

distinction between land and the things fixed or attached to land. Accordingly, Elias, stated that:

> "...it is however important to bear in mind that all the known customary systems of land tenure in Nigeria make a clear distinction between ownership of land and the ownership of things either attached or built on it or otherwise growing on it. The land may be owned by the whole community or by a family or by an individual while "strangers" to the land or even a member of the land owning group may be permitted to build a house or grow crops on it. This follows logically from the indigenous idea that, except in rare cases of individually owned parcels of land due to first cultivation, land is usually owned by a community or family. Therefore, all surface accretions to it by the labours of others normally belong to the latter, provided the activities have had the sanction of those entitled to give it on behalf of the land owing group."

Furthermore, in the case of *Santeng* v. *Darkwa*,[75a] an Akan customary law became a question of dispute. The question really was whether a house built on a family land by one of its members could automatically become the property of the family along with the land. While reversing the judgment of the trial court, Strother Stewart made the following observation:

> "No custom was proved that when a house is built on the site of the remains of a family house, it becomes the family's property. And I know of no such custom...I can find no authority for the stamp of family property; although, of course, the site on which the house is built remains family land".

Invariably, the same customary law principle apples in the case of trees and crops planted by one man on another's land for the planter could pledge such improvements or otherwise dispose of them. This is a universal principle of customary tenure in Africa.

To furnish additional support for the legal position, is the case of *Sule Muhammadu* v. *Audu Ali of Lafia*,[75b] where the appellant successfully sued and obtained declaration of title to a compound which he inherited from his deceased father. The respondent who, prior to this declaration was living in the same compound was evicted out of the compound by the court. The respondent had prayed the court to award him compensation for the houses he had built in the appellant's compound. The respondent complied and on appeal to the Plateau State

---

[75a] (1940) WACA 52.

[75b] (1980/81)1 PCCA30.

Customary Court of Appeal, the fact of the appeal showed that the respondent trespassed when he erected houses on the appellant's compound. The building of the houses became acts of trespass because upon being allowed to be a tenant at will in the compound, his action was inconsistent with the possession of the owner.

By acting in the way he did, the respondent forfeited all his interests in the compound such that on application of the principle of '*quicquid plantatur solo solo cedit*', he would lose outrightly all that he had invested in the houses. As a result of the native law and custom which operates, the respondent was allowed action for compensation.

Essentially therefore, chattels which belong to land are called fixtures. Fixtures include anything that has become so attached to land that it forms part of it. If you buy a ceiling fan, it is a chattel but when it is fixed to the wall, it becomes fixture.

The maxim *quic quid plantatur solo solo cedit* is also applicable to fixtures. Thus if a building is erected on the land and objects are permanently attached to the building then, the soil, the building and the objects affixed to it are all in law, land.

Whether a chattel is a fixture or not is a question of law and the answer will depend upon the mode and the purpose of the annexation; but when once a chattel has been annexed to land, the onus of proving that it is not a fixture lies upon the tenant. The position was clearly put by Blackburn J. in *Holland* v. *Hodgson*[75c]

> There is no doubt that the general maxim of the law is that what is annexed to land becomes part of the land, but it is very difficult; if not impossible to say with precision what constitutes annexation sufficient for this purpose. It is a question, which must depend on the circumstances of each case, and mainly on two circumstances, as indicating the intention, viz the decree of annexation and the object of annexation.

Generally, two tests are applied in deciding whether a chattel has become a fixture or not.

The Decree/Mode of Annexation

A chattel is prima facie a fixture if it is substantially connected with the land or building, e.g. where it is attached to the building by nails or screws even though it may be easy to remove the screws - i.e. the chattel is not merely resting on the ground by its own weight. A thing standing on

---

[75c] (1817) L.R. 7

its own weight on the ground is a chattel and does not become land until it is pierced down more than its weight.

The Purpose/Intention of Annexation

Under this test, a chattel becomes a fixture if it has been attached as a permanent improvement to the land or as part of the architectural design.

In *Vaudeville Electric Co.* v. *Muriset*,[75d] seat secured to a cinema floor were held to be fixtures.

Removal of Fixtures

On the expiration of a lease or tenancy a dispute may arise as to whether a thing brought on the land during the tenancy belongs to the landlord or the tenant. The basic rule is that at the end of the tenancy all fixtures put on the land by the tenant without permission of the landlord, belong to the landlord and become known as landlord's fixtures. However, a tenant will suffer great hardship if items which he had installed himself were called 'tenants' fixtures which may be removed. The law provides three types of fixtures which may be removed by tenants. These are:

i. Trade fixtures
ii. Ornamental and domestic fixtures, and
iii. Agricultural fixtures

Trade fixtures

These are fixtures installed by the tenant for his trade or business, e.g., factory machines, fittings in hotel, petrol pumps fixed in a petrol station.

Ornamental and Domestic Fixtures

These fixtures include windows blinds, refrigerators, etc. which should be removed without causing any substantial damage to the building.

Agricultural Fixtures

A tenant of an agricultural holding who have attached fixtures to the land e.g. shed, or hut may remove them provided he fulfil the following conditions:

i. he must give one month written notice to the landlord

[75d] (1920) 2CH. 74

ii. all rents due be paid and tenants obligations under the tenancy are satisfied by him
iii. no avoidable damage is caused to the land in the removal and any damage must be made good.
iv. the landlord may retain the fixtures if he pays fair price for them.

Sources of Nigerian Land Law

The term source here could be defined as the fountain of authority of a rule of law that is the origin from which a legal rule derives its authority.[76] Thus there has been consensus amongst Nigerian writers[77] that land law in Nigeria is derived from three main sources;[78] the first being Native Law and Custom. Accordingly, the application of customary law in each case is often the one prevailing in the area where the land is situated. There are as many systems of customary law as there are ethnic groups and even within an ethnic group, there may be variations, not in essence but in detail, in respect of the particular localities of the area.[79] The cardinal principle of customary land tenure in Nigeria remains that land belongs to all the people who may be held by families, communities and individuals. The right of access to land is based on the privilege of being a member of the family or community.[80] Acquisition of land under customary law is usually through cultivation and building such grant of which is normally made by the head of the family or community.[81] Where land has been acquired the occupant has what may be called allodial title equivalent to the English freehold against the whole world.[82] Customary land tenure in the past did not know of any payment of

---

[76] See Olong M.A., *The Nigerian Legal System: an introduction* 2nd edition (Lagos: Malthouse Press Ltd, 2009) at p.11.

[77] Ibid.

[78] Egute, *op. cit.*, at p.4.

[79] See Elias T.O. *Nigerian Land Law & Custom* (London: Routledge & Kegan Paul Ltd, 1962) at p.93 where he stated that the evidence which one gets from comparative estimate of the studies of field workers as also of the available data from judicial decisions points to a large measure of common basic principles which underline indigenous systems of land tenure in various parts of Nigeria. See also *Amodu Tijani* v. *Secretary, Southern Nigeria* (1921) AC 399.

[80] See Egute op.cit at p.5. See also the West African Lands Committee 1912, which stated in no less emphatic term that land belongs to a vast family of which many are dead, a few are living and countless number still unborn.

[81] See *Alabi* v. *Doherty* (2005) 32 WRN, *Usiobaifo* v. *Usiobaifo* (2005) 3 NWLR (pp.460-673 *Adedeji* v. *Oloso* (2007) 1 SCNJ p.416, *Awuru* v. *Iledu* (2008) 12 NWLR at p.249, *Anukan* v. *Anukan* (2008) SCNJ at pp.74-75 and *Unity Bank* v. *Bouari* (2008) NSCPR 33 at p.1297.

[82] Egute, *op. cit.*, at p. 5. Egute asserted further that in the past, only wars can dispossess a person from his land or where he could be dispossessed for public purpose which rarely arose under customary law. Nowadays, when land is required by the Government of the Federation, State or Local Government for public use, the land can be taken away and compensation paid to him for the unexhausted improvements.

tribute in terms of a value or even crops after harvest to a chief or any leader as having a proprietary power in land.[83]

The dynamism of customary land tenure stems from its flexibility and adaptability to modern changes.[84] By virtue of section 14(1) of the Evidence Act a custom may be adopted as part of the law governing a particular set of circumstances if it can be noticed judicially or can be proved to exist by evidence. The burden of proving a custom shall lie upon the person alleging its existence.

The principles of customary land tenure can best be described as a situation whereby land belonged to the people, all the people having equal rights of access to the chief or headman having charge of the land, the chief or headman to some extent been in the position of a trustee who holds the land in use for the people and every member being entitled to a piece of the land.[85]

The Received English Law[86]

The received English law remains a source of Nigerian land law which consists of the common law, doctrines of equity, statutes and subsidiary legislations.[87]

The common laws of England comprises the body of those principles and rules of action relating to the government and security of persons and property which derive their authority from solely uses of customs of immemorial antiquity embodied in the judgment and decrees of the courts recognizing affirming and enforcing such usages and customs.[88] Common law again means the law developed by the old common law courts of England precisely the Kings Bench, the Court of common pleas and the Court of Exchequer.[89]

---

[83] Lugard. *The Dual Mandate* (London: 1929) at pp.288-289. In *Dashi & 3 Ors* v. *Satlong & Anor* (2009) 1-2, S.C (pt.11) the Court held that a customary tenancy involves the transfer of an interest in land from the customary landlord or overlord to the customary tenant and which interest entitles the customary tenant to exclusive possession of the land and which interest subject to good behaviour, he holds in perpetuity. Unless it is otherwise excluded, the main feature of customary tenancy is the payment of tributes by the customary tenant to the overlord.

[84] See Osamolu *et al.*, *op. cit.*, at p.10 See also *Lewis* v. *Bankole* (1909) 1 NLR 82, and *Dawodu* v. *Dawole* (1998) 3 FSC 46.

[85] See Lord Halden in *Amodu Tijani* v. *Secretary of Southern Nigeria* (1921) AC (*supra*)

[86] See Egute, *op. cit.*, at p.14 and Osamabor *et al.*, *op. cit.*, at p.11.

[87] See Olong, *op. cit.*, at pp.11-17.

[88] Ibid at p.12. See also Clive Newton, *General Principles of law* 3rd ed. (London: Sweet & Maxwell, 1983) at p. 6.

[89] See Obilade, *The Nigerian Legal system* (Nig: Spectrum Publishing CO, 1993) at p.10.

The doctrines of equity means the body of rules that would before 1875 have been administered by the Court of Chancery.[90] Whilst statutes and subsidiary legislations made on or before October 1st 1960 and still extending to Nigeria equally remains a source of Nigerian land law.

Local enactments relating to land[91]

Several local legislations relating to land in Nigeria abound and they constitute a source of land law in Nigeria.[92]

There are several local legislations relating to land in Nigeria and they constitute a vibrant source of Nigerian land law. A few of such legislations include: Land Tenure Law of Northern Nigeria;[93] Property and Conveyancing Law[94] of Western Nigeria; Land Registration Act;[95] Land Instruments Registration Law;[96] Registration of Titles Law[97] of Lagos State; Law Reform (Contract) Act;[98] Native Land Acquisition Law;[99] Acquisition of Land by Aliens Law,[100] Recovery of Premises Act;[101] Land Use Act;[102] to mention a few. The Land Use Act preserves the existing land tenure systems subject to the limitations created by the Act as regards land holding and the exercise of land rights.

Nigerian Case Law

The pronouncements of the courts in Nigeria also serve as a veritable source of the Nigerian land law. These judicial decisions propound the correct interpretation of both the principles of substantive land law as well as the proper construction to be placed on the various provisions of statutes relating to land[103] in Nigeria.

---

[90] Olong, *op. cit.*, at p.12. The Conveyancing Act 1881, the Wills Act 1837, and the Statute of Fraud 1877 all relate to land and are statutes of general application.
[91] See Osamolu, *op. cit.*, at p.11. cf also Egute at pp.12-14and Egwummou, *op. cit.*, at pp.28-38.
[92] Osamobor, *op. cit.*, at p. 11.
[93] Cap 59 Laws of Northern Nigeria, 1963.
[94] Cap 100, Laws of Western Nigeria, 1959.
[95] Cap 99, Laws of the Federation of Nigeria and Lagos 1958.
[96] Cap 56, Laws of Western Nigeria 1959; Cap 72 Laws of Eastern Nigeria Cap 58 Laws of Northern Nigeria 1963.
[97] Cap 66, Laws of Lagos State 1994.
[98] See Cap 114, Laws of Lagos State 1994.
[99] Cap 80, Laws of Western Nigeria, 1959.
[100] Cap 2 Laws of Eastern Nigeria, 1957.
[101] Now replaced by the Recovery of Premises Laws of the various States of the Federation.
[102] See Cap L5 LFN 2004.The author agrees with Osamolu *et al.*, that although this is the principal legislation relating to land in Nigeria today, it is humbly submitted that there is no justification for separating it as a distinct source of Nigerian Land Law. It forms part of local enactments.
[103] For example in *Idundun* v. *Okumagba* (1976) 10 SC 227, the court propounded the ways by which ownership of land may be established in Nigeria. In *Ekpendu* v. *Erika* (1959) 4 F.S.C. 79., the Supreme Court established the requisite conditions for the valid alienation of family property.

Statute of Fraud Act 1677

Section 4 of the Act provides that no action shall be brought upon any contract for the sale or other disposition of land or any interest in land, unless agreement upon which such action is brought or some memorandum or note thereof is in writing, signed by the party to be charged or by some person by him lawfully authorized. The rationale for this provision is to prevent the possibility of a non-existent agreement between two parties being claimed to exist through perjury or fraud. Its object is to prevent possible fraud on innocent persons engaged in land dealings. The principle in the law (that a contract for sale of land is unenforceable except in writing) is reflected in other legislation on property practice such as the Property and Conveyancing Law of 1959,[104] the Law Reform (Contract) Act of the Federal Capital Territory,[105] the Law Reform (Contract) Law of Lagos State[106] and the Law of Property Law Cap 23 Laws of Abia State 1999.[107] The Federal Capital Territory Act applies to specific real property transactions.[108] Even though these laws require a note or memorandum in writing as evidence of a transaction in a sale of land, "no special form is prescribed for the note or memorandum"[109] and "the terms of the memorandum need not all be contained in one document, but may be spread in many."[110]

See also *Ogunleye* v. *Oni* (1990) 2 NWLR (pt.135) 745, where the Supreme Court laid down the conditions a certificate of occupancy must satisfy to amount to a good root of title.

[104] Section 67 (1) states that "No action may be brought upon any contract for the sale or other disposition of land or any interest in land, unless the agreement upon which such action is brought, or some memorandum or note thereof, is in writing, and signed by the party to be charged or by some other person thereunto by him lawfully authorized."

[105] Law Reform (Contracts) Act Cap.517, Vol.3, Laws of the Federal Capital Territory, 2006. Section 5(2) of the Act provides that no contract to which this section applies shall be enforceable by action unless the contract or some memorandum or note in respect therefore is in writing and is signed by the party to be charged therewith or by some other persons lawfully authorized by him. But by the provisions of subsection 3 of the Act, the requirement of writing shall not (a) apply to a contract for the sale or other disposition of land made under customary law, (b) apply to sale of land by order of a court of competent jurisdiction; and (c) affect the operation of the law relating to part performance.

[106] Section 5

[107] Section 67.

[108] Section 5(1) of the Act states that the requirement of writing shall apply to (a) contract for sale of land, (b) to a contract to enter into a disposition of land being a disposition that is required by any enactment to be made by deed or instrument in writing or to be proved in writing; (c) to a contract to enter into a mortgage or charge on land; and (d) to a contract by a person to answer to another person for the debt, default or liability of a third person.

[109] *Adeniran* v. *Ologunju* (2002) FWLR, (Pt .87), p. 827 at p. 840.

[110] *Ejuetami* v. *Olaiya* (2002) FWLR part 88, p. 955 at p. 974.

Wills Act of 1837

This Act which applies to States of Nigeria that have not yet enacted their Wills law, guarantees the right of any person to make a Will without any restriction;[111] provides for the formal requirements of Wills to be in writing and signed by the testator and attested by witnesses;[112] provided for the competence of witnesses in proving due execution of a Will;[113] and makes provisions for alteration and revocation of Wills.[114] A Will that is not made in conformity with the requirements for making Wills will be null and void.

Conveyancing Act 1881

The Conveyancing Act 1881 applies as law in States that are yet to enact their property laws, notably some states of the former Northern and Eastern regions of Nigeria.[115] The Conveyancing Act applies so long as there is no comparable local legislation enacted by such a state. Some States however have enacted legislation to regulate property practice. Abia State in South-East Nigeria has enacted a comparable law, the Law of Property Cap.23 of 1999. Rivers State has equally enacted a comparable local legislation. The Act of 1881 does not apply to States of the former Western Region because the Western Region of Nigeria in 1959 enacted the Property and Conveyancing Law, Cap.100 of 1959 and as 'Successors-in-law' the States carved out of the former Western Region apply the provisions of the Property & Conveyancing Law.[116]

Nigerian Legislation

Nigerian Legislation, enacted by either the States or the Federal Government regulates property transactions. The most important of the legislation on property practice are:

1. Constitution of the Federal Republic of Nigeria.
2. Land Use Act
3. property and Conveyancing Law
4. Registration of Titles Law

---

[111] Section 3.
[112] Section 9.
[113] Section 14.
[114] Sections 18,20, & 21.
[115] *Supra*
[116] Cap. 100 Laws of Western Region of Nigeria, 1959.

5. Wills Law of the States of Nigeria
6. Administration of Estates Laws
7. Illiterate Protection Laws
8. Land Instrument Registration Laws
9. Land Instruments Preparation Law
10. Stamp Duties Act
11. Companies and Allied Matters Act
12. Town Planning Laws

There are other legislations which deal with property law practice, where the specifics of the transaction require their application. These include the Companies and Allied Matters Act,[117] the Environmental Laws,[118] and the several gazettes of the various states on property practice.[119] The salient features of some of the legislation deserve some treatment here.

Constitution of the Federal Republic of Nigeria

The Constitution of the Federal Republic of Nigeria, 1999 guarantees the right of every Nigerian to won immovable property anywhere in Nigeria.[120] A citizen of Nigeria has the right to own property in any State in the Federation and could apply to the Governor of such State for the grant of a right of occupancy even if he is not from that particular State. This provision was not contained in the previous Constitution of Nigeria, but inserted in the 1999 Constitution as a direct guarantee to stop discriminatory practices in States where a person may be denied immovable property simply because he is not from that State. Accordingly, the Constitution explicitly provides in Section 43 that "subject to the provisions of this Constitution, every citizen of Nigeria shall have the right to acquire and own immovable property anywhere in Nigeria". The Process of acquiring and owning property is incidentally connected with the transfer of property from one party to another. The Constitution also prevents governments from compulsorily acquiring the properties of Nigerians except "in the manner and for the purpose prescribed by law".[121] Even with this, the power of compulsory

---

[117] Where for instance a company needs to mortgage its properties in order to raise capital.

[118] Where for instance, developments of properties are restricted because of fear of environmental hazards.

[119] For example, the destination of lands into urban and non-urban area, pursuant to the provisions of the Land Use Act is contained in States regulations and gazettes to that effect. Section 3 Land Use Act.

[120] Section 43.

[121] Section 44(1).

acquisition does not affect any general law relating to leases, tenancies, mortgages, charges, bills of sale or any other rights or obligations arising out of contracts; or relating to the vesting and administration of property of persons adjudged or otherwise declared bankrupt or insolvent, of persons of unsound mind or deceased persons, and of corporate or unincorporated bodies in the course of being wound-up.[122]

Land Use Act

The Act was first decreed in 1978 by the then military government, and was intended to make lands available for the benefits of Nigerians. The Land Use Act is not a constitutional enactment (that is, it is not part of the Constitution). It is however a legislation that enjoys some special treatment, because the provisions for its amendment can only be effected using the cumbersome process for amending the Constitution.[123] By making all lands within a State tenured, the Act seeks to enhance the principles of leasehold by which the land in each State is vested in the Governor of a State to hold in trust for the benefits of Nigerian within the State. The Governor of a State is a trustee of all lands in a State and all Nigerians are left with the equitable interest in the land and become the beneficial owners of the land subject to other provisions of the Act.[124] The tenor of the Act was to "nationalize" all lands in the country by vesting its ownership in the State and the maximum interest preserved in the hands of private individuals in a right of occupancy.[125] in pursuance of the trust, the Governor may grant to a Nigerian citizen a term of years in a land to hold, use and occupy, subject to payments of rent to the State and the observance of conditions and covenants of the grant.

The grant of a term of years to a citizen to hold, occupy and use the land is a right of occupancy which is the highest and greatest legal interest a holder can have.[126] To certify the grant of a right of occupancy, the Governor grants a Certificate of Occupancy to the holder. A Certificate of Occupancy creates a term of years absolute or a lease for a number of years. A Certificate of Occupancy which is properly issued by a competent authority raises a rebuttable presumption that the holder is the owner in exclusive possession of the land.[127]

---

122 Section 44(2) (c & d).

123 Section 315(5) 1999 Constitution. Section 9(2) of the Constitution provides for process for amendment of the Constitution. See *Nkwocha* v. *Governor of Anambra State* (2001) FWLR part. 48, p.1386.

124 *Abioye* v. *Yakubu* (1991) 5 NWLR (pt.190) p.130.

125 *Kachalla* v. *Banki* (2006) ALL FWLR, (pt.309), p.1420.

126 Section 5(1) Land Use Act, See *Ezennah* v. *Atta* (2004) All FWLR (pt. 202), p.1858, at p.1884.

127 *Ezennah* v. *Attah*, ibid at p. 1884.

Some specific features of the Act are that it –

(a) Vests of all lands in each State in the Governor of the State, "such land shall be held in trust and administered for the use and common benefit of all Nigerians."[128]

(b) Empowers the Governor to grant a right of occupancy and also to grant easements appurtenant to statutory rights of occupancy of Nigerians. The right of occupancy is only for a prescribed period and not infinitum, meaning that the relationship is in the nature of a leasehold only and not freehold.[129]

(c) Empowers the Governor to plan and use of land

(d) Prohibits the alienation of a right of occupancy or any part of it by way of assignment, mortgage, transfer of possession, sublease or otherwise howsoever without the consent of the Governor first had and obtained.

(e) Allows for revocation of a right of occupancy or customary right of occupancy of land on grounds of public interest and payment of compensation in that event.

Registration of Titles Law

The Registration of Titles Law, Cap.166, Laws of Lagos State, 1994 (presently Cap.R4, Laws of Lagos State of 2004) [herein RTL] requires titles to land to be registered as first or subsequent registrations. The principal purpose of the law is for the State to guarantee titles that have been investigated and registered by the Registrar of Titles. Once this has been done, the entries in the register constitute sufficient evidence of title for any purchaser dealing with the land to rely on and determine if the vendor has title to sell the property and the encumbrances that attach to the land. This dispenses with another separate and constant repetition of proof of title by the vendor on every purchase of the land.

Property and Conveyancing Law, Cap.100 Laws of Western Region of Nigeria

This legislation regulates property transaction in most of the States of the former Western Region of Nigeria. Some salient features of this law are:

---

[128] Section 1.

[129] Section 5(1)(a&b)

a) No sale of land shall be enforced except there is a note or memorandum in writing containing the terms of the sale and signed by the person to the charge.[130]
b) All conveyances of land interests in land for the purposes of creating any legal estate are void unless they are made by deed.[131]
c) Where a person executes a deed, he shall either sign or place his mark on it and sealing alone is not sufficient.[132]
d) The rights to create leases are safeguarded so long as certain elements exist in it.[133]

Illiterates Protection Laws

The illiterate protection regime and laws of the various States exist to protect illiterate persons involved in transactions generally.[134] The various States of Nigeria have what are commonly referred to as Illiterate Protection Laws. Example in Ogun State, the Illiterate Protection Law is Cap.47 Laws of Ogun State 1978; in Lagos State, it is Cap.13, Laws of Lagos State 2003; in Kwara State, it is Cap.73 Laws of Kwara State 1991; and in Jigawa State, it is Cap.81, Laws of Jigawa State 1998. The Illiterates Protection Act applies to the Federal Capital Territory, Abuja.[135]

The Illiterate Protection Laws protect illiterate persons in transactions generally and not only in real property transactions; hence, "it is like a very wide umbrella and covers all forms of writing or document written at the request of an illiterate person".[136] An illiterate is a person who is unable to read or write or understand a particular document. In the absence of evidence to the contrary therefore, the fact that a person thumb-printed a document is regarded prima facie evidence that he was illiterate. Any person who shall write any letter or document at the request, on behalf or in the name of any illiterate person shall also write on such letter or other document his own name as the writer and his address.[137]Compliance with the above provision is equivalent to a statement that the person was instructed to write such letter or document by the illiterate person for whom it purports to have been written; and that the document fully and correctly represents his instructions. Again,

---

[130] Section 67(1) PLC.
[131] Section 77(1) & 78(1) PCL.
[132] Section 79(1) PCL
[133] Section 79(2) PCL
[134] For a detailed discuss on illiterate protection in conveyancing see Dadem Y., "Protection of Illiterate Persons in Conveyancing Transactions: Faulting the Laws", in Smith, I.O. (ed.) *Law and Real Property Rights in Nigeria*, University of Lagos, 2008 pp.197-216.
[135] Cap.11, Vol.3, Laws of the Federal Capital Territory, 2006.
[136] *Lawal* v. *Ollivant* (1972) 3 SC 124.
[137] Section 2 Illiterate Protection Law, Cap.67 Laws of Lagos State, 1994.

if the letter or document is purported to be signed with the signature or mark of the illiterate person, it would be assumed that the signature or mark was made by such illiterate person.[138] The importance of the date and address is that if there is any doubt or a denial as to the statements that were made by the illiterate, the writer will be traced to show whether the contents of the document represents the veracity of what the illiterate asserts. In other words, the protection is for the benefit of the illiterate.[139]

The object of the illiterate protection law is to protect an illiterate person from possible fraud. Strict compliance therewith is obligatory as regards the writer of the document. If the document creates legal rights and the writer benefits under it, those benefits are only enforceable by the writer of the document if he complies strictly with the provisions of the law. If a document which does not comply with the provisions of the law creates rights between the illiterate and a third party, evidence may be called t prove what happened at the time the document was prepared by the writer before the parties signed it, but the writer himself cannot adduce evidence on his own to remedy the omission.[140] Further, where the illiterate person is to sign or to make a mark, the document must be read over and explained to him. In practice, this calls for the insertion in the document of what is usually referred to as the Illiterates' Jurat,[141] which is a clause intended to show that the illiterate person had been made to understand the contents of the document before affixing his signature, at the same time providing the particulars of the person who explained the contents to the illiterate person. A typical illiterate jurat is set out below.[142]

The absence of a jurat may vitiate a Conveyance, as in *Itauma* v. *Akpe-Ime*;[143] Ogwuegbu JSC, noted that:

> I have carefully examined Exhibit B. it was thumb-printed by the plaintiff who was described as lessor...The writer failed to write his name and address. He did not sign it either...It is clear from the evidence and on the face of Exhibit B that it does not comply with Section 3 of the Illiterates Protection Law. The object of the law is to

---

[138] Section 2 (a & b).

[139] *Fatumbi* v. *Olanloye* (2004) All FWLR (pt.225) p.150.

[140] *Ezeigwe* v. *Awudu* (2008) All FWLR (pt. 434) p.1529.

[141] A jurat is a certification or deposition before an authority showing that the person signing did so in the presence of an authority; that he appeared before the officer on the indicated date, and that the officer administered an oath or affirmation to the signer, who swore to or affirmed the contents of the document. See *Black's Law Dictionary*, *supra* at 854.

[142] See chapter 4.

[143] Reported in (2000) FWLR (pt.16) p.228; (2000) 12 NWLR (pt.680, p.156.

> protect the illiterate person from fraud. Strict compliance therefore becomes obligatory as regards the writer of such document.[144]

It seems that where there are other evidences to show that the contents of the document were read and interpreted to the maker (apart from the presence of the jurat), then the physical presence of the jurat may be dispensed with. In order words, the jurat is not conclusive evidence that the contents of a document were read and understood by an illiterate person. This point was highlighted in the case of *Edokpolo* v. *Okenhen*,[145] where the court, in interpreting Section 3 of the Illiterate protection Law, Cap.70 Laws of Bendel State 1976, held that the section only raises or provides certain presumptions of law in respect of a document prepared at the request, on behalf, or in the name of an illiterate by any person who shall write on such document his own name as the writer and his address. That the purpose of the provision under Section 3 of the law is to ensure in furtherance to the said protection of illiterate persons, that the writer of such a document is identified or traced. Further, that the Illiterates Protection Law has made no mandatory provision to the effect that the only evidence of interpretation that is legally acceptable by the court is the one on the face of such document. Evidence of the fact that any document is written by person on the instruction of an illiterate, that the contents fully and correctly represent his instructions, that prior to its being singed, it was read over and explained to the illiterate and that the signature or mark thereon was made by such illiterate may either be oral, and such oral evidence is clearly admissible in law; or it may be patent on the face of such a document where the name and address of the writer are indicated as required by law.[146]

Land Instrument Preparation Laws[147]

These laws require that preparation of instruments and documents on sale or transfer of land can only be done by a Legal Practitioner. Accordingly, no person other than a legal practitioner shall either directly or indirectly for or in expectation of any fee, gain or reward, draw or prepare any instrument and any agreement to pay a fee or reward to any person other than Legal Practitioner in consideration of such person

---

144 See pages 174 & 175 of the report.
145 (1994) 7-8 SCNJ (pt.III).
146 Words in italics are for emphasis only.
147 For example Cap. 84 Laws of Kaduna State, 1991.

drawing or preparing any such instrument is void. Such amount paid may be recovered by action by the person who paid the amount.[148]

Land Instrument Registration Laws

Many States in the Federation have laws that require that instruments used in land transaction should be registered.[149] "Instrument" is defined as meaning:

> A document affecting land whereby one party (hereinafter called the grantor) confers, transfers, limits, charges or extinguishes in favour of another party (hereinafter called the grantee) any right or title to, or interest in land, and includes a certificate of purchase and a power of attorney under which any instrument may be executed, but does not include a Will.[150]

In Ogun State and most States in the former Western Region of Nigeria, "instrument" includes a deed of appointment or discharge of trustees containing expressly or impliedly a vesting declaration affecting any land to which Section 27 of the Trustees law extends.[151]

What the legislation ahs done is to fix the meaning of instruments; but in listing them, the legislation uses the word "includes" to import that the instruments are not limited to the ones listed in eh definition, but embraces any document that confers, transfers, limits, charges or extinguishes interest in land. Thus, in the case of *Ogbimi* v. *N.C.L.*,[152] a written letter which attempted to transfer interest in the property in dispute was held to be 'instrument' within the context of the definition of instruments and hence registrable, with Onnoghen J.S.C. noting that "what is material… is not the form the document was written but its contents."[153]

---

[148] See for example Sections 5 and 6 of the Land Instrument Preparation Law, Cap. 84, laws of Kaduna State, 1991. Section 22(1)(d) of the Legal Practitioners Act provides that if any person other than a legal practitioner prepares for or in expectation of reward any instrument relating to immovable property, or relating to or with a view to the grant of probate or letters of administration, or relating to or with a view to proceedings in any court of record in Nigeria, such person shall be guilty of an offence and liable to a fine of an amount not exceeding N200 or imprisonment for a term not exceeding two years or both. "Instrument", in relation to immovable property means any document which confers, transfers, limits, charges or extinguishes any interest in the property or which purports so to do, and 'immovable property".

[149] Examples are Land Instruments Registration law, Cap.L58, Laws of Lagos State, 2003; Cap.83 Laws of Kwara State 1994; Cap.81, Laws of Jigawa State 1998. 'Certificate of Purchase' means a certificate granted by a court certifying that the right, title and interest of a judgment debtor in certain immovable property has been sold to the person named in the certificate.

[150] Section 2 Land Registration Law, Cap.85 Laws of Kaduna State 1991.

[151] Section 2 Land Instruments Registration Law, Vol.3, Laws of Ogun State, 2006.

[152] (2006) All FWLR (pt.317), p. 390.

[153] Section 9(1)(a) Land Registration Law, Kaduna State, 1991.

Registration of Instruments requires that the land be sufficiently described. Thus, "No instrument executed after the commencement of this Law, other than a power of attorney, shall be registered unless it contains a proper and sufficient description...(and) a plan, of the land affected by such instrument".[154] The decision of the registrar on the adequacy of the description and plan of any land in any instrument meant for registration is final, subject to any review by the High Court. The plan in the Instrument is must be signed by a Surveyor. Similarly, an instrument which requires the consent of the Governor or of any public officer will not be registered unless such consent is endorsed on it or the registrar is otherwise satisfied that such consent had been given.[155] A certified true copy of the judgment of a court together with a copy of any map or plan ordered to be filed in that court to which the judgment refers which affects an instrument must be registered by the registrar within two months of the judgment;[156] although the failure to transmit or file any judgment and any error in transmitting or filing any judgment will not affect the validity or effect of such judgment.[157]

The registrar is under duty to allow searches to be made at all reasonable times in any register book, register or file of registered or filed documents in his custody, and he should, upon request, give a certified copy of any entry in any such register or filed document.[158] Every such certified copy can be received in evidence, without any further or other proof in all civil cases. A person conducting a search must be careful since it is an offence punishable with a term of imprisonment for seven years for a person to wilfully destroy or injure or cause to be destroyed or injured, any register books, register or filed document or counterfeit or cause to be counterfeited any part of any such books, register or document or any certified copy or extract, or to wilfully insert or cause to be inserted in any such book, register, file, certified copy or extract any false entry, or to certify any writing to be a copy or extract of any such book, register or file, knowing the same to be false in any part or to forge and counterfeit the seal of any registry office.[159]

Any instrument is registrable and where an instrument is not registered, it has the following effects:

a) it cannot be pleaded;

b) it is inadmissible in evidence as proof of title; and

---

[154] Section 10 Land Registration Law Kaduna State, 1991.

[155] Section 19(1) Land Registration Law Kaduna State, 1991.

[156] Section 21 Land Registration Law Kaduna State, 1991.

[157] Sections 27&28 Land Registration Law Kaduna State, 1991.

[158] Section 30 Land Registration Law Kaduna State, 1991.

[159] Ibid

c) the courts cannot give effect to it to transfer interest in land.[160]

It may however, serve as proof of payment of money with the effect of creating equitable interests in favour of the person making the payment. In the case of *Nsiege* v. *Mgbemena*,[161] the court held that where a purchaser of land or a lessee is in possession of land by virtue of a registrable instrument which has not been registered and has paid the purchase money or the rent to the vendor or the lessor, then in either case, the purchaser or the lessee has acquired an equitable interest in the land which is as good as a legal estate and this equitable interest can only be defeated by a purchaser of the land for value without notice of the prior equity and such registrable instrument can be admitted to prove such equitable interest and the payment of the purchase money or rent.[162]

It is not every document that relates or mentions land that is registrable. It must be one that transfers, charges, or extinguishes some interest in the land. In *Olanrewaju* v. *Ogunleye*,[163] the instrument was simply a "farm cultivation agreement". In *Abu* v. *Kuyabana*,[164] the Instrument (a Power of Attorney was made by the donor) was "to institute, defend, prosecute or take any other legal steps… in my behalf in respect of any landed property owned by me…"[165] In both cases, the courts held that they were not instruments within the context of the definition of "Instruments" in the land instrument registration laws.

The land instrument registration laws also provide protection for illiterate persons involved in real property transactions. For example Section 8(1) of the Lagos State and Instrument Registration law says that:

> No instrument executed in Nigeria after the commencement of this law, the grantor, or one or more of the grantors, whereof is illiterate, shall be registered, unless it has been executed by such illiterate grantor or grantors in the presence of a Magistrate or Justice of the Peace and is subscribed by such Magistrate or Justice of the Peace as a witness thereto.

An agreement for sale of land made under native law and custom is not really required it to be registered. In *Etajata* v. *Ologbo*,[166] the court held that once a document shows that it is a customary agreement of a

---

160 *Akinduro* v. *Alaya* (2007) All FWLR, (pt.381), p.1653; *Anufe* v. *Ogbomienor* (2004) All FWLR (pt.224), p. 2061.
161 (2007) All FWLR (pt.372), p.1769.
162 Ar p. 1801-2.
163 (1997) 1 SCNJ p.144.
164 (2002) FWLR (pt.99), p. 1141.
165 At p.1154.
166 (2007) All FWLR (pt.386) p. 584.

sale of piece of land, it does not therefore fall within the definition of an "instrument" for the purpose of the Land Instrument Registration Laws.

Stamp Duties Act

Stamp duties are a form of taxation paid to the Federal or State Governments on documents such as Conveyances on Sale, Agreements, Contracts, Bills of Exchange, Promissory note, and instruments (Letters and Certificates of Admission, Instruments of Apprenticeship, Insurance Policies). Stamp duties require that the above instruments be stamped. By Section 19 and 22 of the Stamp Duties Act, Cap.58 Laws of the Federation of Nigeria, 2004 (herein SDA) an unstamped instrument will not be admissible as evidence in court. However, a Court, Arbitrator or Referee may permit a defaulter to pay al unpaid duties and penalties on an instrument to enable him to formally tender it in evidence.[167] The Federal Government is the only competent authority to impose, charge and collect duties on instruments specified in the schedule to the Stamp Duties Act where such instruments relate to matters executed between a company and an individuals.[168] In fact, a stamp duty is a matter in the Exclusive Legislative List of the 1999 Constitution. That means, the legal basis of stamp duties belong to the Federal Government. It has however permitted the State Government to collect duties where the party executing the instrument is an individual. Individual residents of Abuja pay their duties to the Federal Government.

Companies and Allied Matters Act

The Act permits registered companies under the Act to mortgage their properties by the creation of debentures over the assets of the company. Section 166 of the Act says that a company may borrow money for the purpose of its business or objects and may mortgage or change its undertaking, property and uncalled capital and issue debentures, debentures stocks and other securities for any debt, liability or obligation of the company. 'Property' in the section includes land or any interest in land which the company has. The provisions of part of vii of the Act regulate the creation of securities by way of debenturing assets of a registered company.

Wills Laws of States

Even though the Wills Act 1837 is an English statute of general application in Nigeria, some States have replaced it with their individual

---

[167] Section 22 of SDA.
[168] Section 4(1) Stamp Duties Act, Cap. 58 Laws of the Federal Republic of Nigeria, 2004.

Wills laws. Examples of Wills laws of individuals states include Wills Law Cap.W2, Laws of Lagos State, 2003, Wills Law Cap.163, Laws of Kaduna State 1991; Plateau State Wills Law, No.2 of 1988; the Bauchi State Wills Law Cap.168 Laws of Bauchi State 1989; the Kwara State Wills Law, Cap.168 Laws of Kwara State 1991; Abia State Wills Law Cap.37 of 1999 and the Jigawa State Wills Law Cap.155 Laws of Jigawa State, 1998. In the Western Region of Nigeria, the Wills law Cap.133, Laws of Western Region of Nigeria of 1959 applies in the States carved out of the region that have not yet enacted their Wills Law.

Some salient features of the Wills Laws of the States are:

1. Freedom to make wills and dispose of estate by every person is guaranteed.
2. The right of testation is sometimes restricted by imposing limitations on the maker of the Will in respect of the disposition of his estate.
3. There are requirements for the validity of a Will.
4. Witnesses are required for making and revoking Wills.
5. There are provisions to ensure that a Will does not lapse as a result of the death of the beneficiaries.

Chapter Two

Concept of ownership

Ownership is the right of exclusive use of property. The exclusivity of the property of the person called the owner.[1] Opinion seems to be divided as to whether land in typical African society can be said to be capable of being owned and or being subject to the seemingly context of ownership *per se.*

Coker[2] feels the idea of ownership in the English parlance is unknown to customary law.[3] So the greatest right which a person can have in land is the right of possession not ownership.[4] According to Nwabueze[5]

---

[1] See Idrisu J., *Understanding Nigerian Land Law*, 2nd Edition (Zaria, ABU Press Ltd, 2008) at pp.12-13 where he further asserted that ownership implies that the owner's title is superior to any other right which may exist on the property or land. The direction of an owner's right is unlimited. His interest exists even when he is not in physical possession of the property and can be inherited by his offspring. Ownership connotes the totality of rights and powers that are capable of being exercised over a thing or property. These are the right to possession, right to derive income from it in cash or kind, the power of management including that of alienation. Traditional concept of ownership was a bundle of rights including rights to *utendi*, i.e., to use or enjoy, *furendi* - i.e., dispose or transfer and *abutendi*, *i.e.*, to abuse, consume or destroy. In Jinadu v. Esurombi Aro (2009) 4 MJSC (pt.111) at 6, the Supreme Court asserted that proof of acts of ownership are ordinarily provided by acts of persons or persons claiming the land such as selling, leasing, renting out all or part of the land or farming on it or on a portion of it or otherwise utilizing the land beneficially. All evidence of ownership provided they extend over a sufficient length of time and are numerous and positive enough. It warrants the interference that he is the true owner. See also *Chukwu* v. *Amadi* (2009) All FWLR (pt.177) at 7189 and *Oko* v. *Okenwa* (2010) 3 NWLR at 407-409.

[2] Coker, *Family Property Among the Yorubas* (London, Sweet & Maxwell, 1966).

[3] See Bryan A.G.; *Black's Law Dictionary*, 7th ed. (London: St. Paul Minn, 1999) at p.1131, sees the term as the collection of rights allowing one to use and enjoy property including the right to convey it to others. Ownership implies the right to possess a thing, regardless of any actual or constructive control. Ownership rights are general permanent and inheritable.

"Possession is the de-facto exercise of a claim. Ownership is the de jure recognition of one. A thing is owned by me when my claim to it is maintained by the will of the state as expressed in the law; it is possessed by me, when my claim to it is maintained by my own self assertive will. Ownership is the guarantee of the law; possession is the guarantee of the facts. It is well to have both forms if possible; and indeed they normally co-exist. Ownership does not always mean absolute dominion. The more an owner for his advantage, opens up his property for use by the public in general, the more does his rights become circumscribed by the statutory and constitutional powers of those who use it; See *March* v. *Alabama* 320 US 501, 506, 66.

[4] Coker, *op. cit.*, See also Egute M.A., *Essentials of Nigerian Land Law* (Makurdi: Onaivi Publishing Company, 2002) at p.33. According to Elias, *Nature of African Customary Law* (London: Manchester University Press, 1956) at p.164, what we have said so far as well as what we shall see

ownership is the most comprehensive and complete relation that can exist in respect of anything. It implies the fullest amplitude of rights of enjoyment, management and disposal over property. To put it the other way round, it implies that the owners' title for these rights is superior and paramount over any other right that may exist in the land in favour of other persons.

Under Customary Law, the term could be used loosely. In *Enimil & Ors* v. *Tuakyi*,[6] the Privy Council asserted that sometimes it (ownership) denotes what is in effect absolute ownership at other times it is used in a context which indicates that the reference is only rights of occupancy. Ownership therefore connotes the totality of relation that may exist with respect to land.[7] The subject of ownership consists of some rights to use and enjoy the land to the exclusion of other persons, which is recognized and protected by law.[8]

The right of the owner is therefore not subject or restricted by the superior right of another person. Ownership covers the totality of rights and powers which are capable of being exercised over land. These rights and powers include the right to make physical use of the land, the right to generate income from the land in terms of cash or service or in kind and the power to manage the land which includes the power to alienate all rights and powers in it.[9]

The right to physical use of the land connotes the indication that within the limits allowed by the law and by the nature of the law the owner is entitled to use it in any way beneficial to him or destroy same. Aside the right to derive income from land, the most conclusive proof of ownership is the right and power to dispose of the land. Given the sophistication of the Nigerian society land has become a good source of income provided it is attached to it the power to alienate or dispose the land i.e. marketability and not physical use remains the most important element of value as regard land.

---

later, will show that the land holding recognized by African Customary Law is neither "communal holding" nor ownership (in the strict English sense of the term), Coker, *op. cit.*, at p.34 maintained that native law and custom does not therefore vest ownership in the strict sense in the family but ascribes to the family the aggregate of the rights which could be described as ownership. Olawoye C.O. *Title to Land in Nigeria* (Ibadan: Evans Books Publishing, 1974) at p.3 disagrees with Coker.

[5] Nwabueze B. *Nigerian Land Law* (Enugu: Nwanife Publishers Ltd, 1972) at p.9.

[6] (1952) 13 WACA. In *Nsirem* v. *Nwakerendu* (1955) 15 WACA 71, the West African Court of Appeal once against had the opportunity of deciding a dispute as to the ownership of land between the appellants and the respondents. It was held, following *Enimil & Ors* v. *Tuakyi* that the word 'owner' is loosely used in West Africa.

[7] Utuama A.A., *Nigerian Law of Real Property*, (Ibadan: 1989) at p.1.

[8] Olawoye, *op. cit.*, at p.1.

[9] Ibid.

Methods of proving ownership of land

There are basically five years of proving ownership of land required from those who claim title to land. These methods were recently restated by the Supreme Court in *Amadi* v. *Chinda & Ors*,[10] where the court held that a party may prove title to a piece of land in any of the following five ways:

(1) by traditional evidence;
(2) by documents of title;
(3) by various acts of ownership, numerous and positive and extending over a length of time to warrant the inference of owners.
(4) by acts of lawful enjoyment and possession of the land; and
(5) by proof of possession of adjacent land by circumstances which render it probable that the owner of such land would in addition, be the owner of the disputed land.

Although ownership of land may be proved by evidence of long and uninterrupted possession the Supreme Court held in *Buraimoh* v. *Bamgbose*, that possession no matter for how long cannot ripen into title or that equity cannot defeat the title of a person whose title or ownership has been admitted or established.[11]

In spite of the Land Use Act,[12] Land is still been held under customary law though ownership or dominion vests in the Governor of a State the pervasive effects of the Land Use Act being the dominion over the owners of the land; the character in which the holders hold such land remain substantially the same.[13] Consequently, an owner of land under customary law still remains an owner of the land in spite of the Land Use Act. But agreeably, he is no longer the absolute owner, as he now requires the consent of the appropriate authority to alienate or dispose of the right and interest in the land in accordance with the Land Use Act. Ownership is therefore the best and highest relationship that a person may have with respect to a property or land. It remains the right of exclusive use of property.

---

[10] (2009) MJSC (pt.1) 1-205, 120. See also *Usung* v. *Nyong* (2010) 2 NWLR. In *Oko* v. *Okenwa* (2010) 3 NWLR at 408, the Court of Appeal asserted that one of the five ways will suffice. See also *Chukwu* v. *Amadi* (2009) All FWLR (pt.472)

[11] See (1989) 2 NSSC 395. See also *Salami* v. *Oke* (1987) 9-11 SC at 63 *Ogunola* v. *Eiyekola* (1990) 4 NWLR (pt.146 at p.632, *Ukaegbu* v. *Nwololo* (2009) 1-2 M.J.S.C at 99, *Atanda* v. *Ajane* (1989) 2 NWLR (pt.111) 511.

[12] Cap C. LFN 2004.

[13] See *Ukeagbu* v. *Nwololo* (*supra*)

The character of possession

The term possession inputs manual custody, physical control, coupled with the intention to exercising such control. Possession denotes physical relation between a person and something in his control. The right to possession is therefore an incident of ownership. Possession may be actual i.e. where the law for certain purposes, considers a person to have possession of a thing even though he does not. Actual possession is against the whole world except the true owner.[14]

A person is said to be in possession of land if he is in physical control of the land and has the intention to control it. The element of intention is vital because control necessarily involves an act of will. The right it possession may however arise not only as an element of ownership but also in virtue of a grant from an owner. In *Shittu* v. *Egbovemi*,[15] the Supreme Court was of the opinion that a trespasser who had obtained possession by force could not validly obtain a claim to same based on such possession. Apart from the fact that possession is an incident of ownership, it is equally an altruism that where ownership of land is in dispute, the law presumes that the person in possession is the owner of such land until the contrary is proved[16] and there cannot be concurrent possession by two persons claiming adversely to each other.[17] A vendor who sold his land to a purchaser cannot subsequently claim a declaration of title to the same piece of land in an action involving a third party. In other words, having sold his land to a purchaser a plaintiff cannot turn around to claim a declaration of title to the same land he has sold.[18] In

---

[14] See Idrisu, *op. cit.*, at p.13.

[15](1998) 7SCNJ. See also *Chukwuma* v. *Ifeloye* (2009) All FWLR (pt.460) 631 & *Ojini* v. *Ogo Oluwa Motors (Nig.) Ltd.* (1998) 1 SCNJ 20.

[16] See *Shittu* v. *Egbovemi* (*supra*)

[17] See the Evidence Act Cap.112 LFN,2004. In *Asher* v. *Hotlock* (1865) 1 QB, the court held that possession is good against all the world except the person who can show a better title. In English Law, possession of land is called seise. It is to be noted that possession in law refers to exclusive possession i.e. ability to exclude the whole world. Where it is not exclusive, the law does not protect it. In *Ayeyiola* v. *Adesola* (1973) NLWR 10, the court held that where two parties are claiming ownership, it is the duty of the trial court to find out which side was in exclusive possession. Section 145 of the Evidence Act Cap. LF LFN puts the burden of proof on a person who is not in possession. Possession ordinarily may be of a temporary nature, whilst ownership is essentially purely a legal concept unlike possession which is essentially a matter of fact. Cf Idrisu J., *op. cit.*, at p.14.

[18] In *Ukaegbu* v. *Nwololo* (2009) All FWLR at 1873, the facts of the case was that the plaintiff based his claim of ownership of the disputed land known as Oru-uhu Egbereuri, on traditional history and claimed he had been exercising acts of ownership thereon. He also claimed that his family was involved in a matter in respect of the land in the Native Court in 1948 and the judgment was in their favour, but the defendants entered the land and felled timbers without their consent. The plaintiff therefore instituted an action in a representative capacity. In the High Court of justice,

Ukeagbu v. *Nwololo*,[19] the court held that when an attempt to prove a root of title fails acts of possession based on the not of title, cannot sustain a claim of title.

The notion of possession can be better understood in the legal expression that possession is ninth-tenth of possession. Acts therefore that portion physical control are important as regards possession. In *Wuta-Ofei* v. *Danquah*,[20] the Privy Council posited that their lordship do not consider that in order to establish possession, it is necessary for a claimant to take some positive steps in relation to the land such as enclosing the land or cultivating it. The type of conduct which indicates possession must vary with the type of land. The erection of pillars on the land is sufficient indication of possession.[21] Again, surveying of land and demarcation of its borders by wooden pegs were sufficient to found possession.[22]

A lodger in a hotel or a boarder in a dormitory does not possess the hotel or dormitory where in he spends the might though he makes use of the hotel or dormitories facility.[23]

Imo state, claiming declaration and injunctive reliefs that, the land is his family property, injunction restraining the defendants from the land and damages for trespass. The defendants also laid claims of ownership to the land. The trial court dismissed the plaintiff's claims. Aggrieved, the plaintiff appealed to the Court of Appeal where a retrial was ordered. Also aggrieved, the defendants appealed to the Supreme Court. The Supreme Court in allowing the appeal held that where title is derived by grant, sale or conquest or inheritance, etc., the pleading should aver facts relating to the finding of the land in dispute, the person or persons who founded the land and exercised original acts of possession. If the pleaded root of title is not established by evidence, it will be futile exercise to go to the essence of possession or acts of ownership. See also *Dabo Dabo* v. *Abdullahi* (2005) All FWLR (pt.255) 1039 (2005) 25 CNJ 76.

[19] (2009) ALL FWLR at 1873. See *Oko* v. *Okenwa* (2010) 3 NWLR at 409, the facts of which were that at the High Court of Enugu State, the appellants sued the respondent claiming a declaration that they are entitled to the statutory certificate of occupancy lying at Isiagu Amechi Awkunana in Enugu South Local Government Area; damages for trespass, perpetual injunction and a declaration of title to the certificate of occupancy granted to the respondent dated 13/8 is null, void and of no effect. The appellants who were members of Umuoko family claimed to own the land from time immemorial and that they inherited same from their forefathers. Later, structures were seen being developed on the land. The trial court found that the appellants failed to establish root of title to the land in dispute and held that consideration of the issue of sale and grant of certificate of occupancy to the respondent would be a mere academic exercise. The Court of Appeal dismissed the appeal and held that it is not sufficient for the plaintiff to say that the land in dispute belong exclusively to his family from time immemorial and stop there. He must show how the family got the land either from some other persons or authority in succession, or that the family found it a virgin land and deforested it. See *Dike* v. *Okoloedo* (1995) 10 NWLR (pt.623).

[20] *Supra*, 2010

[21] Ibid.

[22] See *Alatishe* v. *Sayalu*. In *Yusuf* v. *Adejoke* (2007) 4 SCNJ at pp. 93-94. The Supreme Court held that long possession is not enough to prove ownership. Valid title is needed.

[23] See *Harmond* v. *UAC* (1936) 60. A person in possession can maintain an action in respect of the land against every body except one with a better title. See also the Supreme Court in *Akinterinwa & ors* v. *Oladunjoye* (2000) 5 SCNJ 128.

Chapter 3

Ownership and communal land holding under customary land tenure

Communal land holding has been asserted as the most remarkable principle of customary land law.[1] The observations of Lord Haldane in *Amodu Tajani* v. *Secretary of Southern Nigeria*,[2] that land belonged to the community, village or the family has often being cited to the effect that the existence of communal landholding had never been in doubt. Communal land is land vested in the community as a corporate whole. No individual member of the community could therefore claim ownership of any portion of such land as his own.[3]

Meaning of communal land

Communal means a group of people. This group of people may be a tribe, clan, town or village or an extended family.[4] Communal land in sum refers to any land in which all the members of a community have a common interest, all of whom are jointly, severally and directly liable for debts properly incurred with respect thereto. Judicial attitude seems to favour the notion that a community in law is not a corporate entity empowered to sue or be sued. In *Ekwudo* v. *Efejiake*,[5] the court in

---

1 Nelson D., "Real Property Management in Nigeria," *International Journal of Law and Contemporary Studies*, Vol.3 No.1&2, (Nigeria: The Development Universal Consortia, 2008) at p.85.

2 (1921) 2 A.C. 399 at 404. *Manuel* v. *Manuel* (1926) 7 NLR 101, *Chief Etim* v. *Chif Eke* (1941) 16 NLR, Bajulaiye v. Akapo (1938), *Lewis* v. *Bankole* (1908) 1 L.R. and *Coker* v. *Jinadu* (1958) U.R.

3 The Supreme Court of Nigeria has made serious attempts to introduce the concept of individualism as part of the theory of property ownership in Nigeria. Cf. Olayide A., "Legal Theories of Property. The Land Use Act in Perspective". A paper presented at the National Workshop on the Land Use Act held at the Nigerian Institute of Advanced Legal Studies, University of Lagos, 1990 April 9-11. In *Chukweke* v. *Nwankwo* (1921) AC 399, the court held that the statement of Lord Haldane in *Amodu TIjani* v. *Secretary Southern Nigeria*, to the effect that "the notion of individual ownership is quite foreign to native ideas" is not true for all system of land tenure in Nigeria as there is no uniform customary law tenure. It was then held that there were incidents of individual ownership in many communities in Nigeria. See also *Otogbolu* v. *Okeluwa* (1985) 2 NWLR, 195.

4 Idrisu J., *Understanding Nigeria Land Law*, 2nd ed. (Zaria: ABU Press, 2008) at p.14.

5 (1960) 5 E.S.C. 156.

deciding the legal status of Obosi community held that the Obosi are not a legal entity they are a large number of natural persons. A community therefore has some distinct unit, characterized by the possession of a common territory, language, dialect or kingship.[6]

Ownership of land by the community[7]

Customary law acknowledges the fact that absolute ownership can vest in the community. The Privy Council in *Awodu Tijani* v. *Secretary of Southern Nigeria*,[8] held that the notion of individual ownership is quite foreign to nature ideas. Land belongs to the community the village or the family and not to the individual. In *Lewis* v. *Bankole*,[9] the court held that it was perfectly well known that by strict ancient native law all property was family property. The Court of Appeal, in *Lebile* v. *Rev. Preshec & Ors*,[10] observed that in West Africa, there is a presumption of communal ownership of land and therefore where an individual or group asserts exclusive as against communal rights the burden in against such individual to prove exclusive ownership.

The notion of communal ownership did not favour some early judges who were English men accustomed to the English notions of individual ownership of land.[11]

---

[6] Nwabueze B.O., *Nigerian Land law* (Enugu: Nwamife Pub. Ltd., 1982) at p.4 assessed further that communal land remains that in which common interest or rights are vested in all the members of that community, jointly command rights been defined as rights in or over land referred to as communal right exercisable at a community but shall not include any right exercisable by any person in respect to family land on behalf of the family. See also Utuama A.A., *Law of Real Property* (Ibadan: Shaneson Publishers Ltd, 1989) at p.1.

A community head, the Elesi of Odogbolu sums up the law as regards communal land wherein when he said before the West African Lands Commission in 1908 that land belongs to the vast family of which many members are dead, few are living and countless member are still unborn. But Nwabueze opposes the assertion that it is not true that individual ownership was foreign before the advent of the British. The reason for his opposition was that the very notion of family property implies all individual ownership because an history of family is traced to its founder who just acquired the land. Nwabueze cannot be faulted on this argument. Cf Poriso, *op. cit.*, at p.15. and the court's decision in *Otogbolu* v. *Okeluwa* (*supra*).

[7] Nwabueze *op. cit.*, at p.45 asserted that communal ownership has survived because of three reasons: (i) the kinship and lineage w organization of Nigerian Society i..e. after the death of a head, the ownership continued in the line; (ii) the system of inheritance whereby the estate of a Nigerian who dies intestate revolves upon his children as family property. This applies even where the intestate property was held by him under English Law, See the recent case of *Umaru* v. *Pam* (2010) 2 NWLR at 406; (iii) the Communal ownership retains a firm grip because of the presumption that native lands are communal or family land.

[8] *Supra*

[9] *Supra*

[10] (2003) 3 NSCQR at p.19. See also *Akpan* v. *Udeattu* (1953) NWLR at 279.

[11] In *Lewis* v. *Bankole* (*supra*) a chief in Lagos left three plots, one was a developed on another he built houses for some of his children and the third was a shrine years after disagreement arose between his descendants. Some of them brought an action in court claiming the family compound

In the 3rd Millennium Nigeria, the institution of communal ownership has greatly reclined in import. The emergence of cash economy meant that individuals begun to acquire wealth of a permanent kind, which could be passed from generation to generation. The tendencies of people acquiring land vide personal effort as part of property, starting plantations and permanent houses, other structures became ripe. And with the advent in education communication and transportation, individuals ventured few from their places of birth and so communal and family fives ties became reckoned, urban migration became a phenomenon, and pressure began mounting on available land and brought about the need for increased individual interest in land.

Origin of communal land

Various methods abound by which a community may own a piece of land. One of such methods is by settlement. The first settler or founder of a piece of land becomes the owner of the land and the head of subsequent settlers on the land.[12] The founders of a new settlement might regard the entire land as belonging to the whole community jointly and would not allow individuals to appropriate any part of the land to themselves except as regards occupancy rights which could be acquired by clearing a portion of the land, or by grant from the authorities of the community. The community might regard the land as jointly owned but would permit individuals or villages to acquire separate ownership by grant from the authorities of the community.[13] Land therefore severally remains in the communal ownership but individuals hold right of occupancy. In such instances, communal or family property can never ripen into personal ownership of such property.[14]

---

was family property. The trial judge in his narrow understanding of traditional situations held that by strict native law, all property was family property. He held that as far as he was concerned, the institution communal ownership had been dead. He ended up by holding that the concept of communal and family ownership was engagement to the native justice, equity and good conscience.

[12] In *Titiloye* v. *Olupo* (1991) 2 NLR (pt.191) 344, the court held that it is a notorious fact that the fight settler of the piece of land becomes the owner of the land. See also *Bankole* v. *Pelu* (1991) 8 NLR (pt.211) where it was held that where the plaintiff traces his title to one whose title or ownership has been established, it is not necessary that he should show acts of ownership.

[13] See Nwabueze, *op. cit.*, at p.33. In *Idehen* v. *Playe* (1991) 5 NWLR (pt.191) at 344, it was held that that land in Benin (present day Edo State) belongs to the community for whom the Oba holds same in trust and it is only the Okawuo that can grant to a person individual ownership.

[14] See *Ogboni* v. *Oja* (1996) 6 SCNJ 140 at 155. In *Anyabunsi* v. *Ugwunze* (1995) 7 SCNJ 55, the court held that allotment of family land to its members for farming purposes has the effect of only conferring rights of user on the member.

Another method via which a community acquires ownership of land is by conquest. In time past, when a community is conquered in war, its land passes to the conqueror by right of conquest.[15]

Again, community ownership of land could originate via gift by a subordinate entity wherein the community and vice versa.

Management of communal land

The headmen, chief or traditional ruler of the community personifies it and as such exercises the power of control and management of communal land on behalf of the community. He may exercise these powers in consultation with other senior chiefs or elders of the community. This depends on the traditional authority structure of the community concerned.[16]

The chief is not a trustee in English sense of the word, this is because the title remains vested in the community as a composite entity[17] as the institution of communal land lacks, therefore, the division into legal and equitable ownership which is the fundamental principle of trust property.[18] The right and power of the chief are merely that of a caretaker.[19]

The chief or head or owner of the community holds the land for and on behalf of the community and not in his personal capability as such the Chief or head or heirs and children cannot inherit communal land ruled over by the Chief.[20] The authority of the chief derives from his office and not from any authority or agency given by members of the community. In effect, the position of the Chief in relation to community land is unique because the corporate powers of management are divorced from ownership.

Rights of members to communal land

Members of a community exercise some rights over communal land as members of their community. In the words of the Privy Council,[21] all the

---

[15] In *Mora* v. *Nwabusi* (1962) All NLR 681, the Privy Council held that proof of possession following conquest would suffice to establish ownership.

[16] See Nelson, *op. cit.*, at p.85.

[17] Ibid.

[18] Ibid.

[19] But see the cases of *Ruthermen* v. *Ruthermen* (1937) 3 ACA 178 and *Odukwe* v. *Oguntiyi* (1998) LRN 4001.

[20] In *Omagbemi* v. *Numa* (1923) NLR 17, the descendants of a traditional ruler claimed title to land held by the Chief. It was held that upon the death of the Chief that the Chief never held the land as an individual but that the land belonged to the community and that he was only land. See also *Faddoju* v. *Faddoju* (2000).

[21] *Amodu Tijani* v. *Secretary Southern Nigeria* (*supra*).

members of the community have an equal right to the land. These rights vary from community to community.[22]

Right to a portion of the land[23]

A member of the community has a right to portion of the community land upon which to build and farm. This right being inherent does not depend on the power of the community chief. Upon allocation of a portion, the member allotted does not become the absolute owner of the land. He enjoys exclusive possession. The chief or headmen cannot make an inconsistent allocation to another person without consultation and grant upon the original allocatee. A member can make use and enjoy the land in perpetuity for as long as he uses the land in a manner beneficial to himself and to his community.[24]

Right to share of income

A member of the community has the right to a share of income or profit whether in the form of rents, proceeds of sale or compensation for compulsory acquisition of communal land. On no account should a genuine and bona fide member of the community be excluded from share and account of the income from communal land.[25]

Right to partake in management

A community member has the right to partake directly or indirectly in the management of the community land. He partakes directly if he takes

---

22 In Benin for instance, the Supreme Court held that under Bini customary tenure system, all land in Benin is owned by the community for whom the Oba holds same in trust and it is the Oba who can transfer to any individual the ownership of such land. See *Arase* v. *Arase* (1984) 5 S.C 58. In other jurisdictions a grant of land by the traditional authority vests in the allottee permanent right equivalent to ownership.

23 Idrisu, *op. cit.*, at p.17.

24 In *Adewoyin* v. *Adeyeye* (1963) 1 All NLR 52, the Oni of Ife the paramount ruler of Ile-Ife testified that once an Oni had allocated a portion of communal land to a native of Ife for farming, the allotee enjoyed ownership rights to the exclusion of the community. During the term of the member's occupancy of communal land, he may alienate the land by pledge or loan.

25 In *Odusi* v. *Bolaji* (1962) LCR 217, the plaintiff claimed a share of the income and account of the income paid as compensation on the community land acquired compulsorily by the government. In deciding in favour of the plaintiff, the court held that the chief has refused or failed to give the plaintiffs their share or to render an account to them. The plaintiffs are left in ignorance as to the exact amount due to them and as to the fact from which such amount could be ascertained. In the result, I am of the opinion that the plaintiffs must succeed in their claim against the defendant. See also *Osuro* v. *Anyorin* (1964) 18 NLR 48, where the court held that a member has a right not only to a share of an income derived from the community land but to demand a reasonable account of it when he has a reason to support that there is something dubious.

active part in decision making and consultatory and indirectly, if he takes part in the chief, elders or councillors.[26]

Strangers as regard communal land

A stranger is not entitled to a portion of community land upon which to live or farm is right. The right to appropriate virgin land is the exclusive pressure of the member of the community.

In appropriate cases, however, where the stranger is a refugee or immigrant, he may be granted a portion of communal land as a customary land in return for which he acknowledges the title of the community by payment of customary tributes.[27]

Communal lands and contemporary developments

Communal land holding can be said to be on gradual by steady decrease. The most drastic of the many factors responsible for this phenomenon is the application of state powers of compulsory acquisition under the varied enabling statutes. Again, is the transformation of the hitherto indigenous substance economy as a result, communal land became easily saleable. This development converted many communal lands to individual lands with the attendant grants to individual members of the community. In *Ologbelu* v. *Okoluwa*, the court stated that each member of the community generally within his economic capacity do acquire as he desires interest in a piece or parcel of communal land which he can transmit to his offspring and which he is entitled to protect and prosecute by action a claim to his right against any other member who trespasses and to that extent the interest of the community in the land is displaced or postponed.

Communal land holding, in spite of the momental changes, is still a strong feature of land law in Nigeria. In the third Millennium Nigeria, communal title still exist in relation to sacred bush; stool or chieftaincy lands, communal playing ground, communal farm lands and ponds.[28]

---

[26] In *Archibong* v. *Archibong* (1947) 18 NLR 117, it was held that the requirement of consultation is a requirement of law and not just a matter of convenience by the Chief or elders to be observed or disregarded.

[27] See Ohiyele, P.O., *Modern Nigerian Land Law* (Ibadan: Evans Brothers Publishers Ltd, 1989) at p.40. In some instances where a custom permits, a stranger may acquire title to land by purchase. See *Omongonwan* v. *Okoegbuale* (1986) 5 NLR (pt.40).

[28] See Utuama, *op. cit.,* at p.9.

Chapter 4

Individual land ownership

Defining individual land ownership

Individual land ownership describes any land which is owned by a person in his individual capacity. The person may be a member of a family in who is vested the ownership or title to such land absolutely and that he can dispose of it without let or hindrance.

Individual land ownership may be equated with separate property of the individual which in English parlance is personality.[1]

A distinguishing factor between the interest a person has in his individual land and the interest he has in family land lies in the fact that whereas, his interest in family land is not absolute in the sense that he cannot alienate same by will, gift or sale, his interest in his individual land is absolute or allodia as he can alienate it in any manner he chooses. Whilst, a sale of family can only be valid where there is an agreement to sell between the family head and the principal members of the family.[2]

Origin of individual land ownership

In time past, the notion of separate land of the individual was unknown.[3] But attitudes, judicial opinions, opinions of legal texts writers,

---

[1] James, opines that the term 'separate property' is used to distinguish the individual property of a Nigerian or indeed any person from his joint family property or rather in his interest in the family property. This property acquired by inheritance or gift as property acquired by purchase is his separate property.

[2] See *Awuru* v. *Iledu* (2008) 12 NWLR at 249. See also *Usiobaifo* v. *Usiobaifo* (2005) 3 NWLR (pt.913) at 460-673, *Adeoeji* v. *Olusi* (2007) 1 SCNJ p.416; *Yusuf* v. *Adejoke* (2007) 4 SCNJ pp.53-94, *Anukan* v. *Anukan* (2008) SCNJ pp.74-75 and *Unity Bank* v. *Bouari* (2008) NSCQR 33 p.1297.

[3] See *Amodu Tijani* v. *Secretary Southern Nigeria* (1915-21) 3 NLR 24, and Speed Ag C.C. in *Lewis* v. *Bankole* (*supra*) where he observed that it is perfectly well known that in ancient native law, all property was family property and all real property was inalienable and it is equally well known that a very large portion of the land on which this town (Lagos) is built is not owned by individuals. In *Akpan* v. *Udeatu* (1993) (pt. 279) NWLR, the court observed that in West Africa there is a presumption of communal ownership of land and therefore where an individual or group asserts

colonialism, urbanization, modernization, the force of socio-economic activities have brought individual ownership of land to greater prominence.

In spite of the old notion that individual ownership did not exist, the customs of particular communities even in the early days recognized and accepted the concept of individual ownership of land because of the fact that a family comes into existence through the fecundity of the founder, so on the death of the founder, his personal belongings including land devolves on his successors as family land.[4]

Individual land ownership may arise under customary land in the following ways:

(a) Partitioning of family land

Once family land is partitioned, the joint interest c and the member to whom such land has been given becomes the absolute owner of the land under customary law.[5]

(b) Clearing virgin land[6]

An individual who has the strength and industry may clear a piece of virgin forest and farm on it and acquires interest on it as first settlers.[7]

(c) Survivorship[8]

Survivorship is known as the principle of *jusac crescendis* and it is to the effect that where all members of a family except one dies, the only surviving member will become the absolute owner of the family land.[9]

(d) Grant to an individual

This may arise where a community or family makes an absolute grant to an individual.[10]

---

exclusive as against communal rights, the burden is against such individual to prove exclusive ownership.

[4] See *Umaru* v. *Pam* (2010) 2 NWLR at 406.

[5] See *Buraimoh* v. *Bamgbose* (1993) NLR (pt.304). In *Akamu* v. *Adigun*, it was held that where communal land is partitioned either amicably or through the instrumentality of the court, the individuals hold the partioned portions. See also *Agbomeji* v. *Bakaro* (1998) 61 IRCN 1741.

[6] Idrisu J. *Understanding Nigerian Land Law*, 2nd ed. (Zaria: ABU Press Ltd, 2008) at p.26.

[7] Ibid., See also *Anyebunsi* v. *Uguize* (1995) 7 SCNJ 55.

[8] Idris op.cit at p.26.

[9] The rationale for the application of the principle is that interest in each member of the family is not absolute as no family member can alienate his interest in the property by way of gift, sale or will. So where a family member tries to dispose of family land by will favouring some of his children at the expense of the other children, the act was held a nullity since the basic nature of family property is to remain in the family indefinitely.Cf.*Adewoyin* v. *Adedeye* (1963) All NLR 52, *Fatire* v. *Abiri* (1953) NRNLR.

Alienation of individual land

This individual owner may dispose of the land as the absolute owner, the way he *likes*. Alienation by way of lease or mortgage is governed by statutory provision whilst alienation by way of gift requires no special procedure. But to alienate by way of outright sale the purchaser must be let into possession.

[10] See *Chukweke* v. *Nwankwo* (1985) 2 NLR 195, the court held that an individual has some rights over his land i.e. the right of absolute interest. This entitles him to use the land whether beneficial or wasteful, or even harmful; he can mortgage, lease, pledge, pawn or even dispose of it by outright sale or gift. Secondly, the individual has the right of reversion. This is obtained where the individual owner dies without any male child to inherit his land; the property will be inherited by the next of kin, a father or brothers. If no such exists, the kindred are entitled to the land. The ultimate reversionary right resides with the community who shall then re-allocate the land and lastly there is the right of way; right to pass over the land to another. This exists in respect to land for farming purposes not with residential purposes except with the consent of the owner.

Chapter 5

Family land ownership

Family land is land vested in a family as a corporate entity. In social parlance, the term family refers to a man his wife the individual member of the family therefore has no separate claim of ownership to any part or whole of it. A corollary to this is that a member has no dismissable interest in that property either during his lifetime or under his will.[1] This means that it is only the family that can transfer its title to any person. A purported transfer of family property by a member of the family is therefore void and of no effect.

In *Solomon & Ors* v. *Magaji*,[2] a family head sold family land as his own and on appeal, to the Supreme Court; it was held that the purported sale was void *ab initio* because he had no separate individual interest to transfer to the appellants. In *Ojoh* v. *Kanialu*,[3] the court held that the law is settled that where family property is conveyed as personal property, the purchaser gets no title to the property just as a member cannot dispose of family land by will.

What then is a family?

The term "Family" does not lend itself to easy and precise definition. In one sense, it may be defined as including all persons with common ancestors. Under this wide embrace, the family may accommodate a large body of persons related by blood to a common ancestor. The relationship may be traced through males as in the patrilineal societies or through females as in matrimonial societies. On a restrictive level, the term embraces a household; the man, his wife, the children and probably the dependants who are with him. But in English parlance, the term is restricted to the man, his wife and children.

---

[1] See Nelson D., "Real Property Management in Nigeria", *International Journal of Law and Contemporary Studies* Vol.3 No.1 & 2, Universal Consortia 2008 at p.83.

[2] (1982) 1 SC 1.

[3] (2006) 36 LRCN 1130. See also *Oyebanyi* v. *Okuwola* (1968) NMLR 221, *Fasehun* v. *Fadoju* (2000) 14 WRN 1 S.C.

But from the African perspective, family is a unit comprising the man, his wife or wives and the children. In social parlance, the term "family"[4] signifies a man, his wife or wives and his children though this may constitute the nuclear family. An extended family included a man's nuclear family and all his other relations, affinity and consanguinity.

A family under customary law consists of the children of the founder of the property that is to be held as family land. In *Adeseye* v. *Taiwo*,[5] the Federal Supreme Court held that the term family, for purposes of succession to land, means the children of the founder was are entitled to his property and will hold it as joint family property.[6] In *Nnezianya* v. *Okagbue*,[7] it was held that although widows are generally given living apartments, they cannot as a rule; inherit the deceased husband's land. In *Sareru* v. *Sunmonu*,[8] it was held that the brothers, sisters, cousins or uncles of the deceased founder of the family, do not constitute member of the family.

However, the deceased may by his own declaration, will to enlarge the family thereby including relations. In *Sobesan* v. *Adebiyi*;[9] the deceased founder of the family devised his property to include his heirs as family house. It was held that the will in its entirety chose that the testator intended the world 'family' to include his brothers and sisters and their descendants as well as his own children.

Among the Yoruba, the term family may connote any group from the smallest nuclear family of a man, his wife and children, to several thousands tracing descent from a common ancestor.[10]

In sum, the term family denotes a group of persons bound by blood who are entitled to inherit jointly either in accordance with customary

---

[4] Bryan A.G., *Black's Law Dictionary*, 7th ed. (London: West Group, 1999) at p. 621 sees the term as a group consisting of parents and their children, a group of persons connected by blood, by affinity or by law or a group of persons usually relatives.

[5] (1956) 1 F.S.C 2004.

[6] In *Coker* v. *Coker* (1938), the court stated that it seems well established that the primary meaning of the family is children. In *Richardo* v. *Abel* (1963) 1 All NLR 352, children are generally held to refer to both sexes. But in some societies, female children have been held not entitled to inherit the property of their late father. See *Lopez* v. *Lopez* (1924) 5 NLR 50. In similar vain, a widow is not a member of the family and therefore, has no right to inherit the real property of her deceased husband. See *Akinubi* v. *Akinubi* (1997) 1 SCNJ. But see *Mojekwu* v. *Mojekwu* (1997) 7 NWLR (pt.512) 288 and *Mojekwu* v. *Ejikeme* (2000) 5 NWLR 403, Uke v. Albert Iro (2001) 12 WRN, *Gladys Ada Ukeje* v. *Lois Ukeje & Enyinnaya Ukeje* (2001) 27 WRN 142. See generally Mowoe K.M., *Constitutional Law in Nigeria* (Lagos: Malthouse Press Ltd, 2008) at pp. 504-506.

[7] (1963) 1 All NLR 352.

[8] (1950) 2 FSC

[9] (1941) 10 NLR 26.

[10] See Oputa CJ in *Chinweze* v. *Mazi* (1989) 8 NWLR (pt.99) 254 and the case of *Kazeem* v. *Mosaku* (2007) All FWLR (pt. 359) 1272.

rules of succession or under a will or law which creates a family land ownership.[11]

Origin of family land

Family land ownership may originate by varied ways like by operation of the law, acts of the parties, first settler, conquest, purchase or by gift.

(a) By operation of law or acts of the parties.
This arises where a land owner subject to customary law dies intestate, his self acquired land devolves on his children by family land in accordance with the applicable customary law.

(b) Family land could originate where the family's own ancestors were first to settle on a virgin land and exercised acts of ownership over sufficient length of time numerous and positive enough to warrant inference of exclusive owner.[12]

(c) Conquest may be another way of originating family land. This ordinarily occurs where a family conquers a people; it may appropriate the land of the conquered.[13]

(d) Purchase. This often occurs where family uses funds to purchase or loan a land. In *Nelson* v. *Nelson*,[14] family funds was used to purchase land, the conveyance of which was executed in the favour

---

[11] In *Chinweze* v. *Mazi* (1987), the court gave a parameter of what constitutes a family under customary law.

[12] See *Umaru* v. *Pam* (2010) 2 NWLR. It could also arise by declaration under a will as a testator devised his land to his heirs jointly as family land.

[13] See *Ukaegbu* v. *Nwololo* (2009) 2 All FWLR wherein the plaintiff based his claim of ownership of the disputed land on traditional history and claimed he had been exercising acts of ownership thereon. He also claimed that his family was involved in a matter in respect of the land in the Native Courts in 1948 and the judgment was in their favour, but the defendants entered the land and felled timbers without their consent. The plaintiff therefore instituted an action in a representative capacity in the High court of Justice, Imo State, claiming a declaratory and injunctive reliefs; the land is his family property, injunction retraining the defendants from the land and damages for trespass. The defendants also laid claims of ownership to the land. The trial court dismissed the plaintiffs claim. Aggrieved, the plaintiff appealed to the Court of Appeal where a retrial was ordered. Also aggrieved, the defendants appealed to the Supreme Court. The Supreme Court in allowing the appeal held amongst others that where title is derived by grant, sale, consent or inheritance, etc. the pleading should aver facts relating to the founding of the land in dispute, the person or persons who founded the land and exercise original acts of possession. If the pleaded root of title is not established by evidence, it will be a futile exercise to go to the issue of possession or acts of ownership. In the instant case, the plaintiffs failed to establish their root of title. See also *Oko* v. *Okenwa* (2010) 2 NWLR. Whilst in *Idundun* v. *Okumagba* (1976) 9-10 S.C 227, the defendants who traced their title to the first person to settle on the land in dispute by traditional history was awarded title by the Supreme Court.

[14] See *Mwa* v. *Nwalusi* (1962) All NLR 681. Some writers have argued that the method is barbaric and anachronistic and may not stand the test of legitimacy in modern times.

of a member. It was held that notwithstanding the land was family land.

(e) Gift.[15]This occurs where a family is a donor of unconditional gift of land; this follows the rule that a donor of land under an unconditional gift to a donee cannot recall his title.

Rights of members over family land

Some identifiable members of the family such as the family head, principle members, junior members and other members of the family like the female members, would be considered as to the rights just as the primary purpose of family land is essentially to provide for the needs of the family.[16]

In the wise, members have some basic rights which include the right to be given an allotment for their occupation and use, to have a say in the management, the right of ingress and egress and the right to share in any surplus income.[17]

(a) Family head: right-cum-duties[18]

The position of the family head with respect to the performance of his duties has been likened to that of a trustee in the English sense. However, the strict trustee analogy to a family head as in the case of the chief of the community is misleading.[19] The English trust creates a dichotomy of ownership between legal and equitable ownership vesting in the trustee and beneficiaries, respectively. Family property does not admit of such dichotomy of ownership. The family head has no form of ownership of property vested in him, which he can validly give out as the trustee in the English sense.[20]

The Supreme Court referred to the family lead as a 'manager', in *Akano* v. *Ajuwon*,[21] it reaffirmed that description in the case of *Solomon & Ors.* v. *Mogaji*.[22]

---

[15] (1951) 13 A.C.A. 248.

[16] Nwabueze, op. cit.

[17] See *Thomas* v. *Thomas* (1932) 16 NLR 5, where the right of members of the family was clearly stated.

[18] See Nwabueze, *op. cit.*, at p.13. In *Ajobi* v. *Oloko* (1959) LLR 152, it was held that if a member is med his right of allotment the court will order partition and the land will be sold and the profit shared out.

[19] See Nelson, *op. cit.*, at p.84.

[20] Ibid.

[21] (1982) 11 SCI at 72.

[22] *Supra*

The family head has also been labelled as a representative, agent, caretaker and a fiduciary. Be that as it may, the application of the various analogies to family head in relation to the many of the family property can be explained in terms of a donee of power. As a manager, he has power to direct the affairs of family property. In this capacity, he bears a fiduciary relationship to family property. As such, he is a fiduciary like a judge and must act in good faith in his dealings with family property in the interest of the family. He must neither make secret profits nor take personal advantage.[23]

The Supreme Court in *Ohiaeri* v. *Yusuf*,[24] the facts of which were that the 1st and 2nd respondent, who were the plaintiffs in the High Court of Lagos State sued the appellant claiming various reliefs which included declaration, specific performance injunction and order for possession. The 1st and 2nd respondents also had an alternative claim of ₦150 million being damages for breach of an agreement for the assignment of the property in dispute known as plot 1164, Saka Tinubu Street, Victoria Island, Lagos. The 2nd plaintiff/2nd respondent entered into an agreement with the 1st defendant/3rd respondent in 1982 for the sale of the property in dispute at an agreed price of ₦850,000.00. In pursuance of the agreement, the respondent as purchaser paid to the 3rd respondent as vendor the sum of ₦48, 000.00 representing agreed part payment. In July, 1985, the same 3rd respondent in conjunction with her daughter the 14th respondent who is also the co-administratix of the property conveyed the same property to the 3rd defendant who is the appellant. Out of the 5 defendants sued only 3rd defendant/appellant entered appearance and filed a statement of defence to the action.

After the statement of claim and statement of defence had undergone several amendments, the matter proceeded to trial and thereafter judgment was delivered by the learned trial judge who allowed the plaintiff's respondent's claims and granted most of the reliefs claimed. Learned trial judge also awarded the sum of ₦3,500,000.00 to the plaintiffs/respondents for loss of use of the premise in dispute. The 3rd defendant/appellant's appeal to Court of Appeal was dismissed. The 3rd Defendant/Appellant further appealed to the Supreme Court. Unanimously dismissing the appeal, the Supreme Court held on the status of the validity of the sale of family property without the concurrence of the head of the family that: where the head of family disposes family property without the consent of other members of the

---

[23] *Foko* v. *Foko* (1965) NMLR.3.

[24] (2009) 2 M.J.S.C (pt.11). See also *Ejilemele* v. *Opara* (2003) 8 M.J.S.C.

family, it is still a valid sale and therefore only voidable at the instance of those other members of the family.[25]

Essentially, the headship of a family is determined by the native law and custom of a particular kindred.[26] In respect of this right over family land, he must consent to any alienation of family land. Any alienation without the family head is void. In *Awurui* v. *Iledu*,[27] the Court held that sales of family land can only be valid where there is agreement to sell between the family and the principle members of the family. A family head who sells family property without the consent of the principal members is voidable at the instance of the non-consenting members.[28]

It is the responsibility of the family head to manage and control family land and within his discretion to allocate portions of family land to deserving members of the family. He receives tributes in instances where the family has customary tenants on parts of family land.[29]

The family head is equally the proper person to initiate action in respect of any wrong done to the family's land but if the family head refuses to act, then any other member of the family can sue.[30]

No individual member or collection of members has the legal capacity to enter into contracts for and or on behalf of the family aside the family head. Gladly, when the head goes abusing his powers, the courts would intervene to stop him. In *Vincent* v. *Vincent*,[31] the Supreme Court held that the position of the family head to alienation of family land is very crucial, that he is not a figure head but one whose decision once made must be respected until set aside by another meeting or court of competent jurisdiction.

On ways of recognizing the family head, the court held that: A person can be recognized as a head of a family by three major ways: (a) by operation of law (b) by election by the members of the family and (c) by direct appointment by the founder of the family. He is in most cases the eldest child of each wife.[32]

---

[25] Ibid., at 190.

[26] See *Lewis* v. *Bankole* (1908) 1 NLR 81 where the court held that by Yoruba customs, when a founder dies, the person to be held is *Dawodu* or the eldest son. According to James in Land Law in Nigeria, (Ile-Ife: University Press, 1973), he posited that in some areas, the founder of a family head can be attained by election and yet in some areas, a titled man or the senior titled man who may not necessarily be the oldest male in the family becomes the head of the family. In Igbo culture, the first son is the *opale* or *orokpa*.

[27] (2008) 12 NWLR p. 249.

[28] See *Nzekwu* v. *Nzekwu* (1989) 1 NSCC 581 *Mneanegen gege* v. *Veronica Naide* (2008) 10 NWLR (pt. 988) at pp. 288-481, *Animashaun* v. *Onyekuluje* (2006) All FWLR (pt.340).

[29] See *Dashi & 3 Ors* v. *Sathong & Anor* (2009) 1-2 S.C. (pt.11).

[30] See *Okunbla* v. *Ojawa* (1958), *Emena* v. *Ewa* (1958) 5 NLR 25.

[31] (2008) 18 WRN p.181

[32] See *Lews* v. *Bankole* (1908) 1 NLR 82; See also *Ejilemele* v. *Opara* (2003) 8 M.J.S.C. at 2005.

(b) Principal members and family lands

A principal member basically is the head of a branch of a family. Family here refers to the kindred whilst branch refers to the small family or the nuclear family.[33] The consent of the principal members is required before an alienation of land is made. The consent of the principal members of the family is fundamental to family property.[34]

In *Akure* v. *Kadu*,[35] the appellant applied to set aside an alienation of family land to the respondent by a member of the family without the knowledge and consent of other members. The court held that, for a valid alienation of family land, consent of both the family head and principal members must be in accordance and that the proposed sale was subsequently set aside.

Similarly, in *Alabi* v. *Doherty*,[36]the plaintiffs/ appellants commenced this action against the defendant/appellant claiming possessory rights to the land in dispute setting aside the purposed sale of their land to the defendant/ appellant under Yoruba law and custom. The defendant who was a tenant of the property contended that the land was sold to him by Tiamiyi Ashaniu who was the head of the family.

The respondent's prayer for possession and mesne profits were granted. The Court of Appeal unanimously dismissing the appeal brought by the defendants/appellant held on the principle guiding transfer of title to family land under Yoruba land leave system that:

It is a common ground that title to a piece of land under the Yoruba land tenure system can truly be transferred to a purchaser *by the head of the head of the family and with the approval and consent of the principal members of the family*.[37] A sale by the family head without the consent of the other members of the family is voidable.[38]

(c) Junior members and family land

A junior member is a member of the family who is neither the head of the family nor a principal member. In ordinary parlance, he has no right only

---

[33] James, *op. cit.*, at p.84.
[34]Ibid.
[35] (2008) 12 NWLR (pt.1098) at p. 249.
[36] (2006) All FWLR (pt.299) 1527.
[37] Italics mine.
[38] *Supra.* See also *Animashaun* v. *Onyekwuluje* (2006). All FWLR (pt.340) p.1150 at 1153 where the head of the family granted a deed of lease in 1975 with dependent coupled with a secret lease deal. On discovery, the plaintiffs sued against the shady deal. It was held that under customary law, a transaction for the sale of family land requires consent of all the members of the family or substantial majority of them and such conyeyancing of sale is voidable at the instance of the non-consenting members of the family.

in the form of expectancy i.e. the right only accrues to him when he becomes a principal member.[39]

In *Ojoh* v. *Kamalu*,[40] the plaintiffs/appellants claimed against the defendants/appellants for trespass to their family land and injunction. The plaintiffs/respondents pleaded and gave traditional evidence of ownership of the land in dispute and the respondent claimed having obtained the land from a junior member of the family. Judgement was entered for the plaintiff/respondents on the ground that a junior member has no right to alienate family land. The court held that the appellant acquired no title from such transaction.

(d) Female members and family lands

Basically, the right of a woman over family land depends on her status in the family. If she is the widow of the founder of the family, she has the rights to reside on the family land until she dies provided she does not remarry. This is because customary law does not cover her by the term family so as to enable her acquiring rights and privileges equal to those of the children of the deceased founder.[41] In *Sanni* v. *Makinde*,[42] the Court of Appeal followed the case of *Adeseye* v. *Taiwo* and held that under Yoruba law, all the children whether male or female are entitled to inherit their parts land unless that is evidence to the contrary.

A female member has the right to reside with her husband on their family land but is not entitled to be consulted on management issues or disposition or alienation nor is she entitled to share in any money realized from the sale of the land. Where a marriage is contracted under the Marriage Act,[43] there is no restriction as to the application of the English Will Act.[44] As regards customary law, if a marriage is contracted subject to customary law, the devolution of the deceased land would be subject to the customary law.

---

[39] In *Eyin* v. *Gondiner* (1953) 14 WACA, the West African Court of Appeal held that it is a well established principle of native law and custom that junior members of the family cannot call on the head of the family for an account.

[40] (2006) All FWLR (pt.227) pp.978-982.

[41] In *Nnezianya* v. *Okeagbue*(supra)the court held that although widows are normally given living apartment, they could not as a rule inherent their husbands land, they can stay and enjoy the land because of the interest of the children. In *Chinweze* v. *Magi* (*supra*), it was held that the interest of a wife in the property of her deceased husband is that of a life interest she still cultivates all the husbands' personal or individual land.

[42] (1994) (pt. 348 NWLR 314.

[43] Cap. E LFN, 2004.

[44](1837)

In Yoruba customary law system, a widow typically has no right of inheritance. So also among the Igbo.[45] But modern judicial activism seems to water down the concept of non-inheritance of female members to property of their deceased husbands as been discriminatory on ground of sex.[46]

In *Emeke Mojekwu* v. *Okechukwu Ejikeme*,[47] the Court of Appeal considered the *Oli-Ekpe* custom that enabled a man to perform certain rites and keep one of his daughters unmarried to raise male issues. In this case, the deceased died intestate after performing the rites on one of his

---

[45] In *Akinnubi* (1959) 2 FSC, the Supreme Court stated that it is well settled rule of native law and custom of the Yoruba customary law that a widow under an intestacy is regarded as part of the estate of her deceased husband to be administered or inherited by the deceased family, she could neither be entitled to apply for a grant of letters of administration nor appointed as co-administrators of her deceased husband's estate. In the instance case, there is no dispute over the type of marriage, which was solemnized between the first respondent and her deceased husband. It was a marriage under the Yoruba native law and custom. Rufus Gbadebo Akinnubi died intestate in Lagos. Hence there could be no and there are no dispute over the provisions of the Yoruba native law and custom that a widow could not inherit her deceased husband's property nor could a woman be appointed an administrator of her husband's estate. In *Eze* v. *Okwo* (1959) unreported (Oboko District Court suit 8/59 & Nsukka Customary Court of Appeal suit No.C/531/59), the District Court gave judgment for the plaintiff on the ground that a wife cannot in customary law lay claim to her late husband's land chattels and cannot administer the estate. The court further said that a male relative of the deceased has a right to expel the widow from her late husband's compound if she committed such a breach of custom as would have entitled her husband to divorce her and that by laying claim to the property in disobedience to her late husband's oral instruction that she could be expelled from her husband's compound by the nearest male descendant of the deceased. The case was appealed against. On appeal, the Appeal Court upheld that judgment of the trial court but merely reversed the expulsion order on the ground that the conduct alleged was not serious enough to warrant expulsion.

[46] In *Augustine Nwafor Mojekwu* v. *Caroline Mgbafor Mojekwu* (1997) 7 NWLR (pt.512) 288, the crux of dispute was a property acquired by Kola tenancy by the deceased Mojekwu who was survived by his wife and two daughters. The only son of the late brother now seeks to acquire that property and exercise such rights as the owner of the property against the widow and surviving children of the deceased. He claimed that according to the Nnewi custom, the first son of the late brother in the absence of any male child by the deceased and no surviving brother is entitled to the deceased property. The court questioned whether such a custom was consistent with equity and fair play in an egalitarian society such as ours where the civilized sociology does not discriminate against women? Day after day, month after month and year after year, we hear and read about customs which discriminate against the women folk in this country, they are regarded as inferior to men folk. Why should it be so? All human beings – male and female are born into a free world and are expected to participate freely without any inhibition on grounds of sex apart from being unconstitutional is antithesis to society built in the tenants of democracy which we have freely chosen as a people. We need not travel all the way to Beijing to know that some of our customs including the Nnewi-*Oli-Ekpe* custom relied upon by the appellant are not consistent with our civilized world in which we live today including the appellant. In my humble view, it is the monopoly of God to determine the sex of a child and not the parent. Although scientific world disagrees with the divine truth. I believe that God the creator of human beings is also the final authority of who should be male and female. Accordingly, for a custom or custom of law to discriminate against a particular sex is to say the least an affront on the Almighty God himself, let nobody do such a thing. On my part there no difficulty in holding that the Nnewi Oli-Ekpe custom of Nnewi is repugnant to natural justice and equity and good conscience.

[47] (2000) 5 NWLR 403.

daughters who also died without an issue. The deceased grandchildren in his other daughters sought to inherit his property and were challenged by a distant male cousin. The trial court held in favour of the distant cousin. The Court of Appeal reversed the decision and condemned the custom as inimical and discriminatory practices prescribed in the name of custom. The court noted that the custom was not only unconstitutional; it was contrary to international human rights standards contained in CEDAW.[48]

Some explanatory terms/distinctions as regards family land ownership

(a) Stool land

Stool land in other words is called chieftaincy land, quite often is referred to as royal land is land attached to the office of the head i.e. the emirs, kings, or obis. Stool law is vested in the ruler as a corporate sole.[49] The chief has full control of stool land where a chief does or is disposed; stool land passes to the successor. Stool and does not pass on the family or to the chiefs natural descendants. So the chief enjoys stool land for as long as he remains in the title and allotment is not as of right.[50]

(b) Emergency situations

The pre-eminence of emergency situations as regards family matters under customary land law cannot be overemphasized. Nonetheless, there seems to be no definition of emergency situations where the worth of the family head predominantly comes to play. But it has been argued that borrowing money to pay medical bills for a critically sick member of the family and paying off family debts by pledging family property have all been viewed as emergency situations.[51]

---

[48] See *Uke* v. *Iro* (*supra*) and *Ukeje* v. *Ukeje* (*supra*). In *Uke* v. *Iro* (2001) 17 WRN, it involved a custom which prevented women from giving evidence in relation to issues of title to land which the Court of Appeal also condemned.

[49] Idrisu, *op. cit.*, at p.27.

[50] In *Quarm* v. *Yankah* (1930) 1 WACA 80, the court held that the concept of the stool, that is and has always been accepted in the courts of this country is that it is an entity which never dies a corporate sole like the crown and that while the occupants of the stool may come and go, the stool goes on forever and in *Oyekan* v. *Adele* (1952) 14 WACA 204, the court posited that from this it may be deduced that land vested in the ruler as such is not vested in him in his office.

[51] In *Blowgun* v. *Blowgun* (1935) 12 WACA 290, a case which positioned the import of a family head in Yoruba Custom Principles governing the position of the family head do not differ materially in other parts of the country. The head of the family is in charge and control of a family property. He has to make disbursements out of the family revenue for the family purposes, upkeep of the family

(c) Routine matters

Routine matters can be said to be necessary matters relating to the management and allocation of land. It was argued that monies used for financing family litigation, rebuilding the family house, acquiring chieftaincy title allocate for the family head to enhance prestige can be said to be routine matters.[52]

---

property; funeral, marriage, baptism and ceremonial expenses of members of the family often the entire members, litigation on behalf of the family, education of the children and so on.

[52] In *Foko* v. *Foko* (1965) NMLR 3, the head of the family sold 3 landed properties belonging to the family constituting of 16 branches with the consent of only one branch. The non-consenting members sued to set aside the sale. It was argued that the money was used for (a) financing family litigation (b) rebuilding the family house (c) acquiring a chieftaincy title for the head, which title would enhance the prestige of the Foko family. Items a & b were said not to be routine but c was for personal aggrandizement.

Chapter 6

Alienation under customary law

Alienation of land under customary law in the twenty-first century is not without its attendant challenges. Alienation of family land is not shielded from these ground-shaking challenges. The *Oxford Advanced Learner's Dictionary*, defines land as the solid dry part of the earth's surface.[1]

Alienation according to the *Black's Law Dictionary* is the conveyance or transfer of property to another. It has also been defined as the power of an owner of a property to voluntarily transfer or dispose his interest in the property.[2]

In the olden days, land was inalienable. According to Elias, "land was believed to be the property of the original settler and thus belongs to the past, the present and the future generation to come." He stated further that there is perhaps no other principle more fundamental to indigenous land tenure system throughout Nigeria than the theory of inalienability of land. In the same vein, Coker observed that strict orthodox native law and custom does not recognize sale of land;[3] but following the Supreme Court's decision in *Agblo* v. *Sappor* and which was recently upheld in the case of *Awure* v. *Iledu*,[4] the court recognized the alienability of land and family land in particular.

Family land is land owned by a particular family. A family for this purpose consists of father, his wife or wives and his children. In *Adesanji* v. *Taiwo*, the Supreme Court held that the term family means the children of the founder who are entitled to his property and will hold same as a joint family property. This view has also been expressed in *Usiobaifo* v. *Usiobaifo*.[5] It could also mean the children of the founder of the property i.e. to be held as family property. Therefore, family land refers to a land own by children of a deceased owner.

---

[1] *Oxford Advanced Learner's Dictionary*, 6th edition, 2000, p.662.
[2] Bryan A Garner, *Black's Law Dictionary*, 8th edition, 2004 p.637.
[3] Olong, Lecture Notes, 2008.
[4] (2008) 12 NWLR (pt.1098).
[5] (2005) 2 NWLR (pt.913).

The family appoints the family head who holds the land in trust for the family. He does not own the land. Thus, he cannot alienate it as his own land. This principle has recently been expressed in the case of *Usiobaifo* v. *Usiobaifo*[6] where the court held that though the family land is put in care of the appellant, as the eldest son, he does not become the owner and neither can he alienate same as his own land nor as family property without the concurrence of other members of the family.

The decision in the above case has also been expressed in the latter decision of the court in *Mozie* v. *Mbamalu*[7] where the court held that family land is no one man's property and that a sale of it by a member of the family without the consent of other members of the family will amount to a wrongful alienation. In similar vein, the court held in the case of *Awure* v. *Iledu*,[8] that family land is not owned by the family head and he cannot alienate family land as his own land. Where he does so, such alienation is void at the instance of the principal member.

Acquisition of family land and its relevance to alienation

The mode of acquisition of family land sometimes makes it unfavourable for alienation. Family land can be acquired by purchase, by inheritance, conquest, by grant or by operation of law. Where family inherits a land through their ancestors, it is expected of them to give same to their children so that perpetual ownership will remain in the family, for instance in the celebrated case of *Usiobaifo* v. *Usiobaifo*,[9] family land was given to the children of the deceased by their deceased father. The PW3 testified that the family land was given to the first defendant in joint ownership with his brothers who will be living there according to their seniority in age and that the land was not to be sold. The first respondent gave evidence to the effect that the property in dispute was given to him as his own and thus sold the land without the consent of other members of the family. The court held that the sale was void since the land was not

---

[6] *Supra*

[7] (2006) 15 NWLR 1003.In *Kopek Construction Ltd* v. *Ekisola* (2010) All FWLR (Pt.519) P1025, the court held as to the poser whether one witness is enough in transaction relating to land under native law and custom that a sale of land witnessed by only one witness but having taken other elements of native law and custom into consideration will create an equitable interest in the land which can be converted into legal estate by specific performance. Cf also section 179(1) of the Evidence Act, 2004.

[8] *Supra*

[9] *Supra*

to be sold, as a joint family land. But that if it will be sold at all, the consent of the entire family members must be obtained.

Alienation of family land

It is now a trite law that where there is concurrence between family head and all principal members of the family, family land can be sold. This is the decision of the court in the case of *Awure* v. *Iledu.*[10] The decision was also arrived at by the court in the case of *Animashaun* v. *Onyekwuluje.*[11] In *Farajoye* v. *Hassan,*[12] the court held that upon sale or alienation of family property, all the rights and interest in the said property, reverts or becomes vested in the new owner or the title holder.

Requirement for a valid alienation of family land

There is catalogue decision of the court which is to the effect that certain requirement must be met for alienation of family land to be valid.

The first requirement for the sale of family land has been settled in the case of *Awure* v. *Iledu,* where the court held, *inter alia,* that sale of family land can only be valid when there is concurrence between family head and all principal members of the family. To this effect, the court held that family land can only be sold by the family head or Morgaji with the concurrence of principal members of the family.[13] This is because family land is no one man's property. Thus, the principle in the maxim *nemo dat quod non habet* applies. It is to the effect that one cannot transfer a better title than he has.

Another requirement stated by the court is that the person selling must act in a representative capacity rather in personal capacity. This principle has been rightly expressed in the case of *Ojo* v. *Kamalu.*[14] In this case, a junior member of the respondent granted lease to the plaintiff as personal property. It was held that the purchaser gets no title to the property. This was also upheld in the more recent decision of the Supreme Court in the case of *Vincent* v. *Vincent.*[15] In this case, the court held that the family head is not just a figure head, he is therefore suppose to act in a representative capacity. His decision once made must be

---

[10] (2008) 18 WRN 187.
[11] (2006) 340 All FWLR (pt.1152).
[12] (2006) 16 NWLR (pt.1006).
[13] (2008) 12 NWLR (pt.1098).
[14] (2006) All FWLR (pt.294).
[15] (2008) 18 WRN 187.

respected until overturned by a popular vote at another meeting or court of competent jurisdiction. Thus, in *Animashaun* v. *Onyekwuluje*,[16] the court held that under Yoruba customary law, transaction for sale or conveyance of family land requires consent of all members of the family or substantial majority of them. Such a sale is voidable at the instance of those members f the family who did not consent.

However, the court held that the non-consenting member must act timeously to set aside the lease. But that time does not begin to run until the non-consenting member acquire necessary knowledge of the sale.[17]

The third requirement is seen in the case of *Adedeji* v. *Oloso,*[18] where the court held that the transaction needs to be concluded in the presence of witnesses who witnessed the actual handing over of the property. The principle expressed here has also been upheld in the case of Equenewu[19] where the court held that the transaction must be witnessed by witnesses.

Another requirement for a valid alienation of family land is expressed in *Adedeji* v. *Oloso* where the court held that the purchaser must be let into possession.[20] This principle also has been expressed in the case of Equenewu.[21]

In addition to the principle stated above, the court further held in Equenewu that there must be payment of money or agreed consideration for a sale for a valid alienation to take place.[22] This view was also expressed in the case of *Commissioner L & H Kwara State* v. *Atanda*[23]. In *Ogundalu* v. *Macjob*, where the appellant had not paid in full the purchase price, the court held that there was no sale of land in dispute to him under native law and custom. The court held that where the purchase price of the land is not fully paid, there can be no valid sale notwithstanding that the purchaser is in possession.

In *Commissioner L & H Kwara State* v. *Atanda*, the court held that agreement in writing is unknown to valid sale under customary law and that valid sale comes without it.[24] Similarly, in *Etajata* v. *Ologbo*, the court held that written agreement or registered conveyances are not necessary to affect a valid sale under customary law.[25]

---

[16] *Supra.*
[17] Ibid.
[18] (2007) All FNWLR (pt.356).
[19] (2007) 16 NWLR (pt.1031).
[20] Ibid.
[21] Ibid.
[22] *Supra.*
[23] (2007) 2 NWLR (pt.1018).
[24] Ibid.
[25] (2007) 30 NSCQR.

Void and voidable alienation

In the case of *Usiobaifo* v. *Usiobaifo*,[26] the court held that where a sale is void, it has to be so declared if asked to be set aside but where it is voidable, whether or not it will be set aside will depend upon the facts and circumstances of the case. The court commenting on the twenty-first century alienation, in the instant case, held that, where the principal members of a family sell family land without the concurrence of other members of the family, the sale is voidable. The court also held that where there's a sale or conveyance of family land by the head of the family with some important members but without the consent of the principal members of the family, then, the transaction is voidable.[27]

In *Amodu* v. *Daniel*,[28] the court held that where the father sells his compound in which his children are living, such sale is voidable at the instance of the children. If he wishes to sell same, he must notify them. But that the children should remember they cannot inherit it whilst their father was still alive. In *Usiobaifo* v. *Usiobaifo*,[29] the court held that where a head of the family sells family land without the consent of the principal members of the family, the sale is voidable. The Supreme Court making a distinction between its decision in 1959 in the case of *Ekpendu* v. *Erika* where it held that where a head of the family sells family land without the consent of the principal members of the family, the sale is voidable but in *Adejumo* v. *Ayantegbe*, the Supreme Court extended the legal frontiers that where a head of family sells family land as his own, the sale is void.[30]

Alienation of land is void on the other hand where the family head sells family land as his. This decision has been upheld by the Supreme Court in the case of *Usiobaifo* v. *Usiobaifo*.[31] The Supreme Court held that a sale is void where principal member of a family sells family land as his own. Thus, in the present case, the court held that unimpeachable title can only be transferred by a family to another person or family where the family heads does so with the consent and concurrence of the principal members of the family.[32] The court held that neither the head of the family alone, nor the principal member alone can make any valid

---

[26] *Supra.*
[27] Ibid.
[28] (2005) 2 NWLR (pt.909).
[29] *Supra.*
[30] Ibid.
[31] Ibid.
[32] *Supra.*

alienation or give title to any person with respect to family land.[33] It also held that a head of family not acting as such cannot convey valid title in respect of family land.[34]

Family land can be recovered when it is wrongfully alienated. This principle is richly imbedded in the maxim *ubi jus, ebi remedium* which is to the effect that where there is a wrong, there is a remedy. Thus, in the classical case of *Usiobaifo* v. *Usiobaifo*,[35] the court held that family land is recoverable where the sale is voidable.

On who can sue to recover family land, the court held in *Mozie* v. *Mbamalu*[36] that a member of a family has capacity to sue to protect family property. Indeed, any member of the family whose interest is threatened by the wrongful alienation or wrongful interference with the family property can sue to protect his interest whether with the consent or without the consent of the other members of the family for if he does not act, he may find himself being held to be standing by when his rights were being taken away.[37]

In *Animashaun* v. *Onyekuluje*,[38] the court held that, the non-consenting members of the family to the sale must act timeously to set aside the lease. Where they have waited for 10,20,35 years before acting to set aside the lease, they have delayed but time does not begin to run until the non-consenting members have acquired necessary knowledge of the sale.

An *Encyclopedia of Nigerian Law and Practice*, commenting on the above view, states that the rights of generation yet unborn can be sold and the proceeds squandered; family land can lose its character of family land and come to be land which is owned absolutely by an individual.[39]

Similarly, in *Unity Bank* v. *Bouari*,[40] the Supreme Court held that a member of the family can sue to protect or defend the interest of any property. The court further held that if the member has not the authority of the family, to bring the action, the family would or will of course be bound by the result unless that it is/was estopped from denying that the action was binding.[41]

---

[33] Ibid.
[34] Ibid.
[35] Ibid.
[36] (2006) 15 NWLR (pt.1003).
[37] Ibid.
[38] *Supra.*
[39] *An Ancyclopedia of Nigeria Law & Practice, Sasegbon's Law of Nigeria,* 1st ed. 2005 p.102.
[40] (2008) 33 (pt.2) NSCQR.
[41] Ibid.

When alienation is carried out either through lease, sale, pledge or gift, right and interest in the land becomes vested in the new owner. In *Fayoroye* v. *Hassan*, the court held that upon sale or alienation of landed property, all the rights and interests in the said property revert or become vested in the new owner or in the title holder.

Lease

This is another medium of alienation of land. Here, landed property is given out to an individual on acceptance of consideration.

The landed property is given out on payment of an agreed amount but for a specified period after which the right on the land revert back to the lessor. The lease can be by monetary consideration or otherwise. In *Okoro* v. *Nwachukwu*,[42] a pledge is defined as either a sum of money or something valuable that one person leaves with another person to prove that the former will do something or pay back money that is owed. After the payment of such money, the right reverts back to the rightful owner. The court recognizes lease as a means of alienation.

Gift

This is another method in which alienation of family land can be carried out. Where a family or a donor decides to give out or donate a portion of the family land as an unconditional gift, alienation is considered to be validly done. In such circumstance, he cannot revolt his title. However, the family head must obtain the consent of the principal members of the family to do this. A family member cannot give out family land as a gift. This principle has been expressed in the case of *Orunengimo* v. *Egebe*.[43]

Alienation of family land in the 21st century Nigeria, if in accordance with customary law, it requires that it must enjoy the consent of the family as a whole which has now been taken to mean the consent of the head of the family and the principal members. Where there is a deviation from this path, a calamity is caused.

Family land is generally inherited by the surviving children of the deceased founder to the exclusion of all others not related.

Generally, in Nigeria, family land under the customary law can be alienated principally in four ways as follows:

1. by sale;
2. by gift;
3. by loan; and
4. by pledge.

---

[42] (2007) 4 NWLR (pt.1024).
[43] (2007) 5 NWLR (pt.1058).

It must be noted that alienation in this context has two main characteristics, thus:

(a) Alienation which destroys the nature of the family property;
(b) Alienation which temporarily suspends the rights of the family from the property so that, within the period, the family cannot exercise the usual rights vested on them.

An example of this right is loan and pledge. The cardinal principle of family property is that, the property should be held jointly by the members of the family and none of them has the right or power to alienate family property on his own or at his own will or for his own interest without the consent of the other members having been sought and obtained.[44]

The poser is who are the proper persons to act for the family when disposing its land?

Basically, it is noted that there are three consents required; the consent of the head of the family, the consent of the principal members and the consent of other numbers of the family.

These consents for the purpose of alienation of family land would be emphasized in my subsequent discussion.

Alienation by Sale

To Niki Tobi, sale as a form of alienation denotes an outright purchase of land for money from the grantor by the grantee.[45]

It is the transfer of right of a property in consideration for a sum of money. In *Dateme* v. *Duke*,[46] the court held that a sale or transaction of a parcel of land under customary law is, in law, validly concluded in the following ways:

(i) When payment of purchase price had been made coupled with the actual delivery of the property;
(ii) There is concurrence of the vendor and the buyer;
(iii) The property is handed over in the presence of the witnesses under sale.

The consent required here for family land by way of sale under customary law is that of the head of the family and the principal members. The headship of a family is usually determined by the native law and custom of particular kindred or area for instance in *Lewis* v. *Bankole*, the court note that, by Yoruba customs, when a founder dies, the person to the head is "Dawodu" i.e. the eldest son. While in the Igbo

---

[44] See M.A. Egute, *op. cit.*, at pt.76.
[45] See Niki Tobi, *op. cit.*, at p.54.
[46] (2006) All FWLR (pt.313), 159.

custom, such head known as Opala or Orakpa who is the oldest son. Professor James informed us that, in some areas, the founder of a family head can be attained by election, and yet in some areas, a titled man or a senior titled man who may not necessarily be the oldest male in the family becomes the head of the family.

It is the duty and responsibility of the head of the family to consent to any alienation of the family land. It follows that any alienation without the consent of the family head is only purported and therefore void.

It also within his discretion to allocate portion of family land to its member or stranger when the need arises. In *Vincent* v. *Vincent*,[47] the Supreme Court held that, the position of family head to alienation of family land is very crucial. That he is not figure head but one whose decision once made must be respected until set aside at another meeting or court at competent jurisdiction.

On no ground would the family head claim the ownership of family land or property. In *Usiobaifo* v. *Usiobaifo*,[48] the respondents are of the same family and father with the first appellant. Their father died intestate in 1954. First appellant (elder brother) claimed that, having performed burial rites of their late father, he was exclusively entitled to the ownership of the family land in accordance with their custom. He sold the property to the second appellant without notice to the respondents. Respondents then sued appellant declaration that, first appellant had no right to sell family property and that, the sale was null and void and of no effect whatsoever. The alienation was held to be avoided by the respondents.

The Supreme Court in this case laid down rules or principles governing alienation of family land as follows:

a) Neither the head of the family alone nor the principal members alone can make any valid alienation or grant title to any person with respect to family land.
b) A family head not acting as such cannot convey valid title in respect of the family land.
c) Unimpeachable title can only be transferred from one community to another where the head of the family does so with the consent and concurrence of the principal members of the family or community.
d) The sale of the land by a member who is not the head is void.

---

[47] (2008) 18 WRN, p. 181.
[48] (2005) 3 NWLR (pt. 913) pp.665-669.

e) The sale of the family land by the head of the family without the consent of the principal members is voidable.

Family land can also be alienated through sale with both the concurrence of consent of the family head and the principal members of the same family. A principal member generally is the head of a branch of a family, most especially the large family.

The principal member is used for the purpose of alienation. While branch of family which principal member represents is referred to the small family or nuclear family. It is also used to refer to the division of the kindred for the purpose of consent to alienation, presentation and sharing of the family resources. Thus, a principal member represents his own branch and sharing of action is proposed which requires the consent of the various branches.

It is noted that, where there is no head of the family, alienation by the principal members of their family is valid. The consent of the principal members is fatal or fundamental to alienation of family property. In *Akure* v. *Kedu*,[49] the appellants appealed to set aside an alienation of family land to the respondent by a member of the family can unilaterally family land without the knowledge and consent of other members. The court held that, for a valid alienation of family land, consent of both the family head and principal members must be in accordance; and that, the purported sale was consequently set aside.

Similarly, in *Alabi* v. *Doherty*[50] the plaintiffs/appellants commenced this action against the dependant/appellant claiming possessory rights to the land in dispute, setting aside the purported sale of their land to the defendant/appellant under Yoruba law and custom. The defendant who was a tenant of the property contended that, the land was sold to him by Tiamiyi Ashamu who was the head of the family, in 1778.

The respondents' prayer for possession and mesne profits were granted. The Court of Appeal unanimously dismissing the appeal brought by the defendants/appellant held on the principle guiding transfer of title to family land under Yoruba land tenure system that:

> It is a common ground that title to a piece of land under the Yoruba land tenure system can only be transferred to a purchaser by the head of the land owning family and with the approval and consent of the principal members of the family. A sale by the family head without the consent of the other members of the family is voidable.

---

[49] See (2008) 12 NWLR (pt.1098), p. 249.
[50] See (2006) All FWLR (pt. 299) 1527.

Where a family land is disposed of by the family head or any other members, an account should be made clear to the rest members of the family. In *Etajata* v. *Ologbo*,[51] the plaintiffs/respondents were alleged to have sold portion of the family land without giving account of the sale to the family. The plaintiffs/respondents claimed inter alia, a declaration that, the appellants were holding the proceeds of the sale of the family land in trust for the family, an account of the proceed of the sale to be made to the family and injunction restraining them from further sale of the land without the consent of other members of the family. The relief sought by the plaintiffs/respondents was granted by the court.

Alienation with the consent of other members of the family is not very necessary. A valid alienation of family land or property may be done and the support of law be obtained or not the consent of other members of the family is obtained.

It is clear that, the consent of other members of the family is necessary for the alienation of family property. But, however, if the consent cannot be obtained for good reason, alienation of family property (land) may be valid.

Other members here could be referred to junior members in this context. A junior member is neither a member of the family who is neither the head nor the principal member. It has only rights in the form of expectancy. That is the rights accruable to him only when he becomes a principal member. A junior member cannot alienate a family land.[52] Thus, in *Ojoh* v. *Kamalu*,[53] the plaintiffs/appellants claimed against the defendants/appellants damages for trespass to their family land an injunction. The plaintiffs/respondents pleaded and gave traditional evidence of ownership of the land in dispute, and the respondent claimed having obtained the land from a junior member of the family, and judgement was entered for the plaintiffs/respondents on the ground that a junior member has no right to alienate family land. The court held that, the appellant acquired no title from such transaction.

Validity of sale of family land under customary law

What comes to fore in this case is instances where such alienation of family land made through sale is void and/or voidable. A sale is void when it is declared a nullity by a court and not only bad but incurably

[51] (2007) All FWLR (pt.586) at p.587.

[52] See Egwute, *op. cit.*, at p. 79.

[53] (2006) All FWLR (pt. 227) p.978-982.

bad. But if a transaction is voidable has some life on its own and remains good unitl set aside by the court.

In *Ogundali* v. *Maijob*, on whether sale of land without full payment of price under native law and custom – that when price is not fully paid as in this case, there can be no valid sale.

The sale of the family land without the consent of the principal member of the family is voidable. So also the sale of the family land by a member who is not the head of the family is void. This is the holding in *Ojoh* v. *Kamale*.[54]

The case of *Animashaun* v. *Onyekwuluje*[55] supports the rule of consent of principal members of a family before alienation can be made. Without this consent, any alienation is voidable. In this case, the head of family had granted a deed of lease in 1975 to the defendant coupled with a secret lease deal. On discovery, the plaintiffs sued against the shady deal, it was held that, under the customary law, a transaction for the sale of family land requires consent of all the members of the family or substantial majority of them and that such conveyance or sale is violated at the instance of the non-consenting members of the family.

The requirement of a valid sale under customary law is that, they must be required consents, payment of money and actual handing of the property (land) in the present of witnesses.

Alienation by pledge

According to Elias, pledge (or pawn, as it is sometimes inaptly called) is a kind of indigenous mortgage by which the owner-occupier of land, in order to secure an advance of money or money's worth gives possession and the use of land to the pledge creditor until the debt is fully discharged.[56]

A pledge of land arises between the person called pledger and the other party called pledge and arising from the transaction, radical title in the land resides in the pledge who only has only temporary occupation license or possession.

The pledge provides the pledge (creditor) with security for a loan made to the pledger who is the debtor and the security takes the form of giving pledge possession of the property (land) and enjoyment of profit therefrom by the creditor until the loan is repaid.

Under the customary or indigenous system, however the pledge creditor obtain possession of the land from very inception of the deal and

---

54 *Supra.*
55 (2006) All FWLR (pt.340) p.1150 at 1153.
56 See Elias, *op. cit.*, at p.153.

also enjoys the usufruct of the land for long as it is considered necessary to give his equivalent credit. The pledge may be restricted to the usufructuary enjoyment of the only trees or crops planted on land by him since taking possession of it or he may be permitted to exercise all the powers of an owner-occupier.

If he plants permanent or economic trees like kola, palm, or cocoa trees on the pledged land, he is usually not allowed any compensation or improvement when it comes for him to vacate the land on payment of the debt or satisfaction of the credit by the pledge's exploitation of the land.[57]

The consents of both the family head and the principal members in this way of alienation of the family land is very crucial to the extent that, if such concurrent consent is not available, such alienation is voidable at the instance of non-consenting members. This pledge can be orally made, today however, they are often reduced in writing.

Another fundamental point in this transaction is that the pledge is not entitled to any interest on the loan because of what he gets from the use of the pledged land are in lieu of interest. However, in the modern pledges, interest is sometimes charged.

Alienation by gifts

This is an out-and-out transfer by the grantor, having enough land to spare to the grantee or grantees who usually enjoy perpetuity or tenure.[58] The procedure of making the grant is by no means uniform in all details throughout the country, but the general outline is tame under the customary law as follows: The Chief or the family head as the case may be, will either go in person, or delegate someone else on his behalf to go, with the intended grantee in sight of the paired of the land to the extent of which is roughly demarcated sometimes placing a mound of earth at each of the four corners and sometimes by planting trees in the same positions as evidence of the boundary. Then Kolas are split, gourd of wines are drunk and other viands taken in celebration of the occasion to which those present are expected to witness in any future dispute, since the customary law is unwritten.

The extent of the rights thus acquired by a grantee of the land win doubtless vary according as the land is cultivated or uncultivated, farmland or according to the kind of husbandry practiced in any particularly locality. But, the conditions attaching gifts of family land

---

[57] Ibid.

[58] Ibid at p. 149.

must depend on what has been agreed between the parties and the relevant customary rules.

We have noted Dr. Nabel's observation that, in Nupe land, palm trees are usually held by Chiefs and other family heads to whom rights to the trees may be transferred. The important thing here is that before alienation of family property be made valid, consent of the family members must be sought. Therefore, with the consent of the whole family land could be and was given outright to strangers as well as group members in need of land.

According to *Black's Law Dictionary*, loan is act of lending a grant of thing for temporary use. A thing for the borrower's temporary use especially a sum of money lent for interest.[59]

In the case of alienation of family land through loan, the same said land may be used to secure for a loan collected by the head of the family for the interest of the whole family. The consent of the principal members must be given along with the family head for a valid lease or contract of loan for such alienation. In *Unity Bank* v. *Bouari*,[60] a member of the family entered a lease where he used family land to secure loan, and the other members of the family sued to set aside the agreement on ground of lack of consent.

Where family property is portioned; the property belongs exclusively to the member as it is no more in the family melting pot. As owners of the partiones portion, they have acquired all the incidents of ownership in the sense that they can do anything they like with the property. The owners of the portioned property are not subject to the rights of another person. Because they are the owners, they have the full and final right of alienation or disposition without seeking the consent of another person because as a matter of law and fact, there is no other party's right over the portioned property that is higher than theirs. They have inalienable right to sell the property at any price, even at a give away price. The can even give it out *gratis*, that is, for no consideration.[61]

The Supreme Court held that under customary land law, a court will not order an injunction against a member of a family with respect to family land which has not been portioned.[62] This principle, however, is subject to exceptions depending on the facts in each case.

---

[59] See Brary, *op. cit.*
[60] (2008) 22 NSCQ 1292.
[61] See *Akayepe* v. *Akayepe* (2009) 11 NWLR, p. 224
[62] *Supra* at 222.

Chapter 7

Customary tenancy

Nature of customary tenancy[1]

The term "customary tenancy" represents tenancy, which is rooted in, and is peculiar to native law and custom. It has no equivalent in English law.[2] It is neither a leasehold interest nor a tenancy at will, or a yearly tenancy. The main incidents of such tenure are the payment of annual tributes, not rents by the customary tenant to the overlord.[3] In essence, the customary tenant is not a lessee or borrower; he is a grantee of land under customary tenure and holds such a determinable interest in the land which may be enjoyed in perpetuity, subject to good behaviour on the part of the tenant. He enjoys something akin to *employteusis* a perpetual right in the land of another.[4] A customary tenancy does not amount to an estate in land like a lease under English law, because whereas estates in land under English laws are generally, unconditional and freely alienable. The right of a customary tenant is limited occupancy during good behaviour;[5] secondly, the rights do no include the power to alienate without the consent of the family who granted the tenancy. A customary tenure is therefore no more than a right to occupy a land belonging to another person.[6]

The genesis of this form of tenancy can be traced to the early days of Nigeria's history when it was not uncommon for strangers to come into a

---

[1] See Ehi Oshio P., "Customary Tenancy under the Land Use Act: Alternative Dispute Resolution of the judicial Dilemma," *Modern Practice Journal of Finace and Investment law*, Vol.10 Nos.1-2 2006 at p. 240. See also Idrisu J., *Understanding Nigerian land Law*, 2nd Edition (Zaria: ABU Press Ltd 2008) at p. 46.

[2] Ehi, *op. cit.*, at p. 240.

[3] See *Dashi & 3 Ors* v. *Satlong & Anor* (2009) 1-2 SC (pt.11) and *Nwokorobia* v. *Nwogu* (2009) Vol.271 LRCN.

[4] Ehi, *op. cit.*, at p. 249. See the cases of *Chief Etim* v. *Chief Eke* (1941) 14 NLR 43, *Josiah Agbenghen & Others* v. *Maduku Wagboregbor and Others* (1974) 1 S.C. 1, *Mohammed Ojomu* v. *Salawu Ajao* (1983) & *D.S.C, Bassey & Others* v. *Chief Eteta* (1938) 4 WACA 153.

[5] Idrisu, *op. cit.*, at p.46.

[6] Ibid.

community and buy land either for farming or for settlement or for both. When such land was granted to the strangers by the community, Nigerian customary law would presume a conditional grant.[7]

The principles governing such grants as enunciated by various judicial authorities are now well established. For instance, the land must be used for the purpose for which it was granted and for no other.[8] The tenant is under an obligation to pay yearly tribute to the grantor as an acknowledgement of the latter's overlordship.[9] Neither the tenant nor the overlord can alienate the land without the consent of the other. The grant is usually presumed for an indefinite period subject to good behaviour on the part of the customary tenant.[10] The interest secured by the tenant is one of inheritance[11] and the land cannot revert to the overlord except upon proven misbehaviour on the part of the customary tenant, or on the rare case of the extinction of the tenant and his family.[12]

Ehi,[13] opines that the only real weapon in the hands of the overlord for dealing with the tenant after the grant is his power to forfeit the tenancy. To constitute a ground for forfeiture, the action of the customary tenant must be wrongful, substantial and must relate to the use of the land subject of the tenancy. He,[14] identified grounds for forfeiture which included abandonment, denial of the overlords title to the alienation or attempted alienation of the land without the consent of the overlord, putting the land to uses other than those originally agreed upon, withholding customary dues persistently, wanton waste and lack of effective user. Forfeiture however is not automatic and misbehaviour merely makes the tenant liable to forfeiture at the will of the overlord which nowadays if resisted can only be enforced by reference to the courts.[15]

Defining customary tenancy

Defining customary tenancy like any other term cannot be totally satisfactory. According to Onwuanmaegbu,[16] the term refers to:

---

[7] Ehi, *op. cit.*, at p. 240.
[8] See *Ukwa & Ors* v. *Awa Local Govt. & Others* (1966) N.M.L.
[9] See *Dashi & Others* v. *Satlong* (*supra*).
[10] Ehi, *op. cit.*, at p.250.
[11] See *Oshodi* v. *Dakolo* (1930) A.C. 667; and *Ovie* v. *Onoviobokire* (1957) W.R.N.L.R. 169
[12] Ehi, *op. cit.*, at p.250.
[13] Ibid.
[14] Ibid.
[15] Ibid.
[16] Onwuamaegbu, *Nigerian Law of Landlord and Tenant* (Enugu:)at p. 32.

> The relationship of landlord and tenant which arises where a person who has a right to possession of land, grants (or is deemed to have granted) this right to another who is not legally entitled to use the land, the grant not being incidental to any other existing relationship between the parties, but for a specified period or a purpose which only be definite or general with intention that the use of the land shall revert to the grantor at the end of the period or when the purpose has been fulfilled.

No other definition of the term seems to have battered that of the Supreme Court in the case of *Dashi & 3 Ors* v. *Satcong & Anor*,[17] the facts of which was that it was a case of farmland dispute between the parties which began to the Upper Area Court Pankshin in Pankshin Local Government Area of Plateau State. The appellants who were the plaintiffs at the trial court sued the respondents and claimed declaration of title to a piece of farmland at miler-minting in chip district, an order of perpetual injunction restraining the respondents from further interfering with the farmland in dispute. The respondents as defendants denied the appellants claims against them. The matter went on trial in the course of which the parties called their witnesses to prove their respective cases. The appellant lost at the trial Upper Area Court and their appeal to the Customary Court of Appeal of Plateau State was also dismissed. Dissatisfied with the judgment of the Customary Court of Appeal, appellant's further appealed to the Court of Appeal Jos against it, was also dismissed. Still not satisfied with the overcome of their appeal the appellants further appealed to the Supreme Court. The Supreme Court in unanimously dismissing the appeal held that:

> A customary tenancy involves the transfer of an interest in land from the customary landlord or overlord to the customary tenant and which interest entitles the customary tenant to exclusive possession of the land and which interest, subject to good behaviour he holds in perpetuity. Unless it is otherwise excluded, the main feature of a customary tenancy is the payment of tributes by the customary tenant to the overlord. The status of his exclusive possession is such that it is enforceable against the world at large including even the customary landlord or those claiming through him.[18]

---

17 (2009), *supra.*

18 Ibid., in *Mitini Nyavwaro & Ors* v. *Babiya Ogegede* (1971) NSCC 200 at 211, the court said as per Fatayi-Williams JSC (as he then was) that:

> ...a customary tenant can be in possession and is usually in possession of the land, which he occupies as such tenant: Furthermore, he can institute proceedings against any person (including all or any of the members of the family or community who are his overlords)

The most important or significant insignia of a customary tenancy is the payment of tributes by the customary tenant to the overlord.

Terms associated with customary tenancy

Possession of land

A customary tenant can be in possession and is usually in possession of the land which he occupies as such tenant. He can institute proceedings against any person (including all or any of the members of the family or community who are his overlords) who commits any act of trespass on his land.[19] A tenancy may be granted not only by the owner but by any one who has a right to possession who grants part of such right to another. Where possession or use of land had not been granted, the relationship of landlord and tenant cannot exist.[20]

Not legally entitled to the use of the land[21]

The grantor must not be under any legal duty to grant nor the grantee be entitled to the grant of land as prior right apart from the agreement for tenancy which makes it obligatory that the grantor should give the land to the tenant.[22]

Reversion to the grantor[23]

Upon determination of the tenancy, there must be reversion to the grantor. If there is an agreement excluding right of reversion then tenancy cannot be said to exist.[24] The land cannot revert to the landlord except upon proven misbehaviour to the part of the customary tenant or on the rare case of extinction to the tenant and his[25] family.

---

who commits any act of trespass on his land. See also, *Bianko* v. *Ogwuile* (2000) 4 S.C. (pt.1) 96 (2001) 12 NWLR (pt.726) 235 and *Okulate* v. *Awosanya* (2000) 1 S.C. 107.

[19] See *Dashi & 3 Ors* v. *Satlong & Anor* (*supra*).

[20] Idrisu, *op. cit.*, at p.47.

[21] Ibid.

[22] Ibid. It cannot be regarded as tenancy where the grantor pledges his land for debt owned to the grantor. Cf. Idrisu, ibid. at p.47.

[23] Ibid.

[24] Ibid.

[25] See *Summonu* v. *Disu Raphael* (1927) A.C.

How customary tenancy can be created

Customary tenancy does not require any mode to be created that it does not need to be in writing. It requires the handing over of the land in the presence of witnesses and the grantee must have known the purpose of the grant to the grantor when the grant is being made.[26] So there has to be intention and agreement of the parties involved.

Classes of customary tenancy

According to Idrisu, two criteria have been generally used to classify customary tenancies. These are (a) according to length of the term granted; (b) according to the nature of the conservation given.[27]

Length of term granted

Under this head, there are (a) periodic tenancy and (ii) indefinite long-term tenancy.

Periodic tenancy is the type that repeats itself from one period to another as long as the tenancy continues the overlord and the grant will agree *abinitio* that the grant is for a short definite period. It usually pertains to growing seasonal crops and the tenancy will come to an end upon the harvest of the crop.[28]

Indefinite long term tenancy is of an uncertain duration and is usually granted for the life time of a tenancy usually meant for residential or agricultural purposes. Here no specific period is often set out as it goes up as long as the parties wish, often forever.

According to consideration

The most significant insignia of a customary tenancy is the payment of tributes by the customary tenant to the overlord.[29] But rents too pay an important role as it arises where essentially there is an agreement between the parties who will negotiate the form and the amount of rent to be paid usually in cash. On the overlord, tribute serves a dual purpose of acknowledgement of the grantors title and as an economic return on the

---

[26] Idrisu, *op. cit.*, at p.47.
[27] Ibid.
[28] Ibid.
[29] See *Dashi & 3 Ors* v. *Satlong & Anor* (*supra*).

land of the grantor. Tribute simply consists of kola, drinks or farm produce.[30]

Where there is a customary tenancy by consideration, the following types of tenancies exist:

Service tenancy

It consists of labour service in consideration of the grant made to the customary tenant usually removed on the landlord's farm.

Share tenancy

The landlord stipulates a proportionate share of the produce grown on the land granted to the customary tenant.

Gratuitous tenancy

It arises in situations where the grantee pays no rent, no service, but it exists because both the grantor and the grantee are on friendly terms. However, there may occasional gifts or performances of services by the grantee to the grantor.[31]

Cash tenancy

The increasing economic value of land necessitates cash zoning. The amount of cash or rent to be paid depends on the negotiation and agreement between the parties.[32]

Kola tenancy

The idea of kola tenancy can be found in Edo, Delta and some parts of Igbo land in Eastern Nigeria. Where a grant of kola tenancy is made, the grantee is expected to make annual acknowledgement of the grantors title by a formal gift of kolanuts, drinks, goats, and some measure of farm produce.[33]

Obligation of the overlord

The overlord during the pendency of the tenancy is obliged to perform certain duties and they are:

---

[30] Idrisu, *op. cit.*, at p. 49.
[31] Ibid.
[32] Ibid.
[33] Ibid.

(i) Power to make the grant

Customary law equally respects the principle of *nemo dat quid non habet.* An overlord can only dispose what he has authority to so dispose. The land which he disposes must either have been his private property. If it turns out that the grantor had no power to dispose, the customary tenant will be entitled to compensation for any loss suffered as a result of invalidity of grant.[34]

(ii) Obligation not to derogate from the grant[35]

An act that adversely affects the grantee's interest may be seem as a derogation from the grant. Worse still, where an overlord grants possession to another person who then disturbs the possession of the customary tenant.[36]

(iii) Obligation that the customary tenant should have quiet possession[37]

Quite possession entitles that the customary tenant would enjoy the status of exclusive possession such that it is enforceable against the world at large including even the customary landlord or those claiming through him.[38]

Rights of the overlord[39]

The rights of the overlord during the pendency of the customary tenancy include (a) right of reversion, (b) right to demand for tribute; (c) right of forfeiture.

---

[34] Ibid.

[35] Ibid at p.51.

[36] In *Etim* v. *Eke* (1941) 15 NLR 43, the plaintiffs occupied certain land in Calabar as a customary tenant of the defendants. The plaintiff shared the right to cut palm trees with the defendant. Later, the grantors, granted to some one else the right to enter upon and cut palm nuts from the land. The third party did not only cut palm nuts but also removed cassava, palm nuts including those planted by the plaintiffs. The plaintiffs were successfully in getting an injunction against the defendants land their agents not to interfere with their possession and use of the land granted.

[37] Idrisu, op. cit., at p.51.

[38] See *Dashi & 3 Ors* v. *Satlong & Anor* (*supra*). In *Chikere* v. *Okegbe* (2000) FWLR (pt. 22) 1005 it was held that possession is an incident of customary tenancy. Until the tenancy is lawfully determined, the landlord has no right to enter the land without the tenant's permission unless it was agreed that the landlord should have a right to re-enter. Any unfaithful entry is actionable as trespass. If the entry causes actual damage to the crops planted by the tenant, the tenant may sue for substantial damages caused by the entry, but may only get nominal damages. The tenant may also sue for an injunction to restrain any further trespass to crops planted.

[39] Idrisu, *op. cit.*, at p.32.

(a) Right of reversion entails that at the end or expiration of the tenancy, the landlord has the right to demand for his land back.
(b) Right to demand for tribute: As an insignia of customary tenancy, an overlord has the right to demand for tribute as failure on the overlord's part could be a ground for the customary tenant to use as a shield based on the principles of laches and acquiescence.[40]
(c) Rights to forfeiture

An overlord has the right to forfeiture if the customary tenant misbehaves. Instances of misbehaviour may include burglary, adultery, insolence or turbulence towards the head or chief of the community. But such cases could be punished by fine instead of forfeiture.[41] Thus to constitute a ground for forfeiture, the action of the customary tenant must be wrongful, substantial and must relate to the use of the land. They include abandonment,[42] denial of the overlord's title,[43] alienation or attempted alienation,[44] of the land without the consent of the overlord, putting the land to uses other than those consequently agreed upon,[45] withholding customary dues persistently,[46] wanton waste and lack of effective user.[47]

Duties of the customary tenant

The onerous duty of the customary tenant makes it imperative that he serves the following: (1) obligation not to deny the overlord's title (2) not to alienate without the overlord's consent (3) not to use the land for a different purpose and (4) to pay customary[48] tribute or rent.

Obligation not to deny the overlord's title

A denial of title occurs where the tenant asserts that somebody else other than the overlord is the owner.[49]

---

40 See *Chukwu* v. *Amadi* (2009) All FWLR at 1193.
41 See *Inasa* v. *Oshodi* (1930) 10 NLR
42 See *Bailie* v. *Offong* (1923) 5 N.L.R. 29.
43 See *Sam Taiwo & Others* v. *Adamo, Akinwunmi & Others* (1975) 1 All NLR 41, 2002.
44 *Eyembee* v. *Holmes* (1924) 5 N.L.R. 85
45 *Chief Onyia & Others* v. *Louis Onia & Others* (1985) 3 NWLR
46 Ehi, *op. cit.*, at p.250.
47 See *Lawani* v. *Tadeyo* (1944) 10 W.A.C.A.
48 Idrisu, *op. cit.*, at pp. 52-54.
49 In *Bogay* v. *Macaulay* (1932) 1 WACA 225, the court held that where a customary tenant has denied his landlord's title and claimed that the land belongs to him, he is liable to forfeit his tenancy and be ejected. See also *Okata* v. *Falolu* (1949) 14 WACA 32, there the tenant not only

Not to alienate without overlord's consent

An alienation or attempted alienation by way of assignment, subletting or mortgaging is a breach of the tenants obligation, except where an agreement so provides for detinue without the overlord's permission.[50]

Not to use the land for a different purpose

A customary tenancy would normally exist for a specific purpose of either residential or farm. A tenant who converts one purpose to another would be liable for trespass.[51]

d. Obligation to pay customary tribute

Default in the payment tribute been an insignia of customary tenancy would result to forfeiture.[52]

How customary tenancy can be determined[53]

Essentially therefore, customary tenancy will come to an end in any of the following ways; by accomplishment of purpose, abandonment, notice to

---

denied the landlord's title but also caused a public notice warning the public against having dealings with the landlord. The court held that it was sufficient to warrant forfeiture.

[50] See *Akunne* v. *Ekwuno* (1952) 14 WACA 59, where it was established in accordance with the Prevailing custom in the area that customary tenant were entitled to place sub-tenants and palm wine tappers on the land without the permission of the overlord. It was held that the tenant did not commit trespass in putting palm wine tappers on the land.

[51] See *Chief Onyia and Others* v. *Louis Orilah and others* (1985) 3 NWLR (pt.II).

[52] In *William Momodu* v. *Ojemah & Ors* (1981) the defendants refused to pay rents thereby denying the landlord's title. It was held that the defendants had forfeited their rights. See also Elias T.O., *op. cit.* at p.141.

[53] Idrisu, *op. cit.*, at p. 54, asserted that customary tenancy will come to an end in any of the following circumstances, forfeiture, accomplishment, abandonment, notice to quit and surrender, Olawoye C.O. *Title to land in Nigeria* (Ibadan: Evans Brothers Ltd, 1982) at pp.100-101 expressly provided that the rights of a customary tenant and others enjoying permanent occupational rights in land may be extinguished in any of the following ways; by forfeiture upon misconduct, abandonment and extinction of issues. See cases like *Aman* v. *Bin* (1947) 12 WACA, *Baillie* v. *Offong* (1923) 5 NLR 20, *Ezeilo* v. *Obi* (1960) EWLR 19, *Akande* v. *Akorede* (1971), *Owume* v. *Iyany* (1931) 10 NLR 111, *Ogbakumanwu* v. *Chiabolo* (1950) WLR 507 *Oreso* v. *Jinadu* (1988) LLR 77, *Lawani* v. *Tadeyo* (1944) WACA 37, *Oloto* v. *Dawuda* (1940) 1. NLR 58, *Elefu & Others* v. *Omojewonniya & Others* (1962) 2 All NLR 13, *Dashi & 3 Ors* v. *Satlong & Anor* (2009) 1-2 S.C. (pt.11), (2009) 1-2 MJSC Vol.1&2 and *Nwokowobia* v. *Nwogu* (2009) Vol.172 LRCN. Read further Egwummuo J.W., *Principles & Practice of land law*, 2nd ed (Enugu: Onye ventures Production, 2007) at pp. 352-360 where in sum, he reiterated that customary tenancy may be determined in any of the following four ways; (i) when the tenant denies the title of the landlord and asserts his own title or the title of the third party; (ii) when the tenant abandons his holding; (iii) when the holding falls into ruin either by natural causes or through neglect of the tenant (iv) where the tenant dies without a successor.

quit, merger, surrender, forfeiture and extinction of ownership by adverse possession.

Accomplishment of purpose

The land must be used for the purpose of which it was granted and for no other.[54] Where its purpose is accomplished, as for instance a customary tenancy for farming purpose, would terminate at the end of the harvest having harvested the crops. It should be borne in mind that unless the tenancy is reviewed else the tenant would quit the land.[55]

Abandonment

Idrisu,[56] sees abandonment as the voluntary relinquishment of land by the customary tenant without intending to transfer title to any particular person or does nothing to show an intention of continual occupation. Mere absence of possession is not sufficient to constitute abandonment. The intention to relinquish must be accompanied by some overt act or failure to act which carries the implication that the tenant neither claims nor retains any interest.[57] In *Dim* v. *Enemou*,[58] the Supreme Court stated that abandonment is a matter of intention and can be shown either by proving facts from which to draw such intention or by inference which is not the case here or by direct and explicit evidence of the party concerned, there is again no direct nor explicit act of abandoning the land in dispute here by the defendant and his kinsmen themselves. In the instant case, there was no proved fact to enable one to draw such inference. In fact, on the contrary, the cause of action in this case as per the plaintiff's claim is borne out of the presence of the defendant and his kinsmen on the land in dispute, in spite of the alleged abandonment and moving out of the said land. The plaintiff's pleadings and evidence here have shown that the defendant and his kinsmen have continued to farm and reap economic trees on the land in dispute without leave of the plaintiff; these are clearly acts inconsistent with plaintiff's claim of defendants and his kinsmen having abandoned the land in dispute. The defendant and his kinsmen as can be seen have not done so.[59]

---

[54] See Ehi, *op. cit.*, at p.350. In *Iraogbara* v. *Ufomadu,* (2009) 1 NWLR at 390, the Supreme Court held that where there is no evidence of customary tenancy between two parties so the question of forfeiture does not arise.

[55] Idrisu, *op. cit.*, at p. 55.

[56] Ibid.

[57] Ibid.

[58] (2009) M.J.S.C. (pt.1) at 158.

[59] In *Benjamin Ezeilo & Ors* v. *Sam Obi & Anor* (1960) iv ENLR 19, the Roman Catholic Mission were granted a customary tenancy of a plot of land in which they built a church and a new school,

Olawoye[60] stated that where land has been granted for a specified purpose, the right of occupation of the land subsists so long as the land is used for that purpose. Use of the land for any other purpose will be construed as abandonment notwithstanding that the grantee is still in possession.[61] This point was illustrated by the decision of the Supreme Court in *Ukwa & Ors* v. *Awka Local Council & Ors*,[62] a land in dispute was granted in 1939 by the plaintiffs to the people of Awka for a central market called Eke Odemigbo. The site of Eke Odemigbo market was not popular with sections of Awka and, as a result another site was established there in 1949. In 1952, the Awka Local Council began to administer the area of Eke Odemigbo, made grants of portions of it and collected rents from the grantees. It was held that as the land had being abandoned as a market, the plaintiffs were entitled to resume possession of it.

Notice to quit[63]

In situations where a customary tenancy can be ended by a notice to quit, the notice should be reasonable. Notices given in between period may not be acceptable. The customary tenant may himself give the overlord a sufficient notice of his intention to so quit.

In the absence of such a stipulation, the land prescribes various lengths of notices from the weekly tenant to the yearly tenant,[64] and these are:

(i) In the case of a tenant at will or a weekly tenant, a week notice;
(ii) A monthly tenant a monthly notice;
(iii) Quarterly tenancy, a quarter's notice; and
(iv) In the case of a yearly tenancy, half a year's notice.

---

later they were granted a new site on which they built a new church and a new school. They discontinued the use of the old site for eight years. The grantors then re-granted the site by the CMS who immediately pulled down the remnant of the RCM's buildings and began to build up their own church. It was held that they were liable for trespass. There has been no abandonment by the RCM since there was no intention to abandon the site. There was evidence that throughout those eight years they had been using the land as a burial ground and had been collecting money in order to develop it. See also *Baillie* v. *Offong* (1923) 5 NLR 29.

60 Olawoye, *op. cit.*, at p.109.

61 Ibid.

62 (1966) NMLR 41. A sale by the Customary tenant amounts to abandonment, see Nwebueze, *op. cit.*, at p.262.

63 Idrisu, *op. cit.*, at p. 55 argues that notice to a quit applies essentially to indefinite tenancies which were not intended to be of perpetual direction. Therefore tenancies for a specified period or indefinite tenancy of perpetual duration cannot be determined by notice to quit.

64 See Section 8(3) Abuja Section 14(2) Lagos Section 8(1) Recovery of Premises Edict 1994, the Plateau State Rent Control & Recovery of Premises Law, 1998 and the case of *International Polymera Systems Ltd* v. *Glover* (2002) 7 NWLR (pt.765) 124.

A notice to quit may be given at anytime before the date of expiration of the current term of tenancy but such notice shall not be effective if the time between the giving of the notice and the time when the tenancy is to be determined is less than those respectively set out in the various recovery laws.[65]

Merger

A merger ordinarily occurs where a tenancy becomes vested in the present customary tenant by the reversion immediately expectant on the term. When it happens, the tenancy ceases to exist and is merged in the reversion by mostly an outright sale of the land to the customary tenant thereby extinguishing the relationship of customary tenant/overlord.

Forfeiture[66]

Ehi[67] asserted that the only real weapon in the hands of the overlord for dealing with the customary tenant after the grant is his power to forfeit the tenancy. To constitute a ground for forfeiture, the action of the customary tenant must be wrongful, substantial and must relate to the use of the land subject to the tenancy. Forfeiture however, is not automatic, and misbehaviour merely makes the customary tenant liable to forfeiture at the will of the overlord which nowadays, if resisted can only be enforced by reference to the courts.[68] The Nigerian courts have often been willing to grant relief against forfeiture, such as fine, except in cases where refusal to grant forfeiture would tend to defect the ends of justice. Whether or not forfeiture will be ordered by the court will be on the seriousness and or repetitive nature of the acts of misbehaviour complained of.[69]

Olawoye[70] feels that the principle of customary law in Nigeria is that a customary grantee of land is only entitled to occupy the land during his good behaviour, unless the grant is intended to be absolute. Forfeiture thereby is the loss of land by the customary tenant as a result of a breach of customary obligations occasioned by the customary tenant.

---

[65] See *NCNC* v. *Oyewole* (1998) 7 NWLR (pt.565) at p. 340.

[66] Idrisu, *op. cit.*, at p.57 See forfeiture as the loss of land occupational or possessory right, by the customary tenant to his overlord as a result of some breach of tenancy obligations. Forfeiture remains the commonest way in which customary tenancy would come to an end.

[67] Ehi, *op. cit.*, at pp. 250-251.

[68] Ibid., at 251.

[69] Ibid.

[70] Olawoye, *op. cit.*, at pp. 100-101.

Surrender[71]

According to Idrisu,[72] a tenancy may come to an end by giving up the term to the immediate reversion i.e. by giving back the land to the overlord. Accordingly in customary law, it occurs when the customary tenant performs an act inconsistent with the continuance of the tenancy.[73] Consent of the overlord is essential to effect a surrender, it is so because if the consent is not given, the customary tenants purported surrender will amount to abandonment of the land in question.

Extinction of ownership by adverse possession[74]

According to Olawoye,[75] adverse possession is one that is inconsistent with that of the owner, i.e., one that is not derived from the owner. A customary tenant cannot be said to be in adverse possession even if he remains in possession without paying rent or tribute. But where the customary tenant transfers the land to a purchaser absolutely enabling the purchaser to go into occupation of the land, his possession will be adverse to the overlord, since the customary tenant has no right to transfer. So also a void disposition of the land would give rise to adverse possession, reason being that the sale being void, the possession of the purchaser is logically inconsistent of the transaction. For an adverse possession to bar the right of the overlord, it must be open and unconcealed. It is immaterial that the squatter is aware of the true state of the title to the land.[76]

Forfeiture re-defined

Idrisu asserts that the real basis of the misconduct or misbehaviour which renders the tenancy liable to forfeiture is the challenge to the title of the overlord.[77] Thus, denial of an overlord's title is one of the gravest breaches that a customary tenant can commit. Native law gives the owner

---

[71] See Idrisu, *op. cit..,* at p.56.
[72] Ibid.
[73] Ibid. For instance, where the grantee denies possession of the land before the accomplishing of the purpose and the overlord accepts possession of it with the consent of the customary tenant, the overlord grants the whole of the land to a third party.
[74] See Olawoye *op. cit.* at pp.111-112.
[75] Ibid.
[76] See *Ado* v. *Wusu* (1940) 6, WACA and *Dania* v. *Soyemu* (1937) 13 NLR 143.
[77] Idrisu, *op. cit.*, at p.57. See also the Supreme Court's decision in *Bamgbegbin* v. *Oriare* (2009) 13 NWLR at 375-376.

of the land the right to recover possession against a tenant who wrongfully claims ownership.

Olawoye[78] opines that the real foundation of the misbehaviour which involves forfeiture is the challenge of the overlord's title which may take one of the following forms;(i) refusal to pay rent or tribute or to render the customary services stipulated (ii) denial of the overlord's titled.[79]
The overlord does not have the right to enforce forfeiture immediately even though the tenant misbehaved. The overlord must as of necessity seek the assistance of the courts for a declaration of forfeiture before he can resume possession, meaning that forfeiture is not automatic. Again forfeiture has to be specifically pleaded.[80] In *Dashi & 3 Ors* v. *Satlong & Anor*,[81] there was a case of a farmland dispute between the parties which began at the Upper Area Court, Pankshin in Pankshin Local Government Area of Plateau State. The Appellants who were the plaintiffs at the trial court sued the defendants and claimed declaration of title to a piece of farmland at Miler-Minting in Chip District an order of forfeiture and order of perpetual injunction restraining the respondents from further interfering with the farmland in dispute. The matter went on trial in the course of which the parties called their witnesses to prove their respective cases. The appellants lost at the trial Upper Area Court and their appeal to the Customary Court of Appeal of Plateau State was also dismissed. Dissatisfied with the judgment of the Customary Court of Appeal, Jos against it was also dismissed. Still not satisfied with the outcome of their appeal the appellants further appealed to the Supreme Court raising five issues for determination of the appeal all of which were clearly hinged on the question of proof of title to the farmland in dispute between the parties. One of the issues was whether the appellants proved that the respondents were customary tenants in respect of the land in dispute and

---

[78] Olawoye, *op. cit.*, at pp.100-101.

[79] See *Oloto* v. *Dawoda* (*supra*), *Ashogbon* v. *Odutan* (1935) 12 NLR, *Onisiwo* v. *Bamigboye* (1947) 7 WACA 69.

[80] In *Ogbakumanwu* v. *Chabolo* (1950) NLR 507, the plaintiffs granted a customary tenancy to the defendants. The plaintiffs claimed damages for trespass on the ground that in 1944, the defendant had denied their title by claiming ownership of the land in an action of declaration of title instituted by the defendants. Plaintiffs claimed that the defendant had forfeited his tenancy rights by bringing the 1944 action. The present action was instituted in 1949. The court held that it would be inequitable in the circumstances to order forfeiture. It further held that even on the assumption that the institution of the suit in 1944 would involve the defendant in forfeiture as the landlords, have not asked him to quit, the defendants was not a trespasser. In *Coker* v. *Jinadu* (1958) LLR 77, where the tenants refused to quit in response to a quit notice from the owners, they would still not be guilty of trespass unless and until a declaration of forfeiture had been made by the court.

[81] (2009) 1.2 S.C. (pt.11)

are therefore entitled to an order of forfeiture? Unanimously dismissing the appeal the Supreme Court held that:

> A customary tenancy involves the transfer of an interest in land form the customary landlord or one show to the customary tenant and which interest entitles the customary tenant to exclusive possession of the land and which interest, subject to good behaviour, he holds in perpetuity. Unless it is otherwise excluded, the main feature of a customary tenancy is the payment of tributes by the customary tenant of the overlord. And the state of his exclusive possession is such that it is enforceable against the world at large inclusive even of the customary landlord or those claiming through him.

Forfeiture can be enforced vide forceful re-entry and action for recovery of possession. In *Irase* v. *Oshodi*,[82] it was held that where the customary tenant or family member to whom family land has been allotted for occupation alienates his to a stranger he has by implication set up a claim of ownership, as it is clear that it was the owner of the land, who can make a valid grant of it to another. Here the grantors families forcibly exit their tenants without first obtaining a court order, the grantor applied that they were justified in forfeiting the tenancy such the tenants had purported to sell the land. The Privy Council accepted that the grantor is legally entitled to re-entry using reasonable force.

But action for recovery of possession is the safest method of enforcing forfeiture. Idrisu[83] argues that the overlord should bring an action in court and should not attempt to forcibly eject his tenant. A landlord should not wave or condone any breach of the interest to succeed in his case.[84]

---

[82] (1934) AC 94
[83] Idrisu, *op. cit.*, at p.59.
[84] Ibid.

Chapter 8

Pledge

Definitional clarification

Pledge as a practice is common in many parts of West Africa and most regions in Nigeria especially in the eastern part of the country, where people have no other means of wealth but their land. Invariably, therefore, the sale of land is often forbidden by native custom, rendering pledge to the only means of raising money. A pledge is an indigenous institution developed by the customary law of Africa. Idrisu[1] sees it as a kind of traditional mortgage by which the owner-occupier of the land in order to secure an advance of money's worth gives possession and use of the land to the pledge creditor until the debt is fully discharged.

Onwuamaegbu[2] describes the term as an indigenous mortgage and by it an owner of land grants possession and use of such land to a person known as a pledge creditor or pledgee in order to secure the payment of an advance of money or money's worth made by the pledge to the borrower known as a pledgor. To Olawoye,[3] a pledge can at best be said to be:

> When an owner of land transfers possession of his land to his creditor as security or rather, in consideration of a loan in order to obtain the maximum benefit as consideration for making the loan.

Accordingly, therefore, Tobi,[4] see the term as sometimes been referred to as pawn in general parlance and asserted further that before a loan secured with land can qualify as a pledge, the land in question must be in possession of the pledgee.

The *Black's Law Dictionary* defines the term as a bailment, pawn or deposit of personal property to a creditor as security for some debt or

---

[1] Idrisu J., *Understanding Nigerian Land Law* (Zaria: ABU Press Ltd, 2008) at p.63. See also Elias T.O., *Nigerian Land Law* (London: Sweet & Maxwell) at pp.153-154.

[2] Onwuamaegbu M.O., *Nigerian Law of Landlord & Tenants* (Enugu) at p.30.

[3] Okwoye C.O., *Title to Land in Nigeria* (Ibadan: Evans Brothers Ltd, 1974) at p.49

[4] Niki T., *Cases and Materials on Nigerian Land Law* (Lagos: Mabrochi Bros,1997) at p.64.

obligation.[5] *Osborn's Law Dictionary*[6] defines the term as the transfer of the possession (but not ownership) of a chattel as security for the payment of a debt or performance of an obligation.

Essentials of a pledge

The term pledge could be impliedly used as meaning a pawn which invariably is the same as a promise, vow, an agreement, undertaking, security or guarantee.[7]

Essentially, therefore, under a pledge, the debtor and pledgor makes physical or constructive transfer of the property to the creditor as security until the debt is paid, such that possession remains with the pledgee but legal ownership remains with the pledgor, meaning that the security for the property takes the form of giving the pledgee possession of the land and enjoyment until the loan is repaid.[8]

---

[5] Bryan A.G., *Blacks Law Dictionary* 7th Ed. (London: St. Paul Minn. 1999) at p.1175.

[6] Sheila B., *Osborn's Concise Law Dictionary*, 5th edition (London: Sweet & Maxwell, 2001) at p.289. Robinson M,. *Chambers 21st Century Dictionary* (India: Willed Chambers Ltd, 2004) at p.1066 defined a pledge as something left as a security with someone to whom one owes money, etc. Nich S, *The Nigerian Law Dictionary* 1st ed. (Zaria: Tameda Publishing Co. Ltd, 1996) at p.251 defined pledge as the transfer of the possession of a chattel s security for the payment of debt or performance of an obligation, on default, the chattel may be sold. Layi A; *Law & Practice of Banking* (Ibadan: Heinemann Educational Books Plc, 1999) at pp.216-717. See pledge as a situation where the debtor and the pledgor make physical or constructive transfer of his property to his creditor (the pledgee) as security until the debt is paid such that possession remains with the pledgee but legal ownership remains with the pledgor. He further stated that pledge was for a long time a most popular form of security but its application is diminishing rapidly nowadays and it is almost resorted to import finance to the extent that an average branch banker rarely comes across it. Pledge has been given different names in different societies but the main ingredient that the pledged has always been a common factor. It was known as '*iwota*' in Yoruba '*olu*' in Igbo and *jinginsin kuru* in Hausa, pledge was the only form of security in borrowing arrangement among the populace generally in Nigeria until the wide adoption of the British system of mortgage, the British author and jurist tagged it as Native Mortgage.

[7] See *Ahmameku* v. *Ihetiva* (1995) 2 NWLR (pt.350) at 758.

[8] Lord Ezle observed in the case of *R.* v. *Smith* (1885) that the practice of pledge is very common amongst the various communities in West Africa especially the Eastern part of Nigeria since the majority of them are farmers the only way of meeting with some of their pressing needs is by pledging their land. In *Mbubu* v. *Obari* (2003) FWLR (pt.150) the court said that a pledge of land arises between the person called the pledgor and the other party called the pledgee. Arising from the transaction radical title to or in the land resides in the pledgor. The pledgee has only temporary occupation licence or possession. See *Onobruchere* v. *Elegine* (1986) 1 NWLR (pt.19) 799 wherein the plaintiffs claimed, *inter alia*, a declaration of title to a piece of land. it was not disputed that they were the original owners. Whilst they pledge the land under customary law to the defendants, the latter pleaded that the land was said to them and not pledged. It was held that in customary law the pledgor retains the radical title which is not extinguished by the pledge. The pledgor has the right of redemption and it does not matter for how long the land has been pledged. Once a pledge, always a pledge.

A remarkable essential of a pledge is the transfer of possession on conclusion of the bargain.[9] In *Halliday* v. *Holgate*,[10] the court stated that there are three kinds of security: the first a simple lien, the second a mortgage passing the property out and the third a security intermediate between a lien and a mortgage - that is, a pledge whereby contract of deposit of goods is made security for a debt, and the right to the property vests in the pledgee so far as is necessary to secure the debt. It is true that the pledgor has such property in the article pledged as he can convey to a third person, but he has no right to the goods without paying off the debt and until the debt is paid, the pledgee has the whole present interest. Egwumuo believes that the above mentioned premise is equally applicable to a pledge of land.[11] Consequent upon the diversification of economic activities in the country resulting in the establishment of mushroom banks in the rural areas, the phenomenon of customers pledge has gained prominence as such banks now accommodate the pledge of security for lending.[12]

In the days of yore, pledge agreements were done informally, without the need for writing or documentation, this was due to the fact that pledge contracts were developed out of mutual trust and good faith. These internal pledge agreements were impregnated with grant consequences which necessitated the formalization of pledge contracts where proper documents are written, signed and sealed to enhance its efficacy and expectation.

The object of a pledge contract covers a variety of items; amongst them is land, animals such as cattle, sheep, rams, goats, locust beans, trees, banana, plantation onceat, palm trees and cocoa trees.[13]

A debt owner under a pledge is something independent for which the pledge exists to secure. Therefore, the debt remains demandable whatever may happen to the security. A pledgee can sue for the repayment of the loan should the pledgor default in the land transaction.[14]

---

[9] See Egwummuo J.N., *Principles and Practice of Land Law* (Enugu: Onye Ventures Ltd, 2004) at p.367.

[10] (1868) LR 3 Erch.299 at p.302.

[11] Egwummwo, *op. cit.*, at p.308.

[12] Ibid.

[13] In time past, especially in the eastern and southern part of Nigeria, human beings were used as objects of pledge; they were used as slaves, servants, maids. They were used as objects or chattels, either in payment of levies and taxes levied on them by the chief or warlord or even exchanged as money worth for the payment of debts or tributes.

[14] See Nwabueze, *op. cit.*, at p.273. Ollenni N.A., *op. cit.*, at p.107, elaborated further on the principle of pledge under customary law, which he asserted that the real essence of a pledge is that the pledge transaction vests in the pledgee only a right to possession of the land and the enjoyment of the profits thereof; it does not give him title to the land, title remains in the pledgor. But where the pledgor defaults in the repayment of the debt, a number of options are open to the pledgee to

Reasons for pledge

Various reasons have been adduced why people pledge their land or properties and these are:

(i) To pay taxes or fines imposed on the impoverished peasants farmers, either by their overlords, chiefs, Emirs or the government. Most communities in the past pledge their lands or its usufruct to raise money to discharge their obligation.

(ii) A land could be pledged by its owners in order to obtain cattle, sheep, rams or goats for the payment of bride-price. In typical traditional settings, a family may pledge land in order to obtain animals for sacrificial purposes to appease the gods of the land or other goods where there is one epidemic or disease or scarcity by drought.

(iii) A pledge may be contracted either because the pledgee wants to raise monies either for the payment of bride-price or to repay a debt owned by his grandfathers or siblings or where he wishes to engage in any form of trade.

(iv) Again, pledge contract may be carried out on the basis of friendship and not necessarily for private gain. This warrants the pledgor to pledge his land without collecting loan of money or money's worth from the pledgee because of their mutual friendship, the pledgee enjoys the fruits of the land as long as that relationship exist unabated. Generations may pass bye before any attempt at redemption is made for they reason it is often advisable to include the male children of both families, as there is no definite time frame within which the agreement is to last or the said land is to be redeemed. For once a pledge, always a pledge.

(v) Though may not be tenable nowadays but in time past human beings were pledge as means of repayment of debts or loans owned to the creditors who were the pledges, these persons so pledged could be made, housemaids, house boys, they would be made to serve their masters for a period of time or for some number of years in which the debt may be discharged at the end of such waiting periods.

---

recompense himself. These are; (a) the pledgee may assign the pledge to another person, who steps into the very shoes of the pledgee and acquires his right of possession and enjoyment of the land. he does not acquire the title tot eh land. (b) if another person pays the loan on behalf of the pledgor, he acquires possession of that land and the enjoyment thereof; he becomes the new creditor of the pledgor; that is to say, the land can be repledged by the pledgee. cf Egwummuo *op. cit.*, at pp. 308-308.

Comparison between a lien, mortgage and pledge[15]

(a) Unlike mortgage and pledge which are formal securities, alien is an informal security. What this means is that at the time the party took possession of the property on which it later sets up alien,[16] there was no intention on the part of either parties that the other party was depositing it as security and the right of lien arose only by operation of law. On the other hand, pledge and mortgage requires prior agreement or intention on the part of the parties that the property involved is being passed as security.[17]

(b) Lien, being an informal security does not require any document to create it since the parties do not consciously intend that it be a security. A pledge may be created orally;[18] too but it may also be created in writing,[19] mortgage can also be created without a formality once the document of title has been surrendered.

(c) Any type of property which is capable of being physically or constructively transferred can be the subject or object of pledge. In the not too distant past, human beings had been pledged. Landed properties especially farmlands and developed properties, were later applied as pledge. Mortgage on the other hand, has been used on properties which are capable of being transferred constructively through documents of title like landed property although conceptually any property may be mortgaged.[20]

(d) The question of who has the possession of subject matter could be a basis for the distinction between a pledge and a mortgage.[21] In *Adjei* v. *Chief Dabanka*,[22] a leasehold land was granted by the plaintiff to

---

[15] See Layi A., *op. cit.*, at pp. 216-218.

[16] Bryan A.G., *Black's Law Dictionary*, 7th ed. (London: St. Paul Minn., 1999) at p.933, defines a lien as a legal right or interest that a creditor has in another's property, casting usually until a debt or duty that it secures is satisfied. Typically the creditor does not like possession of the property on which the lien has been obtained. On the types of lien read further Bryan, ibid., from pp.933-936.

[17] Layi, *op. cit.*, at p. 217.

[18] See Idrisu, *op. cit.*, at p. 63, see also Layi, *op. cit.*, at p.217.

[19] Idrisu, *op. cit.*, at p.63.

[20] Layi, *op. cit.*, at p. 216.

[21] Ibid.

[22] (1930) 1 WACA 63. In *Amoo* v. *Adigun* (1957) 2 WNLR at 35 the plaintiff claimed an account of rents collected by the defendant during his possession of the plaintiff's shop as pledgee in respect of a loan made by the defendant to the plaintiff. The court held that the transaction was an indigenous mortgage or pledge of land and that the plaintiff is entitled to credit for the defendant's exploitation of the premises whilst in possession. See also *Nwagwu and another* v. *Okonkwo and others* (1987) 3 NWLR (pt.60) 314, where the court held that where there is a pledge of land the land is redeemable however core it may be in the possession of the pledge. The court further held that a custom which permits the redemption of a pledge land with a human being is repugnant to

secure a debt owned the defendant on a condition that the plaintiff will remain in possession of the land but possession will pass to the lender only if the borrower defaults on loan repayment. The West African Court of Appeal held that the essential element of a pledge is the transfer of possession to the pledge at the time of the agreement and as the borrower in this case remains in possession after the agreement, the contract between the plaintiff and the defendant is a mortgage and not a pledge. The court further laid down what can be seen as a rule for resolving conflict between claimants as to whether a transaction is a pledge or a mortgage and the answer lies on whose possession the property immediately lies. If the property immediately lies with the person giving out the security i.e. the borrower, the agreement is a mortgage but if the possession lies in the person to whom securities is given, i.e., the lender, then it is a pledge.

(e) Pledge remains merely a possessory security the ownership lies with the pledgor and where the pledgee fails to take either actual or constructive possession, there is no pledge.

(f) A pledge has no automatic right of sale, but he can exercise his common law right. On default, he can obtain judgment against the debtor and proceed to obtain a 'fi-fa' order against the pledged property to be able to sell it.[23] In *Ikeanyi* v. *Adigbogun*,[24] the court held that a pledgor has the right of redemption and it does nto matter for how long. However, once the pledgee files an action and the court sets a definite time for redemption, the pledgor's right to redeem will terminate on the expiration of the time.

Rights of a pledgee[25]

A pledge has the following rights: (i) right to usufructory, i.e., right to enjoyment of the land, (ii) right to any agreed interest on the loan and (iii) right to sue to protect the property.

---

natural justice equity and good conscience and is unenforceable by the courts and *Ebiassah* v. *Ababio* (1946) 12 WACA 106, where it was held that the native custom that a mortgage debt in possession can be ejected as soon as the mortgage debt has been paid was not repugnant to natural justice and equity although the mortgagee had been in undisturbed possession for possibly sixty years. Cf also *Ogundiran* v. *Balogun* (1957) WRNLR, 51.

[23] Layi, *op. cit.*, at p.218.

[24] (1958).

[25] See Idrisu, *op. cit.*, at p. 64.

(i) Right of enjoyment of the land

The right to use and enjoyment of profits or fruits belonging to another is known as usufruct.[26] The pledgee by this right is entitled to the use of only those trees or crops planted on the land himself or the pledgee may be permitted to exercise all the powers of an owner-occupier. Even when he plants permanent or economic trees on the pledged land, he may not receive any compensation when the time comes for him to vacate the land.

(ii) Right to an agreed interest on the loan

In time past, under customary law, the pledgee was not entitled to any interest on the loan but in modern time, pledgee's interest is sometimes charged.

(iii) Right to sue to protect the pledged property

The pledgor cannot sue when the pledgee is in possession, unless the pledgor can show that there is real not hypocritical threatened permanent injury to the property. This is because the possessory right resides in the pledgee whilst the pledgor has the reversionary interest.

Duties of the pledgee[27]

Primarily, the pledgee has the duty to manage and account for the pledged property.

i. Manage

The pledgee is required to manage and take care of the pledged property as he performs the duties of an owner-occupier. He is therefore required to act with reasonable care that would include the act of good management even if it means the pledgee expanding money and labour to take care of the property.

ii. Account

The pledgee has the onerous task of accounting since he enjoys the fruits of the land. But in strict customary law parlance he is under a liability to

---

[26] Ibid., at p. 64.
[27] Ibid., at p. 65.

account for the profits he had made on the land as the purpose of possession is not to have the pledge land as security but to have it as interest on the amount borrowed.[28]

Perpetual redeemability of a pledge

Aside the fact that there is the intent of possession and enjoyment of the profits of the pledged land as its peculiar essentials, the pledgee can never acquire the pledged property. The pledgee cannot be heard that he believed himself to be the true owner nor can he argue that he has acquired title of the land by virtue of his improvements or acquiescence on the part of the pledgor. A pledge remains perpetually redeemable no matter how long the pledge has lasted. Once a pledge always a pledge with the resultant effect being that a pledge is perpetually redeemable.[29]

Again, it should be noted that redemption cannot be postponed by agreement. Even if the pledgor agreed not to redeem the land before a certain date, the pledgor is not bound by such agreement and he can redeem the land at any time by tendering the debt due.[30]

Due to some recent developments, the strict adherence to this rigid rule and principle of the customary maxim of "once a pledge always a pledge" with its consequences of perpetual redemption of the pledged property and that redemption can ever be postponed or delayed by whatever agreement, is seriously posing a very great difficulty.

Since this principle makes a non-sense of the foreclosure and the rule of laches and acquiescence, this allows the pledgor to sleep over his rights of redemption for a very long time, thus, this silence and inaction in

---

[28] Ibid at p.65. In *Daprah* v. *Poku* (1950), the West African Court of Appeal stated firmly that the essence of a native mortgage is that he gets possession and enjoys the profits without accounting for him. But in *Amao* v. *Adigun* (1957) 2 WNLR 55, the plaintiff executed a memorandum on 15 October, 1987, wholly the mortgaged his shop at Ibadan who thereupon entered into possession of the shop until the loan was repaid. He then hired the shop to a retailer. The plaintiff claimed an account of rents collected by the defendants during his possession as pledge and payment of any amount due on the token of such account. The trial judge held that the plaintiff is entitled to credit of the entire defendant's exploitation of the shop.

[29] In *Agbo Kuti* v. *Addo Kofi* (1933) WACA 284, wherein a land was pledged in 1809 to secure a loan of 6s 6d (65k), it was held that the land could be redeemed in 1926 by paying back the 65 6d. Notwithstanding, the lapse of 57 years. The lapse of time is not a bar to recovery of the pledge. The pledgee's occupation of the land is permissive and not bound by presumption. He can't plead acquiescence against the pledgor. See also *Nwagwu & Anor* v. *Okonkwo & Anor* (1987) 7 SCNJ 72, it was held that where there is a pledge of land, it may be in the possession of the pledge, all that is required is evidence of the history of the pledge, and in many traditional evidence is admissible.In *Okoye* v. *Obiaso* (2010) ALL FWLR(Pt.526) p.489, the court held that a pledge cannot ripen into ownership

[30] See Idrisu, *op. cit.*, at p.16.

settling the debts for time immemorial often gingers or stimulates the pledgee the desire to making permanent improvement and structures, only for the so called pledgor to wake up from his slumber one day to want to redeem the land or the pledge object leaving such developer without any adequate compensation based on the rule of "one a pledge, always a pledge" a rule which is a source of most legal conflict these days.

The problem generated by this customary law maxim of pledge received judicial notice in the case of *Iwuchukwu* v. *Anyanwu*,[31] where the Court of Appeal observed that this practice is not in line with the concept of reasonableness it however noted that:

> A pledge is actually a transaction in the nature of a contract and contractual obligation, and ought to be performed within a reasonable time, where time has not been stipulated.

The court ended up with a hope that the Supreme Court will soon reverse the position of this customary law of pledge. It is hereby submitted that to meet with this modern day realities, it is high time the customary maxim of "once a pledge always a pledge" with its concomitants be reformed to meet modern day transactions and contractual obligations where time and reasonableness will be of essence.

Absence of written documents as evidence

As other customary practices, pledge agreements were mostly unwritten, more so pledge contracts are sometimes contracted purely on the grounds of friendship and good faith by both parties. In the absence of any written document, a person alleging pledge must prove the following as was held in the case of *Chief Marcus Ndoro & Others* v. *Ndeezia Planwii & 3 Others*.[32] He must:

(a) Prove the title to the land of the person pledging;
(b) He must prove the pledge itself;
(c) He must know the parties to the pledge;
(d) He must know the witnesses, time and circumstances of the pledge;
(e) Consideration and term of the pledge.

For these reasons the need for proper writing and documentation of relevant information were overlooked, that customary agreements are non-script as such, issues relating to determination of title in a dispute

---

[31] (1993) 8 NWLR (pt.311) at 307.

[32] (2005) 5 NWLR (pt.812).

over a piece of land purported to be an object of pledge arises, to interpret the argument by impression becomes a Herculean task, for non-availability and, or documentation of any evidence as suggesting the existence or otherwise of any agreement of such nature.

Pledge agreement could be orally created with only witnesses of both practices in attendance, whereas, man has a short lifespan as death is inevitable. Where both parties and their witnesses are deceased and the pledgor's heirs which to claim back their land, and the pledgee's heirs defaulted by contesting the title of the said land. According to Section 146[33] on the presumption of ownership says:

> Where the question is whether any person is the owner of anything of which he is shown to be in possession, the burden of proving that he is not the owner is on the person who affirms that he is not the owner.

Based on this evidence rule of the presumption of ownership where the onus of proof is shifted to the defendant as was held by the court in the case of *Ezeudu* v. *Obiangwu*,[34] where there was a dispute over the ownership of a plot of land in possession of the plaintiff, but the defendants contended that although, the plaintiffs has been in possession, but they were not in possession as owners but as pledgee. Therefore, it is obvious that without any available document of evidence and witnesses to affirm or testify, it becomes very difficult for a pledgor (claimant) to prove and establish his claim of title.

Equally, it is a settled law that in a dispute over ownership of a piece of land, whoever is in possession is deemed to be the owner until the contrary is proved, as was held by the Supreme Court in *Anyabunsi* v. *Ugwunze*.[35] This position of the law always give the pledgee greater changes of retaining or claiming ownership, since they are always in possession and in view of the fact that absence of sufficient document and available proof to substantiate the pledgor's claim and to disprove that of the defendant, (the pledgee's) in this case.

The problems identified above posed a lot of difficulties in redeeming pledged land and other objects if not impossible, where the witnesses and the original parties to the pledge itself are all deceased and therefore renders their claim unmeritable and inadmissible for lack of evidence thereby jeopardizing their chances and attempt of redeeming the pledged land or property, even though they were the legal and true owners.

---

[33] Evidence Act Cap.112, Laws of the Federation of Nigeria.2004..

[34] (1980) 2 NWLR (pt.21) at 208.

[35] (1995) 1 SCNJ.55.

Unauthorized alienation by the pledgee

According to Nchi,[36] alienation is the transfer or disposition of property by an aliener to an alienee. Once the pledgor grants his interest in the land to the pledgee, he owes the pledgor the duty not to derogate from any of his obligation, that is, by not alienating any part, or whole of the pledged property in his trust without the consent of the grantor. Thus, any alienation either by way of an assignment, mortgage, re-pledging, sub-letting, leasing etc. is void.

Certainly due to high value and demand for land as a result of modern trend, it mounts pressure on the pledgee and in their craze or quest and craftiness for money, many a times they fraudulently disposed of some portion of the pledged land or properties, sometimes it could either be by subletting, leasing or outright sale without the consent of the pledgor.

Hence, this has culminated in the protracted subject of endless court litigation which is very rampant in our courts, asking for declaration of title and so on. These unending conflicts amongst the parties concerned can be seen in the case of *Da'arap Rentur Tanko* v.*Keben and Anor*,[37] where a piece of land was granted by W to X, and after several years, X died and Y his heir inherited the land, which he now alienates some plots of the pledged land to his son-in-law. It was held that Y cannot alienate the land without W's consent and authorization. Therefore, Z, the son-in-law, lost out the land to W its original owner.

Any act or attempt to alienate a portion or whole of the pledged property by the pledgee is viewed with disdain and seriousness, since it's an act of flagrant disobedience and derogation which is a great threat to the pledgor's title. This is predicated on the fact that once the debt is paid, the same size and length of the pledged property lent out is expected to be re-conveyed to the pledgor or his heirs. Therefore, any act of derogation of the pledgor is dangerous, if it is not promptly detected and challenged.

The pledgor may one day be confronted with an occupier or a trespasser who could avert that the pledgor's right of title in the land has been acquiescence or may be a bona-fide purchaser for value; or in other words, has tolerated acts adverse to his title as was right pointed out by S.P.O. in the case of *Onisiwo* v. *Fagbenro*,[38] a position which is concurred by the expression of the people that:

---

[36] Nchi S.I., *op. cit.*
[37] (Unreported) CV45 99 Grade I Areas Court, Mangu.
[38] *Ramsden* v. *Dyson, supra* (1954) NLRP.

> Secret and indiscriminate alienation of pledged land by the pledgee nowadays constitute a serious problem to the real land owners in Mangu and its environs. This singular act makes a very difficult for strangers to loan out their land, as many of these loaners or borrowers loaned in the past are never retained, sure their were no written evidences to prove.[39]

Any purported act of alienation of a pledged property during the subsistence of a pledge contract by the pledgee is null and void *ab initio.* This is because the principle of *nemo dat quod non habet* will always apply.

---

[39] Ibid.

Chapter 9

The law of property: definition of terms

The term "property" is used in a number of different senses. In its meaning it describes the subject-matter generally ascribed to the "law of property". In this sense, "property" means any right capable of being transferred from one person to another, or in other words any right valuable in the commercial sense. The law of property thus includes all rights over tangible things, but it is not limited to such rights. Contractual rights that are assignable is not limited to such rights. Contractual rights that are assignable and other choses in action are property in this wide sense.[1]

"Property" is also used in a narrower sense to refer to valuable rights *in rem,* i.e., which are enforceable against people generally for rights in *rem*. Such a right is usually referred to as a "proprietary right".

In a third sense, "property" is used, chiefly in relation to the sale of goods, as equivalent to the "ownership" of things. Thus, the Sale of Goods Act 1979 refers to the property in goods being transferred from seller to buyer.

As is explained elsewhere, "ownership" normally refers to those interests which in general comprise the most complete sets of bundles of rights that a person may have over things. "Property" in this sense is, therefore, a particular kind of "proprietary right".

Classification of property

In English law the main division of property is into real property (or realty) and personal property (otherwise referred to as personality of chattels which is a word derived from "cattle").

Real property consists of all freehold as opposed to leasehold interest in land. *Personal property* is subdivided into chattels real and chattels personal. Chattels real are leasehold interests in land; these interests are classified as personalty solely for historical reasons; they are, in fact,

---

[1] See Clive N., *General Principles of Law,* 3rd edition(London: Sweet & Maxwell,1983) at p. 319

inseparably connected with realty and that is why they are called chattels real. Chattels personal or pure personalty (in that they have no connection with realty) are further subdivided into choses in possession and choses in action. Choses in possession are rights over tangible movables such as tables and chairs. Such rights may be enjoyed by the physical possession of the movables. Choses in action are rights such as debts, copyrights or patents which may be enjoyed or protected only by the bringing of an action.[2]

The realty/personalty division is illogical, at least in so far as it makes leasehold interests personalty, and is due to the realty classification of actions into real actions and personal actions. A real action was an action where the successful plaintiff would recover the thing in issue itself; "real" comes from the Latin word *res*, meaning "thing". In realty law only freehold estates in land were protected by real actions. Thus, if A had a freehold estate in land and was wrongfully dispossessed by B, A had a real action against B in which the court would order B to return the land to A. Hence freehold interests in land became classified as realty. All other actions, including the action to protect a leasehold interest, were personal actions. In such an action the successful plaintiff could never insist on the specific restitution of a thing in issue. The defendant always had the option to pay damages or pecuniary compensation in lieu of restoration. All property protected by personal actions was called "personal property".[3]

The starting point is 1066 when all land was vested in King William I by right of conquest. Very soon afterwards, William I started to grant out rights over his land to his most senior followers. These became his tenants-in-chief. The tenants-in-chief were themselves able to make sub-grants to others in respect of the whole or part of the land that they had received from the king and the persons who received grants from the king and the persons who received grants from the tenants-in-chief were able to make further sub-grants and so on. In respect of a particular plot of land the person at the bottom of the scale, the actual occupant, was called a tenant-in-demesne; and all the grantors in the chain between the tenant-in-demesne and the king were called mesne lords (mesne = intermediate). This process of making grants and sub-grants was called "subinfeudation". Every grantor was the lord of his grantee; the lordship was called seignory; and the numerous relationships of lord and man that

---

[2] Ibid.

[3] Ibid.

existed between the grantors and their tenants were the hallmark and basis of the feudal system.

Every grant, moreover, was made upon certain terms and for some period of time. The terms on which a tenant held from his lord were defined by the doctrine of tenure: the duration of his interest by the doctrine of estates.[4]

1. Doctrine of feudal tenures

Every holding of land, or tenure, was originally for a freehold estate, and it is important to stress that the doctrine of feudal tenures has always applied only to tenures for a freehold estate.

From the beginning all tenures for freehold estates were subject to certain terms and were classified according to the nature of those terms. There were two basic types of tenure: free tenures and unfree tenures, the distinction depending upon the degree of certainty of the tenant's duties. There were numerous kinds of free (or freehold) tenures. For example there was knight-service, which required the tenant to supply horsemen to his lord annually for 40 days; sergeanty, which involved personal service as a butler, carver or the like; and socage, which eventually required a small, sometimes nominal, payment.

Unfree tenures varied from manor to manor, but were evidenced by a copy of the Roll of the manorial court on which they were entered. Hence, they became known as "copyhold tenures".

Certain incidents flowed from each type of tenure. For example, a standard incident of socage tenure was escheat whereby the rights over the land were forfeited to the superior lord if the tenant died without an heir.

The Statute Quia Emptores 1290 enacted that if C held the fee simple interest in Blackacre of B and granted that interest to D, C would drop out of the picture altogether and D would hold of B. Thus, further subinfeudation in respect of the fee simple was prevented, and eventually the present position emerged whereby most tenants in fee simple hold immediately from the sovereign. Moreover, when copyhold tenure was abolished by the 1925 legislation all legal estates of freehold became held by socage tenure, the modern name for which is freehold tenure.

2. Leasehold tenure

The doctrine of feudal tenures applied only to freehold estates in land. to begin with leaseholds were not regarded as estates and the question of the doctrine of tenures applying to them simply did not arise. When in the

[4]Ibid.

sixteenth century leaseholds did become regarded as estates they were still not fitted into the system of feudal tenures.

But the leasehold was now an estate and that meant that there had to be a holding of land or tenure. The tenure existing between a lessor and lessee, who may be conveniently referred to as leasehold, was, however, outside the old feudal classification into free and unfree tenures. Leasehold tenure must therefore be kept distinct from the feudal tenures applying to land held for freehold estates.

3. The doctrine of estates

The doctrine of estates classified interest in land according to their duration. The interests so classified were called "estates". Two distinct classes of estates emerged: freehold estates and leaseholds. This classification still exists today and is of great importance.

Freehold estates

The hallmark of a freehold estate is that it of uncertain duration. There are two kinds of freehold estates, *fee* and *life*.

(i) ***Fee*:** the word "fee" denotes that the estate is inheritable and capable of lasting forever since in theory it is possible for the relevant heirs never to fail. There are two types of fee:

Fee Simple: This is the largest of all the estates. Since the early fourteenth century the rule has been that a fee simple will endure as long as the tenant entitled to it for the time being died leaving an heir. ("Heirs" eventually came to include any blood relations; originally ancestors were excluded). From a very early time it has been freely alienable.[5]

Fee Tail: The fee tail is a lesser interest than the fee simple. It will last only so long as the original grantee has lineal descendants (i.e. sons and daughters and their sons and daughters and so on, but not brothers' or sisters' children) of the type specified in the grant. Moreover, such descendants of the original grantee will inherit the interest even though the original grantee has tried to dispose of the interest to someone else. Suppose, for instance, A who has a fee tail, alienates it to B and then dies leaving one son C. C inherits the interest and can claim it from B. The fee tail is, therefore, alienable only to a limited extent.

If the matter had rested there, the fee tail would have provided a ready method for tying land to a family for generation after generation. Tying land in that way, thereby taking it off the market, has always been considered undesirable. Consequently, from the fifteenth century a person entitled to a fee tail has been able to "bar the entail" at least if he

[5] Ibid.

had the consent of the person entitled to the possession of the land or if he was in possession himself. "Barring the entail" results in turning an interest in fee tail into an interest in fee simple which as has been stated, is freely alienable.

(ii) ***Life:*** A life estate lasts until the death of the person for whose life the estate was given in the original grant. Such an estate is of uncertain duration because it is, of course, not known when the relevant person will die. There are two kinds of life estate:

(a) The ordinary type, to which the unqualified term "life estate" usually refers, is where the measuring life is of the tenant himself, as where the grant is "to A for life".

(b) An estate "*Pur autre vie*" (for the life of another) occurs where the measuring life is that of someone other than the tenant, as where the grant is "to A for the life of B".

Leasehold estates

The characteristic of a leasehold estate is that it is of a duration that is certain or capable of being rendered certain, e.g. a lease for seven years will expire at the end of seven years from its creation; a period tenancy such as monthly tenancy may continue indefinitely, but either the grantor (the lessor, the landlord) or the grantee (the lessee, the tenant) may bring the tenancy to an end on a specific date by giving the other party the required notice of termination (which is one month's notice in the case of a monthly tenancy).

A leasehold interest was originally regarded not as an estate in land, but as a mere contractual right to occupy land which right was protected by a "personal action" against the other contracting party and not by "a real action" for the recovery of the land itself. It is because of this that leaseholds were, and still are classified as personalty.

Remainders and Reversions

If A has an estate, for example a fee simple and grants to B an estate of shorter duration than his own, e.g. a life estate, A is said to retain his fee simple interest in reversion because, although A will not enjoy the and so long as B's estate endures, the right to immediate possession of the land will revert to A when B's estate terminates, i.e. on B's death. In such a case, A is said to be a *reversioner.*

If, however, A disposes of his entire interest by means of two successive grants, e.g. "to B for life then to C in fee simple", the right to possess the land is said to remain away from A, C's interest is termed a remainder and C is a remainderman.

A grant may involve several successive remainders: but there can only be one reversion, e.g. in a grant by A "to B for life, remainder to C for life, remainder to D for life, remainder to E in tail", C,D and E are all remaindermen: A is the reversioner.

The person who enjoys the immediate right to possess the land has an estate "vested in possession". Such vested interest must be distinguished from contingent interests... Contingent interests are not present and existing estates at all; they are interests that might or might not become vested or present estates depending on the outcome of certain events. For example, if A makes a grant "to B for life remainder to C in fee simple if C attains the age of 21:, C has a contingent interest; he is not intended to acquire a vested estates unless he reaches 21. The law relating to the validity of contingent interest is, and always has been, extremely complex.

4. Legal and Equitable interests

So far the situations envisaged have been straightforward situations, such as where A holds the fee simple estate in Blackacre and makes a conveyance "to B for life to C in tail remainder to D in fee simple". In such a situation, the common law courts recognized the existence of estates or interest in B, C and D and because these interests were recognized at common law, they were legal (as opposed to equitable) estates or interest.

For a number of reasons, however, it became the practice during the thirteenth century for a landholder, A, to convey his land "to B to the use of C". The common law took no notice of A's intention that B should hold the land for C's benefit. By about 1400, however, protection for C, the intended beneficiary, became established in the Court of Chancery. The Statutes of Uses 1535 partially succeeded in destroying this equitable protection; but the lawyers found a way round the statute by changing the form of conveyances, grants "unto and to the use of B in trust for C" coming to have the same effect as the previous "to B to the use of C".

So originated the concept of the trust, the basic effect of which was that the Court of Chancery acknowledged that at common law the land was vested in B but as a matter of conscience constrained B to act in accordance with the grantor's intention to benefit C and to comply with the trust reposed in him. B, the person holding the legal estate on trust for C, became called a trustee, and C, the person for whom the trustee held the legal estate, was the beneficiary or *cestui que trust.*

The result of this was that the beneficiary obtained an equitable interest or estate with the rights of enjoyment of the land that made him far more like the "owner" of the land than the trustee in who was vested the legal estate. Moreover, the Court of Chancery applied to such equitable interests the common law rules as to duration. Thus, it came about that a trustee might hold the legal estate in Blackacre, for example, in fee simple on trust for A for life, for B in tail and for C in fee simple.

What difference did it make to a person whether his interest was said to be legal or equitable? The most important difference was that in general, a legal interest was enforceable against everyone, whereas an equitable interest was enforceable against everyone except a bona fide purchaser of a legal estate for value and without notice (of the equitable interest).

This distinction may be illustrated as follows: Suppose A, the holder of the legal estate in fee simple over Blackacre, granted to B by deed a legal lease over part of Blackacre and by means of a contract in writing passed on C an equitable lease in another part of Blackacre. Whilst A retained his interest in Blackacre, both B and C were in a very similar position, although any remedy that C sought was bound to be equitable and therefore discretionary (See p.294). If, however, A transferred his legal estate in Blackacre to P, the main difference between B's legal right and C's equitable right would become apparent. P would take subject to B's legal interest in any event, even though he had had no notice of it. But P would take free of C's equitable interest if he could show that he was a bona fide purchaser of the legal estate for value and without notice actual or constructive of C's interest.

1. Tenure

(i) Feudal Tenures

All land is still held ultimately of the Crown and virtually all legal estates in fee simple are now held immediately of the Crown.

As will be seen the only freehold estate that is today capable of existing as a legal estate is the fee simple absolute in possession; all such legal estates are now held by freehold tenure. In practice, freehold tenure is of no importance: no services are exacted and no incidents of any significance survive. The incident, escheat for want of heirs, was abolished by Section 45 of the Administration of Estates Act 1925. If the holder of a fee simple absolute in possession dies intestate leaving no relative entitled to succeed under the Administration of Estates Act 1925, the land now passes to the Crown as *bona vacantia.*

Tenure in relation to freehold estates is therefore of a largely theoretical importance.

(ii) Leasehold tenure

This non-feudal tenure that exists when a person has a leasehold estate is of much greater practical importance. The rent service required by the landlord of his tenant is usually the main reason for the creation of a lease.

2. Legal and Equitable Estates

By Section 1 of the Law of Property Act 1925 only two types of estate are now capable of being legal estates. These are:

(i) *An estate in fee simple absolute in possession.* A estate in fee simple is absolute if it is not subject to any conditions and is in possession if it takes effect immediately and is not in remainder or in reversion.

(ii) *A term of years absolute.* The Act provides a complex definition of this interest. It will suffice to state here that "the expression 'term of years' includes a term for less than a year, or for a year of years and a fraction of a year or from year to year". Every other estate (including the fee simple not absolute or not in possession, the fee and the life estate) can now be only an equitable interest.

3. Contract and Conveyances

Formal requirements

Although an interest in land may be acquired by adverse possession, the more usual methods must comply with certain formalities. The following are the main rules:

(i) To convey a legal estate a deed is generally required, although a legal lease may be created without any formality if the lease takes effect in possession for a term not exceeding three years at the best rent reasonably obtainable without taking a fine.

(ii) A declaration of trust respecting any land must be manifested and proved by some writing.

(iii) A disposition of any already existing equitable interest or trust must be in writing.

(iv) A contract to transfer an interest in land cannot pass a legal estate: in equity, however, there may be specific performance (see p.295) of such a contract provided it is evidenced in writing or supported by a sufficient act of part performance. Moreover, since equity regards as done that which ought to be done, a contract to transfer an interest in land duly evidenced in writing or supported by an act of part performance at once creates an equitable estate. A contract for the sale or lease of land is called an estate contract.

A defective attempt to grant a legal estate such as the fee simple absolute in possession will nevertheless create an equitable estate provided that it can be read as a contract evidenced in writing or supported by an act of part performance.

Words of purchase and words of limitation

When there is a formally valid grant, who acquires what kind of estate depends upon terms of the grant technically known as "words of purchase" and "word of limitation".

"Words of purchase" define the person (or persons) to whom the interest is granted and who is called a "purchaser", e.g., "to A".

"Word of limitation" limits the interest granted to a purchaser: that is to say, they define the estate that he has been granted. The following special rules exist specifying the words that must be used to create the various estates:

(a) By the Law of Property Act 1925, in a conveyance of land the grantee takes the "fee simple or other the whole interest which the grantor had power to convey in such land, unless a contrary intention appears." Accordingly, provided that the grantor holds the fee simple, a grant simply "to A" with no words of limitation will convey the fee simple interest to A.

(b) A fee tail can be created only by the use of one of a limited number of expressions, e.g., "to A and the heirs of his body", "to A in tail".

(c) In order to create a life estate words indicating that intention must be used, e.g. "to A for life", "to A until he dies".

Buying and Selling a House

The subject "Buying and selling a house" covers two main types of transaction. First, there is the situation where A has a fee simple estate in land of freehold tenure and wishes to sell it. The transfer on sale of such an interest is popularly called "a sale of a freehold residence"; the term "freehold" indicating both the quality of the tenure and the quantity of the estate.

Secondly, there is the situation where A has a leasehold interest for a fixed period with a number of years still unexpired. The transfer for value of such an interest is commonly referred to as "a sale of a leasehold property".

The considerations relevant to each transaction are similar but not identical. The following is a short account of the procedure for the transfer on sale of a freehold residence. There are invariably two main stages in the transaction:

(a) *The Contract of sale:* Unless the equitable doctrine of part performance applies, the contract will not be enforceable unless it is evidenced by a sufficient memorandum in writing. Normally, a draft contract is prepared by the vendor (or the vendor's solicitor) and sent to the purchaser (or his solicitor) for approval. The purchaser then signs the contract and returns it to the vendor. This is the offer. The vendor communicates his acceptance by signing a counterpart document and sending it to the purchaser. The binding contract is thus usually formed by an exchange of documents usually referred to as "exchange of contract", although that is somewhat misleading as there is, of course, only one contract. The purchaser is not usually willing to enter into a binding contract until:

(i) he is sure that he has enough money to complete the purchaser (a mortgage advance may be required or he may have to sell a house that he already owns);

(ii) the property has been surveyed;

(iii) certain searches have been made (e.g. to make sure that there are no plans for the compulsory purchaser of the house, for its demolition, or for developments in the neighbourhood that might detract from its value); and

(iv) certain inquiries have been made of the vendor in respect of the property.

Although it would be unusual for a binding contract to be made before these matters have been dealt with, it is quite common for the parties to sign a contract "subject to contract" as soon as they are agreed in principle. Such a conditional contract has no legal effect and either party can withdraw with impunity.

(b) *Completion*. The second main stage is completion which takes place when the vendor (or his solicitor) delivers to the purchaser (or his solicitor) the duly executed conveyance. In practice completion usually takes in the office of the vendor's solicitor.

Completion should take place on the date fixed for it in the contract, or if there is no such date, within a reasonable time after the date of the contract. Normally completion occurs about five weeks after the date of the contract. Such an interval is necessary to enable the purchaser to investigate fully the vendor's title and to prepare the draft deed of conveyance which is sent to the vendor for approval. The deed includes the following parts:

(i) Commencement (e.g. this conveyance...)

(ii) Date (the deed operates from the time when it is signed, sealed and delivered by the parties, no matter what date is inserted in the conveyance).

(iii) Names of the parties.

(iv) Recitals (narrative recitals deals with the past history of the property; introductory recitals explain the purpose of the present deed).[7]

---

[7] Ibid.

Chapter 10

An overview of the effect of Land Use Act on customary ownership of land

No legislation promulgated in this country has elicited so much controversy, so much criticism, so much divergence in the interpretation of its provisions and so much discourse in the academic and business circles as the Land Use Act, 1978.[1]

Criticisms[2] and evaluation of that have been numerous; some have been mild whilst others have been in the extreme. Looked at from the point of view of pure jurisprudence, it is easy to condemn it as a piece of legislation which has not been rooted in the national consciousness of the Nigerian people and which as a result would die a natural death.

It is pertinent to consider the pre-enactment era of the Land Use Act 1978. Before the enactment of the Act there were two systems of land tenure. This system is regulated by either English statutes of general application enacted in England before 1st January, 1908, statutes enacted by local legislature or colonial statutes made expressly applicable in Nigeria.

With the exception of the ten northern states which had acquired a semblance of nationalized system of land tenure as far back as 1916[3] by

---

[1] See Justice Nnamani, A., "The Land Use – 12 Years After" NIJ, (1991) p.105, some academic writers have taken the view that the title of the Act is misleading as it gives the impression that the Act is a unified Federal Code covering all aspects of land usage within the Federation of Nigeria, and covering the utilization of land, as governed by Local Town Planning Authorities when in fact the provisions of the Act do not regulate and control the use of land, but rather they spell out the type of interests obtainable in land, the mode of acquisition and the quantum of rights exercisable therein.

[2] Smith, I.O., "The land Use Act: Twenty Five Years After" *Department of private and Property Law, Faculty of Law, University of Lagos*, Akoko-Yaba, Lagos-Nigeria, 2003, p.49, writing on the 10th Anniversary of the Land Use Act, the Editorial Board of the Journal of Private and Property Law, Vols. 8&9, had this to say on the Act "Its birth like that of a child born to family in a state of barrenness raised all hopes. But has since been a troublesome child". Also in July 1985, the Chief Justice of Nigeria made a statement during a television interview which is remarkable for its condor what he said is that what the statute seek to achieve is difficult to understand. That statement attested the enormity of problems encountered by counsel and the court in the application of LUA, 1978.

[3] Land and Native Rights Act 1916, Cap 96, Laws of the Federation of Nigeria, 1958.

virtue of a statute which was mandatory, the people in the southern part of Nigeria had always had a choice as to the form of acquisition and/or vesting of land. Under customary law, three categories of persons are capable of holding land, but until the second half or the century two of such bodies could hold or own land. These are the community and the family. In later years, it becomes possible for an individual person to acquire and had interest in land although whatever interest he might.

Have acquired soon dissolved into the family melting pot and the land became (and still becomes) family property once again on the death of the original owner.[4]

Thus under customary law, family is the focus of land holding not only in Nigeria but also in many parts of West Africa. Eventually, every inch of the Nigerian soil now purported to vest in one Governor or the other apparently belongs to a Nigerian family.

Apparently, the Act was promulgated to reform and bring serenity into the chaotic land tenure system in part of Nigeria where the position was unacceptable also the Act was enacted to curb the problem of uncertainty of title and the difficulty encountered by government in getting land for development as a result of this it became very imperative that the government must intervene through legislation to court and reform these and other areas of the customary land tenure that needs to be reformed.[5]

As earlier noted that before the commencement of the Act, land in the states of Nigeria were owned by communities and individuals. This ownership has been extinguished by the Act. Though the previous owners lost ownership rights, they retain the right to occupy and use the land; that is to say right to customary land is diminished not extinguished.[6]

Furthermore, the definition of Customary Right of Occupancy under Section 50 of the Act clearly recognizes the existence of customary rights over land. Section 50 defines Customary Right of Occupancy to mean: the right of person lawfully signs or occupying land in accordance with the customary law.

---

[4] *Ogunmefun* v. *Ogunmefun* (1931) 10 NLR 82.

[5] Smith, I.O., *Practical Approach to Real Property Law in Nigeria* (Ecowatch Publication Ltd, 1999) p.69.

[6] Section 5(2) Hereinafter LUA) See also *Edibiri* v. *Daniel* (2009) 2 NWLR (pt.11126) p.428, where the court held that the Land Use Act never set out to abolish existing titles and rights to possession of land. rather, where such rights or titles relates to developed lands in Urban areas, the possessor or owner of the right or title is deemed to be a statutory grantee of occupancy under Section 34(2) of the Act and if it is non-urban area the owner is deemed to be grantee of a right of occupancy by the appropriate Local Government under Section 36(2) of the Act.

The same section also defines occupancy as:

> Any person or community lawfully occupying land under customary law and a person using or occupying land in accordance with the Customary Law.

The whole power of revocation of Customary Right of Occupancy (which includes a deemed grant) under Section 28 of the Act carries clear implication that such right survived the promulgation of land Use Act, as Nnaemeka Agu JSC observed in *Abioye* v. *Yakubu*.[7]

> That if such customary rights are abolished by the Act, there would be nothing left to be revoked.

Also, reading Section 34 and 35 together, one will come to an inescapable conclusion that the Act preserves Customary Land Tenure because Section 35(1) provides, *inter alia,* that Section 34 of this Act shall have effect notwithstanding that the land in question was held under a leasehold whether Customary otherwise.

Beside the above sections of the Act, the Supreme Court has also in plethora of authorities held that the Act preserves and protects the Customary Land Tenure.[8] In *Abioye* v. *Yakubu,*[9] Karibi-White JSC (as he then was) constituting Customary Land Right after the Land Use Act held that:

> Land is still held under Customary Tenure even though dominion is in the Governor.

The most pervasive effect of the Land Use Act is the diminutions of the plenitude of the powers of the holders of land, the character in which they hold remain substantially the same. This position is also confirmed by the Supreme Court in the case of *Ogunleye* v. *Oni*.[10]

Persons in occupation before the coming into effect of the Land Use Act 1978

Section 34 and 36 of the Land Use Act contains transitional provision on Land in urban and non-urban areas respectively. Section 36 of the Act has received a judicial pronouncement of the apex court on the Supreme Court of Nigeria in *Abioye* v. *Yakubu* where Bello CJN said:[11]

---

[7] (1991) 5 NWLR (pt.190) 130.

[8] See *Dzungwe* v. *S.H. Gbishe* (1985) 2 NWLR (pt.8) p.528. See also *Edibiri* v. *Daniel* (*supra*).

[9] *Supra.*

[10] (1990) 2 NWLR (pt. 135) 745.

[11] *Supra* at p. 229. The learned Chief Justice went further to say "...one would observe that the Act did not expressly divest and extinguish the Customary Rights of owners of agricultural land in

> In my view, it is transparent from the dissection of the subsection that in clear and ambiguous words the Act notwithstanding the definition of a "holder" under Section 50, made the customary owner who was in actual possession and using the land at its commencement a beneficiary of the dissected in his actual possession and use at the commencement of the Act.

In the same vein, the learned Chief Justice said:[12]

> A customary tenant has acquired the right to occupy and use land from its customary owner on terms under customary law which included the owner's right to tributes, the continual recognition by the customary tenant of the reversionary right of the owner and the right of forfeiture. Consequently, in the absence of express provision in the Act divesting the customary owner.

Thus, in *Dashi* v. *Satlong*,[13] the Court held that it is not the intention of the lawmaker that the Land Use Act be used to divest citizens of their traditional titles to land. Rather, the Acts is meant to strengthen ownership that derives existence through traditional history. It is for that reason that the Act recognizes the existence of the title of a customary land owner over his parcel of land as a deemed holder where such land existed before the commencement of the Act.

Furthermore in *Adole* v. *Gwar*,[14] the court held that the power of the Governor of a State to grant statutory right of occupancy or customary right of occupancy by the appropriate body must not be exercised whimsically such as to deprive someone who had lawful right or title to a parcel of land prior to the promulgation of the Land Use Act. Hence, they made transitional provisions for the preservation of the interest in land held by persons prior to the coming into being of the Act by virtue of Section 34(1), 5 and 6 thereof. The said provision generally protects the interest of a person in the land held by him prior to the coming into being of the Act. Nnaemeka Agu JSC on his part, said:[15]

---

non-urban areas as it did in respect of under developed land in excess of half hectares in urban areas. See also *Edebiri* v. *Daniel* (*supra*).

[12] Ibid. at p. 2293.

[13] (2009) 5 NWLR (pt.113) p.566.

[14] (2008) 11 NWLR (pt. 1120). it was further held that Section 34 of the Land Use Act recognizes the title of persons who were on the land before 1978 when the Act came into being. If the land wasdeveloped by such persons, they are deemed holders of Statutory Rights of Occupancy issued by the Governor by virtue of Section 34(2) and (3) of the Act. The rights come into existence automatically by the operation of the law. In *Olagunju* v. *Adesoye* (2009)4M.J.S.C.(Pt.1) at p81, the supreme court held that the grant of a statutory right of occupancy automatically extinguishes all existing rights in respect of a parcel of land over which it was granted. See section 2 7 5 of the Land Use Act, 1978.

[15] (1990) 4 NWLR (pt.135) 745.

> No section of the Act which expressly abolished these customary rights and obligations over agricultural land was referred to us. Although arguments were inferential particularly from the interpretation of Section 36 of the Act and word holder and occupier in Section 50 on the contrary concern provisions of the Act clearly show that its intended that existing right shall continue.

So it can be said with certainty that since there is no express provision in the Act revoking or amending the respective rights of customary landlord and customary tenants, then their respective status and rights must continue under the Act subject only to the provision on the Act. Also, in the case of *Ogunleye* v. *Oni*,[16] Belgore JSC delivering the judgment of the Supreme Court said:

> The Land Use Act is not a magic wand and it is being portrayed to be a destructive muster that has also swallowed all rights on land and that the Governor or Local Government with mere issuance of a piece of paper, could divest families of their homes and agricultural lands overnight with a rich holder or certificate of occupancy driving tenant with bulldozers and canes.

He concluded that the law as it is that in areas not declared urban by State Government, everybody remains where he has always been as if the new Act has vested in him a Customary Right of Occupancy.
The various dicta of the Justice of the Supreme Court mentioned above clearly stated the position of the law in Nigeria that where a person from time immemorial had been in continuous possession and occupation of the land in dispute as the owners thereof right up to the 29th March, 1978 then, he is vested with the Right of Occupancy in respect of the land in dispute as the occupier, holder and customary title owner thereof by virtue of Section 36(2) of the Act.

The need for Governor's consent before the alienation of land under the Land Use Act

Since the decision of the Supreme Court in *Savannah Bank Ltd* v. *Ammel Ajilo*,[17] there has been endless controversy over the consent provision of the Land Use Act, the apparent inelegance of its drafting and consequent hardship meted out by its interpretation on its victims sometimes

[16] Smith, I.O., *op. cit.*, at p. 325, 50, until the Right of Occupancy of the person is revoked by the Governor under Section 28(2) of the Act for overriding public interest, no grant can be made by the Governor to a third party over the same piece of land and any certificate issued by the Governor will be illegal and invariably defective.

[17] (1989) 1 NWLR (pt. 97) p.305.

occasioned crocodile tears, etc.[18] The consent of the Governor to alienation of interest in land in Nigeria has its philosophical basis in the concept of ownership.[19] Its potentials are so great that in recent times it has become the focus of governmental policy.[20] Since alienation is one of the incidents of ownership, one can therefore alienate his interest in land without the consent of anybody.[21]

However, with the introduction of the Land Use Act, the radical title in all lands comprised in every state became vested in the Governor as a trustee for all Nigerians and the erstwhile absolute owner of rights and interest in the land retained a limited right, which he can no longer alienate or dispose of as he wishes contrary to the contents of ownership.[22]

Hence, Section 21 read together with Section 22 provides that:

> It shall not be lawful for any Customary Right of Occupancy or Statutory Right of Occupancy or any part thereof to be alienated by assignment, mortgage, transfer of possession, sublease or otherwise however without the consent of the Governor first had and obtained.[23]

Thus, in *B. Mangfang (Nig.) Ltd* v. *MLSOI Ltd,* the court, held that Section 22(1) of the Land Use Act 1978 is clear and unambiguous. The section clearly prohibits the holder of a Statutory Right of Occupancy from alienating his right of occupancy or any part thereof by assignment, mortgage, transfer of possession, or otherwise without the consent of the Governor first had and obtained. It was further held that the holder of a statutory right of occupancy is certainly not prohibited by Section 22(1) of the Land Use Act 1978, from entering into some form of negotiation which may end up with a written agreement for presentation to the Governor for his necessary consent.[24]

---

[18] Examples are: Hon. Justice Nnamani: "The land Use Act – 11 Years After" 2 GRBPL No.6 (1989) p.31, A.A. Utuama: "The Crocodile Tears in *Savannah Bank* v. *Ajilo and Ano*" 2 GRBPL No.7 (1989) p.29.

[19] See the Land Use Act , *op. cit.*, at Section 22. Ownership is of both legal and social interest, hence the court utilize the ideal in such a way as to give effect to views of changing individual and social interests.

[20] See R.W.M. Dias, *Dias Jurisprudence* (5th Edition) Chapter 14 p.22.

[21] This was the position in the Southern Nigeria before the promulgation of the Land Use Act 1978. The only consent needed was the consent of the family head if it was a family property or consent of the landlord if it was a leasehold land with assignment covenant.

[22] Smith, I.O., *Practical Approach to Law of Real Property in Nigeria*, Ecowatch publication Ltd (1999) p. 69.

[23] Land Use Act 1978.

[24] (2007) 14 NWLR (pt.1053) p. 114.

Furthermore, it was also held in *U.B.N. Plc.* v. *Ayodare & Sons (Nig.) Ltd* that by virtue of the provisions of Section 21, 22 and 26 of the Land Use Act, Cap.202, Laws of the Federation of Nigeria 1990, a holder of a statutory right of occupancy who wishes to mortgage the property by assignment must first obtained the consent of the Governor of the State where the land is situate before carrying out the mortgage transaction.[25]

Also, in *C.C.C.T.C.S Ltd* v. *Ekpo*,[26] it was held that Section 22(1) of the Land Use Act, 1978 clearly provides that it shall be unlawful for a holder of a right of occupancy to alienate some or any part thereof by assignment, mortgage, and transfer of possession, sublease or otherwise without the consent of the Governor first had and obtained.
By the tone and tenor of the provision, it is clear that the said provision is mandatory. It makes obtainable the Governor's consent a precondition for the validity of any alienation of the Right of Occupancy under the land Use Act 1978.

Nonetheless this decisions was recently affirmed in *U.B.N. Plc.* v. *Astra Builders Ltd,* that by virtue of Section 22(1) of the Land Use Act, 1978, it shall be unlawful for a holder of a certificate of occupancy granted by the Governor to alienate his right of occupancy or any part thereof by assignment, mortgage or transfer of possession, sublease or otherwise howsoever, without the consent of the Governor first had and obtained.[27] It was further held that by virtue of the Section 26 of the Land Use Act 1978, any transaction of any instrument which purports to confer on or vest in any person interest or right over land other than in accordance with the provisions of the Land Use Act Section 22 of which provides for Governor's consent is null and void.

Notwithstanding the consent provision has generated a lot of controversies among writers and erudite scholars and they have variously suggested that the Land Use Act be amended to remove the consent provision. Prominent amongst the scholars is Adigun and Utuama who share the same opinion when they said that:

---

[25] (2007) 13 NWLR (pt. 1052) p.1052. It was further held that by virtue of Section 22 of the Land Use Act, it is incumbent on the Governor to give consent, but in situations where the Governor cannot give the consent himself, Section 45(1) of the Act creates an avenue where by the Commissioner for lands can exercise the power to do so in the event that the Governor delegates the power of consent.

[26] (2008) 6 NWLR (pt. 1083) p.369. It was further held that the consequence of the unlawful act of alienating a Right of Occupancy without the requisite consent of the Governor is what is stated under Section 26 of the Land Use Act, 1978. It makes the transaction null and void. Section 26, in declaring such acts as null and void used the word shall which makes the provision mandatory and not directory or discretionary. Thus, alienation made contrary to the provision of the Act shall be null and void which means null and void for all purposes.

[27] (2010) 5 NWLR (pt. 1186) p.10.

The operation of consent provision of the Act has made land transaction more difficult and less economic... consequently capital formation has not been satisfactory so also is the general development process in the country".[28]

Governor's power of revocation of statutory right of occupancy and customary right of occupancy

There was a great cry of the people and of their wives against their brethren ...that we have mortgaged over lands vineyards and houses, ...neither is it our power to redeem them, for other men have our lands, and vineyards.[29]

One of the basic social problems confronting many African countries today is how best to fashion appropriate land redistribution policy that would be equitable and fair as well as ensure the security of tenure and access to land including the payment of full, fair and equitable compensation to expropriated land owners.[30]

Land Rights are becoming contentions issues for a number of reasons. First, land is an indispensable natural resource God ever endowed on man. The ability to own, control and use land is not only an important expression of both private and proprietary right[31] but a measure of economic wealth and power[32] secondly, there are strong tensions between customary and statutory forms of land law and ownership, intensified during the era of military regime. These pressures are influenced by the desire of government to control land resources in the state since the discharge of governmental responsibility necessarily and

---

[28] Smith I.O., *op. cit.*, at p.228.

[29] Smith I.O., *op. cit.*, at p.246. The above quotation aptly describes the mode of the people on the magnitude, scale and impact of the Land Use Act in general and in particular, the power to revoke proprietary interest in land by the Governor and disposes them of their land.

[30] Ibid. Aside from the property rights, other notable social problems prevalent in many African State include poverty, political instability, environmental degradation and unemployment. See also Gutto, S.B., "Land, Property Rights, the Decolonization Process and Democracy in Africa.

[31] Access to land involves access to the mineral resources and other productive users to which land may be used. However, ownership of land excludes the ownership of mineral resources as those resources are vested in the Federal Government. See the Constitution of the Federal Republic of Nigeria 1999, See generally Smith I.O., op.cit. at p.247.

[32] This is consistent with the similar view earlier expressed by Prof. Omotola where he asserted, "Every person requires land for his support, preservation and self actualisation...land is the foundation of shelter, food and employment. Man lives on land during his life and upon his demise, his remains are kept in it permanently. Man has been aptly described as a land animal." Omotola J.A., "Law and Land Rights within Nigeria". Test of Inaugural Lecture, (Unilag Press, 1988) at p.1.

implicitly involves the manipulation and use of land for diverse social, economic and political considerations.[33]

Nonetheless, constitutionally, private property can be compulsorily acquired provided "prompt compensation is paid and the right of access to court to challenge the question of compensation payable is not denied."[34]

The Constitution does not define those circumstances when land may be compulsorily acquired by the statutory framework. For the revocation of property right in land is well articulated in the Land Use Act. The Act provides for the revocation of existing proprietary interest in land for "Overriding Public interest" "and for public purpose." Such revocation must also comply with the statutory procedure for revocation. The Act further classified overriding public purpose depending on the nature of interest held by the land owner; where the interest is covered by a Statutory Right of Occupancy, overriding purposes, requirement for mining or oil pipeline and where the grantor alienates the land without consent of the Governor.[35] He may also revoke a Statutory Right of Occupancy on the ground of a breach of any of the provisions implied in a Certificate of Occupancy or any term contained in the certificate or any special contract made under Section 8 of the Act.

The key word here is the revocation of land for "public purpose." The term "public purpose" is a question of fact and depends on whether under certain conditions, public interest exists or not. The term is nebulous and dynamic depending on the social changes and social policy of the day. In India, the Supreme Court in *State of Bihar* v. *Kemeshawar Singh*, remarked that "with the onward match of civilization our notions as to the scope of the general interest of the community are fast changing and widening, with the result that our old and narrow notions as to the sanctity of the private interest of the individual can no longer stand the

---

[33] See Fundamental Objectives and Directives Principle of State Policy, Constitution of the Federal Republic of Nigeria 1999,(As Amended, 12th Jan, 2011) Chap.11.

[34] The preamble of the Land Use Act read "whereas it is in the Public interest that the Right of all Nigerians to the land of Nigeria be asserted and preserved by Law. And whereas it is also in the public interest of all Nigerian to use and enjoy land in Nigeria and the natural fruit thereof in sufficient quantity to enable tem to provide for the sustenance of them and their family should be assured, protected and preserved". See also Nigerian Urban and Regional Decree, Section 75(1). See item 60 of the exclusive legislative list.

[35] The procedure for revocation of interest in land is as laid down in Section 28(b). Revocation is signified under the hand of a Public Officer dully authorized in that behalf by the Governor and notice thereof given to the holder. The latter 25 title is extinguished on the receipt by him of the notice or such later date as may be stated in the notice. Where land is required by the Federal Government, the Governor is obliged to revoke a Right of Occupancy if a notice is issued by the Head of State or on his behalf if he declares the relevant land to be require by the Government for public purpose.

test of time and most necessarily give way to the broader notions of the general interest of the community.

However, what constitutes public purpose is defined in Section 50 to include the use of land for (a) Exclusive Governor's use or for general public use, (b) Use of anybody corporate directly established by law or by anybody corporately registered under the Companies and Allied Matters Act established by Government; (b) Sanitary improvement of any kind (d) control over land contiguous to any part or over land the value of which will be enhanced by the construction of any railways, road or other public work or inconvenience about to be provided or provided by the Constitution; (e) Development of telecommunication, electricity, rural development or settlement, industrial and agricultural development and educational and other social services.

However, generally, every power has legal limit howsoever wide the language of the empowering Act. The power granted by Section 28 to the Governor to revoke the proprietary interest in land is not without limitation, circumscription or procedural guides, which must be observed. In the interpretation of the Land Use Act, particularly as it affects the revocation of interest of private citizens the courts have given a restrictive interpretation to the provision of Section 28. The judicial attitude towards revocation case is not to attack the interest of the statutory power of the Governor to revoke interest in land and acquire land for public purpose but on the strict compliance with statutory procedure to revoke. The litmus tests to which the revoking authority must satisfy are: whether the land sought to be acquired falls within the statutorirly defined purpose and whether the acquiring authority followed the laid down procedure for acquisition, where both question are answered in the affirmative, the court will validate the revocation. Thus, in administrators/executives of the estate of *General Sani Abacha* v. *Eke-Spiff,*[36]where the first respondent's Right of Occupancy was revoked and the same land re-allocated to Major General Sani Abacha,[37] could not be assimilated to an action taken in the overall interest of the public. Major General Sani Abacha in this context was an ordinary citizen. Also, no notice of revocation was served to the first respondent.. Failure to serve on the first respondent, the notice of revocation smacked of fraud. Consequently, the 3rd and 4th respondent breached the provisions of Section 28(1)(4)(c) of the Land Use Act.

---

[36] (2009) 2 NWLR (pt.1070) p.153. See also *Okeowo* v. *Attorney-General of Ogun State* (2010) ALL FWLR(Pt,540) p. 1209 and *Maiyegun* v. *Gov. of Lagos State* (2010) All FWLR (Pt.542) p. 1704

[37] See *Peenock Investment Ltd.* v. *Hotel Presidential* (1983) 4 NCLR 122 at 168.

The reason for strict adherence to the statutory procedure could be gleaned from numerous authorities decided by the Supreme Court and Court of Appeal first, an act that seeks to deprive an individual his property should be strictly construed against the acquiring authority.[38] Secondly, the right to expropriate private interest necessarily implicates the right of the person to be expropriated.

Consequently, the person being denied of his property has the right to know that his property is being taken over by the government. Applying the age long principle of *audi alterem partem*, such individual should be adequately informed of the government's decision to acquire his property. Thus, in *Adole* v. *Gwar*,[39] the court held that by virtue of Section 28(1) of the Land Use Act, the legislature did not intend capricious or arbitrary revocation of Right of Occupancy granted under Section 5(1) and (2) of the Act by the Governor or any appropriate authority. Both subsection (h) and (3) of Section 28 define what overriding public interest in the case of Statutory Right of Occupancy and Customary Right of Occupancy mean.

To effect a lawful acquisition of land, the notice of acquisition must be issued to the public by the Governor and the notice must clearly indicate that the land intended to be acquired is for no other thing than for public purposes. Section 28(5) of the Act spells out the grounds for revocation of a Statutory Right of Occupancy. And to ensure the control of the power to revoke a Right of Occupancy in respect of a parcel of land, Section 28(6) of the Act says in an unmistaken term that the right to revoke shall be signified under the hand of a Public Officer duly authorized in that behalf by the Governor and notice thereof shall be served on the holder personally.

Lastly, for a valid revocation of Right of Occupancy, whether statutory or that of a deemed holder, section 29 of the Act makes the prior payment of compensation to the holder a *sine qua non*.

Furthermore one of the most contentious aspects of the revocation power and which has been widely abused by the Governor and Public Officers is where there is failure of purpose which could otherwise in many ways arise where the land was used for any other purpose other than for which it was acquired like the granting in the instant case by the acquiring authority to private individuals.[40]

---

[38] Ibid. In *Ononuju* v. *A.G Anambra State* (2009)10NWLR, the court held that revocation of a right of occupancy can only be valid, if notice of same is served on the owner or occupier of the property, that publication in Gazette of the notice of revocation without personal service of same on persons concerned does not make the revocation valid.

[39] *Supra.*

[40] *Abacha* v. *Eke-Spiff, supra.*

The second pattern is where private citizens are divested of their land under Section 28 but the Governor later relocates or uses the land for private interest. The question flowing from these scenarios is whether the land should be allowed to revert to the original owner or the Governor should be allowed to hold onto the land in trust until when the acquired land will be required for similar public purposes. Furthermore, does individual who utilize such land for socially beneficiary purpose qualifies as public purpose? The answer to this question will depend on the broad interpretation of the term "public purpose".[41] Generally the Land Use Act has been widely touted as creating trust in favour of the citizen. Section 1 of the Act was interpreted to constitute trust in favour of the Governor for the over all benefit of Nigerians.[42] The nature of this trust has also generated valuable comments. However, in *Ajibulu* v. *Lawson*,[43] the Court of Appeal rightly came to the conclusion that a property ostensibly acquired for public purpose but later directly or indirectly diverted to serve private needs does not amount to valid acquisition. The acquiring authority cannot rob Peter to pay Paul by divesting one citizen of his interest in a property and vesting same in another.

Also, compensation is one of the key issues in any analysis of revocation power. First of course; compensation provides fairness to the person who is harmed by the revocation or government action. The classic rationale for compensation is that, in fairness and justice, one individual should not be forced to bear the burden that ought properly to be borne by society as a whole.[44] Secondly, compensation tends to limit government action. Even though bureaucrats enjoy the benefits of spending other people's money, their action are constrained by their agency's budget. Finally, the payment of compensation helps to encourage the resolution of social problems by private, voluntary contractual arrangement than by regulation.

However, in estimating the compensation to be given for any land or any estate or interest, the determining factor is the estimated market value of the property at the time the acquisition is made under the Land Use Act. The provision of compensation is stipulated in circumstances stated in Section 28(2)(a), (3)(d), (5)(a),(b) and Section 34(5) and (6).

---

[41] Smith I.O., *op. cit.*, at 261.
[42] See the Judgment of Uwais JSC in *Solati* v. *Sheju* (1986) 1 NWLR (pt.15) 158 at 209.
[43] (1991) 6 NWLR (pt. 915) 44.
[44] Smith I.O., *op. cit.*, at 263.

Effect of the Act on the jurisdiction of court with respect to land matters

It is to be noted that the Act itself provides for jurisdiction to entertain proceeding in respect of Statutory and Customary Right of Occupancy under Sections 39, 41 and 42 respectively. Under Section 40 of the Act, proceeding pending in any court in respect of title to any land, on the commencement of the Act whether at the court of first instance or on appeal were to be concluded with the exception that any order or decision of the court shall only be in respect the entitlement of either of the parties to the proceeding to a Right of Occupancy, whether Statutory or Customary in respect of such land. Section 39(1) of the Act gives exclusive original jurisdiction in respect of any land the subject of a Statutory Right of Occupancy and other matters connected therewith to the High Court. Under Section 41, an Area Court or Customary Court or other Court of equivalent jurisdiction in a state shall have jurisdiction in respect of a Customary Right of Occupancy while proceedings for the recovery of rent payable in respect of a Customary Right of Occupancy may be taken before a Magistrate Court of competent jurisdiction.

A constitutional question that has arisen in respect of these provisions is whether Section 41 of the Act which gives jurisdiction over Customary Right of Occupancy with the omission of the word exclusive in that Section could be interpreted to mean that the High Court has concurrent original jurisdiction with the Area of Customary Courts. The question was raised before the High Court in the early days of the Act. Judicial opinion was divergent on the issue. In *Otunba Chief Bola Adewunmi* v. *Ogunbowale & Others*, Balogun J. decided that with the combined effect of Section 1(3) 4(8)(b) and 274(3) of the 1999 Constitution, no existing law or any Act of the National Assembly or a law enacted by a House of Assembly or a law enacted by a House of Assembly of a State shall oust or purport to oust the jurisdiction of the Court of law or of a judicial tribunal established by law and that the High Court of a State has jurisdiction to hear or determine any dispute concerning or pertaining to the validity of a Right of Occupancy granted under the land Use Act 1978.The question was considered in *Sadikwu* v. *Dalori*[45] and *Oyeniran* v. *Egbetola.*[46] These two cases decided by the Supreme Court gave effect to the jurisdiction of Courts as provided under Sections 39(1) and 4 of the Act. The Court stated categorically (Per Wali) JSC in Sadikiwu's case

[45] (1996) 5 NWLR (pt. 447) p. 151.
[46] (1997) 5 NWLR (pt. 504) p. 122. See also *Salati* v. *Sheju* (1986) 1 All NLR 53,

that the original jurisdiction of the High Court in respect of a Customary Right of Occupancy is specifically excluded by the provision of Section 41 of the Act.[47]

It has been posited that the fact that the word "exclusive" is omitted in Section 1 of the Act does not mean that the High Court and the Area or Customary Court have concurrent original jurisdiction which argument sound persuasive. This argument is further buttressed by saying that by any stretch of imagination a High Court cannot be described has a Court of equivalent jurisdiction with an area of Customary Court as in *Oyeniran* case.[48] However, the dictum of Kutigi JSC that where there is no Area or Customary Court, a High Court being other court of equivalent jurisdiction under Section 39(1) of the act shall have original jurisdiction has been rejected by the duo of Ezejiofor, SAN and Okafor SAN.[49] Base on the reasons earlier stated, it is the writer's view[50] that the duo are correct not on the question whether the High Court has original jurisdiction in relation to Customary Right of Occupancy but to the extent that a High Court cannot be regarded as other Court of equivalent jurisdiction under Section 39(1) of the act notwithstanding the Supreme Court's decision that the High Court of a State has no original jurisdiction in proceeding relating to a Customary Right of Occupancy.

However, in *Raimi Agunde and Others* v. *Busari Alagbe & Anor*,[51] the Court of Appeal held that the Land Use Act is not an integral part of the Constitution and that it comes within the provision of any other law under Section 1(3) of the Constitution of the Federal Republic of Nigeria 1999, such that any provision of the Land Use Act contrary to the Constitution shall to the extent of the inconsistency be void. The Court reasons that by virtue of Section 272(1), the State High Court has unlimited jurisdiction and Section 41 of the Act delimiting the jurisdiction of the State High Court runs contrary to Section 1(3) of the 1999 Constitution and is to the extent of the inconsistency void and it was accordingly declared null and void. The Court held that the High Court has concurrent jurisdiction with the Customary or Area Court over the right to the Customary Right of Occupancy.

---

[47] (1986) 1 NWLR (pt.15) 198 per Karibi-Whyte, JCA which supported the decision in *Sadikwu* and *Oyeniran cases.*

[48] *Supra.*

[49] Smith I.O., *op. cit.*, at 42.

[50] Ibid.

[51] (1996) 5 NWLR (pt.447) p.151.In *Francis Idjakpa* v. *Ajigbereno* (2010)ALL NWLR at 1431,,the Court of Appeal held that even if land is situate in a non-urban area, the High Court would still have jurisdiction to entertain the suit.

Chapter 11

The Nigerian Land Use Act, 1978: x-raying emerging controversies

Some observers believe that the Land Use Act, 1978 remains the most controversial enactment in the Nigerian legislative history. According to Irikefe JSC (as he then was) in *Chief R.O. Nkwocha* v. *Governor of Anambra State*,[1] "The Land Use Decree...is indisputably the most impactful of all legislations touching upon the land tenurial systems of this country before and after full nationhood..."

Similarly in the words of Olatawura JSC, in *Abioye* v. *Yakubu*:[2]

> As far as I can remember, no enactment of parliament or Decree by the Federal Ministry Government has generated as much controversy. The Act has been vilified, reviled and criticized. It is undoubtedly an unpopular law because of its revolutionary provisions which have affected certain families and individuals whose source(s) of income or livelihood were from the sales of land which include lease and various grants under the customary land tenure.

Academicians and judges alike disagree among themselves as to the nature, implications and application of the Land Use Act. For instance, there have been serious debates amongst academicians on some vital issues. The issues are the problem of constitutional incorporation, expropriation and ouster clause controversies.[3]

Constitutional incorporation controversy

Until recently, there were conflicting judgments emanating from various High Courts in Nigeria on matters arising from the Land Use Act. Their verdicts are varied on the following questions amongst which are: i)

---

[1] (1984) 6 S.C. 362 at 363.

[2] (2000) 1 N.I.I.C. 1 at 155.

[3] See Acheneje, A., S., The Nigerian Land Use Act, 1978: Some Emerging Controversies. *Journal of Contemporary Legal Issues.* Publication of Idah Branch, Nigerian Bar Association, 2009 at p. 60.

whether or not the Act is an Act of the National Assembly or part of the Constitution of the Federal Republic of Nigeria; ii) and whether or not the Land Use Act survived under the 1979 Constitution.

In response to the two questions above, the court in the unreported case of *Unmar Ali and Company* v. *Commissioner of Land and Survey, Borno State*,[4] held that the Land Use Act is part of the Constitution of the Federal Republic of Nigeria. This decision was based on the provisions of Section 274(5) of the 1979 Constitution (now section 315(5) of the 1999 Constitution of the Republic of Nigerian, as amended), which provides that:

> Nothing in this Constitution shall invalidate the following enactments, that is to say the... Land Use Decree 1978...and its provisions shall continue to apply and have full effect in accordance with their tenor and to the like extent as any other provisions forming part of this Constitution and shall not be repealed except in accordance with the provisions of Section 9(2) of this Constitution.

The thinking of the court was that if the provisions of the Land Use Act should have equal force as the provisions of the Constitution and be repealed in the same way as the provisions of the Constitution, then it should be part of the Constitution.

On the other hand, the court in the case of *Aina and Co. Ltd* v. *Commissioner for Land and Housing, Oyo State*,[5] held that the Act was an existing law by virtue of Section 274(4)(b) of the 1979 Constitution, hence, an Act of the National Assembly. It must be noted that the constitutional controversy of the Act became eminent when it was doubtful whether the words "Military Governor" as during the civilian regime where there was no military without the Act and Constitution being amended to remove the "Military" since by virtue of Section 274 of the 1979 Constitution, the Act was part of it. Thus, in the case of *Chief R.O. Nkwocha* v. *Governor of Anambra State*,[6] the Supreme Court cleared the air on the issues and laid the matter to rest once and for all. The case was a reference made to the Supreme Court by the Court of Appeal by virtue of Section 259(3) of the 1979 Constitution.

The main question for resolution was whether the Governor of Anambra State is the authority to exercise the power or functions vested in or exercisable by the Military Governor under the provisions of the Land Use Act (Decree).

---

[4] Unreported Suit No.Bon/8/2/81, delivered on 4th March 1982.
[5] Unreported Suit No.OYHC/1/434/81.
[6] (1984) 6 S.C. 362.

The question itself arose from the exercise by the civilian Governor of Anambra State of the powers of revocation under Section 28 of the Act in respect of plots No.17 and No. 09 independence layout, Enugu, the leasehold interest which were assigned to the plaintiffs by a deed of assignment registered as No. 40 at page 40 in volume 1043 Land Registry at Enugu. The Supreme Court, Per Kayode Esho JSC held, *inter alia*, that:

> The State Governor succeeded to the powers of the Military Governor under the Land Use Act and has power to revoke a right of occupancy for overriding public interests and such other statutory or public powers which obviously without any further assurance were vested by the Act in the Military Governor;
>
> In view of the provisions of Section 274 of the 1979 Constitution, the Land Use Act is not an integral part of the Constitution. It is an ordinary statute which became extra-ordinary by virtue of its entrenchment (S.275(4)) in the Constitution, for if the Act has been made a part of the Constitution, it would not have been necessary to insert in sub-section(s) of Section 274 the words – "nothing in this Constitution shall invalidate" as the draftsman of the Constitution cannot make the Constitution to invalidate part of itself, nor would it be necessary to have in sub-section 6 of Section 274 that the Act shall continue to have effect as a "Federal enactment";
>
> That the tenor of the Act, as a single piece of legislation, is the nationalization of all lands in the country by the vesting of its ownership in the state leaving the private individual with an interest in land which is a mere right of occupancy, and which is the only right protected in his favour by law after the promulgation of the Act; and
>
> Once the import of Section 274 and Section 276 of the Constitution is separated, it would be clear that there is no conflict in the Act and the Constitution nor in the provisions of the Constitution in relation to the Act. It is the same organic law of the land that has provided for the status of the Act and made it a Federal enactment which the president can modify that has also made provision for the executive administration of the Act.

The above holding is far-reaching and binding throughout the country and settled most of the squabbles on the status of the Land Use Act and its relationship with the Constitution. Even though the decisions conform to the literary interpretation of Section 274(6) of the Constitution, it has an inherent implication. It implies that the president or the National Assembly can, by enactment, confer duties on the Governor a situation unacceptable in a Federal system of Government, which incidentally was decried by the same Justice Kayode Esho JSC., in

Ogun State v. *The Federation*,[7] where he held that "it has always been my contention that the bedrock of Federalism lies in each tier of government being a master in its own domain."

This, it appears, makes the constitutional incorporation argument of the Land Use Act more tenable, for the State Governors in a democratically elected government would readily accept duties assigned to them from the Constitution than duties issuing out from the executive president or the National Assembly. Support to this contention was given by Bello JSC in *Attorney General of the Federation* v. *Attorney General Bendel State & 18 Ors*,[8] where he said:

> I will also amplify the view that the dicta...that the National Assembly cannot unilaterally confer power or impose duty on a state functionary is a correct statement of the principles of constitutional law in a Federation. This principle found expression in our Sections 4 and 5 thereof.

In view of the above, the incorporation of the Act into the Constitution should not create controversies as the intention was simply to preserve its provisions from being amended as an ordinary law by State Governors given the importance of land to the citizens of this country and to the three tiers of government at large. The implication of the incorporation has been that the Act cannot be amended without the Constitution being amended. It is in line with this that the Act has been amended since 1978 thus leaving so many sections obsolete. There is, therefore, the urgent need to amend the 1999 Constitution so that the Act can also be amended if it must play its leading role as the sole unified document that regulates land use in Nigeria. If not, then many critics might still interpret the constitutional incorporation of the Land Use Act as controversial.

Expropriation controversy[9]

Black's Law Dictionary defined expropriation as a "governmental taking or modification of an individual's property rights especially by eminent domain."[10]

The word could also mean the act usually of a state in enforcing the compulsory surrender of private property for the purpose of the state or

---

[7] (1982) 3 NCLR 202.
[8] (1983) 6 S.C. 32.
[9] Acheneje, *op. cit.*, at p. 62
[10] Bryan A.G., *Black's Law Dictionary*, 7th edition, (London, West Group, 1999) p. 602.

for the overriding interest of the state without the payment of compensation.

There have been arguments and counter arguments as to whether or not the Land Use Act nationalized interest in real property in Nigeria. A state could expropriate individual property by exercising its power of "eminent domain" which is the sovereign power of a state that authorizes fair compensation to the other. Thus, the words nationalization and expropriation will be used interchangeably in this work to connote the deprivation of those interests in real property, which constitute proprietary rights under the Act.

An examination of Section 1 and other relevant sections will be done to show how such sections have created controversies amongst judges and legal writers. Section 1 therefore provides that:

> Subject to the provisions of this Act, all land comprise in the territory of each State in the Federation are hereby vested in the Governor of the State and such land shall be held in trust and administered for the use and common benefit of all Nigerians in accordance with the provisions of this Act.

Commenting on this Section, Ogundare J. in *Akinloye* v. *Oyejide*,[11] maintained that the word "vested" in Section 1 of the Act has the effect of transferring to the Governor of the State the ownership of all land in that state. On the literal reading of the Act, the judge was also of the view that the intelligible result is to deprive citizens of this country of their ownership in land and vest it in the respective State Governors. He equally rebutted the presumption that the lawmakers do not desire to confiscate the property or to encroach upon the rights of persons, as according to him, the provisions of the Act were clear and unambiguous. This interpretation was supported and accepted by the Supreme Court in *Nkwocha* v. *Governor of Anambra State*,[12] as representing the correct interpretation of the Act.

On the contrary, a brilliant academic and legal writer, Professor Omotola J.A., contended that this view is incorrect, maintaining that Section 1of the Act is ambiguous and its meaning could be correctly deduced by reference to other Sections of the Act. He was of the view that an examination of some provisions of the Act shows that there is no expropriation of the real property as Section 1 cannot be read in isolation save as is provided in Section 34(5) and (6) regarding the quantum of interest in undeveloped land that can be held by any person within the

---

[11] Unreported Suit No. HCJ/9A/83 decided on 17th July 1981 in the High Court of Ijero, Ondo State.
[12] (1984) 6 S.C. 362.

urban area of a state. He contended further that Section 28, which gives the Governor power of revocation, will be unnecessary if it is true that he is already an owner in the sense under Section 1 as there will be nothing to revoke.

He continued that the essence of Section 28 is not to diminish the proprietary rights over land vested in the Governors under Section 1 but to facilitate the recovery of lands granted or consented to under the relevant provisions of the Act by the Governor as 'owner' of the land. Thus, the researcher submits and agrees with Omotola's views.

On the other hand, Egute[13] maintains that even though Section 1 has vested all the land in the State Governor, Nigerians are left with the equitable interest in the land and have become beneficial owners of the land subject to other provisions of the Act. He equally maintains that the word 'trust' as used in Section 1 simply means that the Governor holds the land as a trustee for the beneficiaries, who are Nigerians and not in his private capacity as the owner and the word 'trustee' as used in Section 1 is not as high as it is under English law where the trustee is sometimes vested with the legal title of the property. Thus, Section 1 has created a bare trust and no more. Accordingly, the Supreme Court in the case of *Madam Salami & Ors.* v. *Oke*[14] held that although the Land Use Act vests all land in each state in the Governor of that State, the land is held by the Governor in trust and administered for the use and common benefit of all Nigerians in accordance with the provisions of the Act.

Consequently, the Act has not taken away the right of customary owners to enjoyment of the tributes. Rather, it left them untouched. As a result, the power that is vested in each Governor is the administrative power to control and proprietary interest. In line with the foregoing arguments, it is contended that the Act, specifically Section 1, did not or has not expropriated the land in Nigeria. It has simply vested the land in the governor of each state for administrative purposes only.

Furthermore, according to Section 34(2) and 36(4), where a piece of land is developed in urban and non-urban areas respectively, such lands shall continue to be held by the person in whom it was vested immediately before the commencement of the Act as if the holder of the land was the holder of a statutory or customary right of occupancy. Comparing and contrasting the above provisions with Section 1 of the Act, it would not be apt to say that Section 1 nationalized all land would amount to taking away such lands from the holders *ab initio*.

---

[13] *Op. cit.*, at p. 113.

[14] (1987) 4 NWLR (p.63); See also *Aigbonna* v. *Suleja Local Government and Ors* (1985) HCNR 847.

Thus, it can be seen that whatever the merit of the Supreme Court decision in *Nkwocha* v. *Governor of Anambra State*,[15] to the extent that it was decided that all lands were nationalized, does not adequately reflect the true spirit of the Act as it appears to be too sweeping to say so. Therefore, it follows that if "A" grants "B" a lease for 20 years before the promulgation of the Act, "B" would be deemed to have obtained his 20 years lease with the consent of the Governor under Section 22 of the Act. Such a lease would be "any encumbrances or interest valid in law" under Section 34(4) of the Act. By virtue of Sections 1, 21, 22 and 34(4), "A" and "B" would be tenant and subtenant respectively to the Governor. "A" is the 'holder' while "B" is the 'occupier'. It is probably in this revolutionary move, that the Act can be viewed to have nationalized all land within a state and turned all land owners into tenants.

It should be noted that when interpreting the provisions of the Land Use Act, great caution must be exercised in looking back into the history and state of land law in Nigeria, unless the provision in question is of doubtful import, or the words used have acquired technical meanings different from their natural meanings which could be resolved by reference to previous state of the law. Thus, in *Bank of England* v. *Vagliano Bros*,[16] when such difficulty arises, one has to "…examine the language of the statute and ask what its natural meaning is, uninfluenced by any consideration derived from the previous state of the law."

With respect to Section 34(5) and (6) regarding the quantum of interest in undeveloped land that can be held by any person within an urban area of a state, the correct position of the law is that, the Act converts such holders to tenants of the Governor with respect to half hectare of the land and such holders are entitled to statutory right of occupancy in respect of such lands.

Also important is the provisions of Section 11, which provides that the Governor or any public officer duly authorized by the Governor in that behalf shall have the power to enter upon and inspect the land comprised in any statutory right of occupancy or any improvements effected thereupon at any reasonable hour in the day time and occupier shall permit and give free access to the Governor or any such officer so to enter and inspect.

Furthermore, under Section 14, the occupier of land shall have exclusive possession against all persons except the Governor. In other words, the Governor has "concurrent possessory right" with all

---

[15] *Supra*
[16] *Supra*

proceedings pertaining to title to land or interest therein, pending before the courts at the commencement of the Act, the court shall not recognize any higher interest or title than the right of occupancy. Sections 21-23 similarly firmly establish the Governor's supervision and surveillance over all land in the State.

There is no denying the fact that some of the Sections of the Act, for example, Section 36 may be irksome, rightly or wrongly, to a number of traditional or customary landowners or landlords. However, as stated by the Supreme Court in the *Abioye* case, it is the duty of the judge construing the provisions of a statute, not to so construe it by making nonsense of it but to do so as not to defeat the manifest intention of the lawmaker.

Ouster clauses controversy[15]

The controversy relates especially to the provisions of Section 47(2) dealing with the duty of compensation by the Governor. The provisions of Section 47(2) are quite clear and unambiguous and plain in ousting the jurisdiction of the courts to inquire into any question concerning or relating to the amount or adequacy of any compensation paid or to be paid under this Act.[16]

But before the promulgation of the Act in 1978, the 1963 Constitution had provided in Section 31 as follows:

> No property, moveable or immovable shall be taken possession of compulsorily and no right over or interest in any such property shall be acquired compulsorily in any part of Nigeria, except by or under the provisions of the law that;
>
> requires the payment of adequate compensation therefore;
>
> gives to any person claiming such compensation or right of access, for the determination of his interest in the property and the amount of compensation to the High Court having jurisdiction in that part of Nigeria.

Similarly, the 1979 Constitution, which was the first to incorporate the Land Use Act into its provision and the current Constitution of Nigeria 1999, have provisions which guarantee access to the courts by an aggrieved person. For instance, Section 44 of the 1999 Constitution provides as follows:

---

[15] Acheneje, *op. cit.*, at p. 65

[16] Ibid.

> No moveable property or any interest in an immovable property shall be taken possession of compulsory and right over or interest in any such property shall be acquired compulsorily in any part of Nigeria except in the manner and for the purposes prescribed by a law that among other things: i) require the prompt payment of compensation; and ii) gives any person claiming such compensation, a right of access for the determination of his interest in property and amount of compensation, to a court of law or tribunal or body having jurisdiction in that part of Nigeria.

It is noteworthy that while the 1963 Constitution provided for "adequate compensation", no such language was used by both the 1979 and the 1999 Constitution which simply provide for "prompt payment of compensation" and this is seen to be controversial.

It is crucial to mention here that both the Public Land Acquisition ordinance[17] and the Land Tenure Law, 1962 (all repealed) provided for payment of compensation and access to the courts by aggrieved persons to challenge the amount of compensation that was payable where their rights were revoked for overriding public interest. There was no provision similar to Section 47(2) ousting the jurisdiction of the courts to inquire into any issues involving adequacy of compensation.

In view of the above, the vexed question can be put differently. What is the constitutional validity of the provisions of Section 47(2) and similar conflicting provision of the Act? Firstly, the maxim – *generalia specialibs non-derogant* (where a general intention is shown in the same statute, which is incompatible with a particular intention then, the particular intention must be construed as an exception to the general intention). This maxim has the effect of validating the conflicting provisions by the Act as sections 36(1) and 44(1) of the 1999 Constitution, which deal with fair hearing and access to court respectively are general provisions which are applicable subject to the exceptions created by the Constitution itself. This contention is justifiable by the use of the phrase "subject to the provision of this Constitution" at the beginning of Section 272(1) of the 1999 Constitution, showing that it is a general provision that does not foreclose exceptions.

The same rule applies to the provisions of Section 315(5)(d) of the Constitution, which delimits the jurisdiction of the High Courts and, thereby, confers validity on Section 47(2) of the Act thereby unfortunately vesting the Land Use and Allocation Committee with powers to resolve disputes on issues of adequacy of compensation instead

---

[17] No. 17 of 1917 (later known as the Public Lands Act). Cap.167 LFN & Lagos, 1958.

of a resort to the courts whose independence is more guaranteed than that of the Land Use and Allocation Committee.

It is actually the view of most scholars, however, that the courts in Nigeria have not been firm and fair in their dealing with the issue of ouster clause created by Section 47(2) relative to the provisions of the Constitution. Egute,[17] for instance, argues "it is unfortunate that the courts as the last hope of the ordinary man have often failed in this regard to either increase or reduce the amount of compensation payable whenever there is a dispute." This was also the view of Yakubu.[18] In his appraisal of the decision of the Chief Judge of Kaduna State in the unreported case of *Dada* v. *Governor of Kaduna State.*[19] The court in deciding the case avoided the determination of the amount of compensation but simply said, in accordance with Section 40 of the Constitution that the appellant was entitled to compensation. This court dodged the real issue, leaving the amount of compensation to the appropriate land officer. But on further appeal to both the Court of Appeal and Supreme Court, consolation seemed to have come as both courts agreed that the court has the power to assess the amount and adequacy of compensation.

Before the Court of Appeal and Supreme Court decision in the foregoing case, the trial judge in *Commissioner of Lands* v. *Ideye*,[20] had similarly relied on the award made by the Land officer and avoided deciding on the amount or adequacy of compensation as sought by the plaintiff.

In *L.E.D.B.* v. *William*,[21] the then Supreme Court equally shied away from the real controversy, holding that the agreed value in similar cases afforded a reasonable good guide for assessment of compensation.

Even though Section 47(2) of the Land Use Act remains unsatisfactory, it is valid and effective. It is hoped that the issue will be laid to rest anytime an opportunity is presented and it is only then that the much needed succour of landowners whose properties are compulsorily acquired for public purposes will get the needed respite from the courts, the alternative is an amendment to expunge Section 47(2) of the Act.[22]

---

[17] Acheneje, *op. cit.*

[18] Ibid., at p. 66

[19] Suit No.KDH/186/81 decided on 31st December, 1982.

[20] (1938) 14 NLR 109.

[21] (1963) 1 All NLR 267.

[22] Acheneje, *op. cit.*, at p67

Chapter 12

The Land Use Act, 1978: a curse or blessing?

A major development in Nigerian land law and conveyance was the enactment of the Land Use Act, 1978. The Land Use Act of 1978 was promulgated into law on the 29th of March 1978. The law was revolutionary in essence and was meant to reassert the right of all Nigerians to the land of Nigeria.[1] The preamble to the Land Use Decree (now Act) succinctly stated that:

> Whereas it is in the public interest that the rights of all Nigerians to the land of Nigeria be asserted and preserved by law;
> "And whereas it is also in the Public interest that the rights of all Nigerians to use and enjoy land in Nigeria and the natural fruits thereof in sufficient quantity to enable them to provide for the sustenance of themselves and their families should be assured, protected and preserved.

The whole essence of the Act was to make land readily available to all Nigerians.[2] The followings are therefore the principal objectives of the Act:

- To remove the bitter controversies, resulting at times in loss of lives and limbs which land is known to be generating;
- To streamline and simplify the management of ownership of land in the country;
- To assist the citizenry irrespective of his social status to realize his ambition and aspiration of owing the place where he and his family will live a secured and peaceful life;
- To enable the government to bring under control the use to which land can be put in all parts of the country and thus facilitate planning and zoning programmes for particular uses.[3]

---

[1] See the *Land Use Act: A Time for Review* by Emeka D. Eleh, Volume 6 of *the Economy* of June 2001 at p.29

[2] See Raimi A.L., "The Land Use Act,1978; A Blessing or Curse" *Ikeja Bar Review,*Vol 1 Pt1&2 2007 at 80

[3] See the Address to the Press by the Military Governor of Lagos State, Commander G.N. Kanu on the Lagos Land Use Law delivered on 25th of May 1978.

The Land Use Act was one of the existing laws entrenched in the 1979 Constitution (now 1999 Constitution) by the Obasanjo-led military regime.[4] Since the promulgation of the Act in 1978 a lot of controversies have been generated in the real property law in Nigeria. While some people regard the Act as a blessing to Nigerians, others have contrary view. To the latter, the Act is a curse and its enactment was quite unfortunate. There is therefore the need for a critical appraisal of the Act.

The pre-1978 statutory intervention in land law and land administration in Nigeria

Before the enactment of the Land Use Act, 1978, statutory intervention in land administration in Southern Nigeria had been in the areas of public ownership of land, planning control, control of dispositions and reform of customary law.

In the area of public ownership of land, some of the earliest legislation introduced by the colonial administration dealt with the acquisition of land for public purposes. The first of such legislation was the Public Lands Ordinance of 1876. It was a legislation of the Gold Coast Colony. By then, Lagos was part of the Gold Coast Colony. The 1876 Act was re-enacted with modification as the Public lands Acquisition Act of 1917.[5] This Act later became a Regional (and later State) law following the introduction of the Federation Structure. This legislation empowered the government to acquire land compulsorily for public purpose subject to the payment of compensation to the expropriated owners.

The power to acquire land compulsorily was also given by some other statutes such as the Town and Country Planning Laws, which allowed the compulsory acquisition for schemes of development. This usefulness of the power of compulsory acquisition was that it enabled government to gain access to land undeterred by conflicting claims to the land.[6] The State land Act or Laws empowered the Government to grant leases of State land to private individuals.

On planning control, a restriction on land use for town planning purpose was seriously attempted for the first time in Nigeria when the Lagos Town Planning Ordinance 1928 was passed. It established the

---

[4] Other existing laws entrenched in the Constitution, by the Military Administration were: The National Youth Service Corps Decree 1993, the Public Complaints Commission Act and the National Security Agencies Act.

[5] Cap.167, Laws of the Federation of Nigeria – Lagos, 1958.

[6] C.O. Olawoye, "Statutory Shaping of land Law and Land Administration up to the Land Use Act" in J.A. Omotola, ed., The Land Use Act: Report of a National Workshop (Lagos: Lagos University Press, 1982) p.15.

Lagos Executive Development Board (L.E.D.B.) and charged it with the responsibility of developing town-planning schemes with the general object of securing proper sanitary condition, amenity and convenience within the town area of Lagos.[7] In 1946, the first countrywide town and country planning statute was enacted.[8] Under the Nigeria Town and Country Planning Ordinance of 1946, the Governor-General constituted the General Planning Authority for the country. He was charged with the responsibility for securing controlled development through the preparation of planning schemes all over the country.[9] Following the introduction of the Federal Structure, the Act became a Regional (later State) law.[10]

The policy of control of dispositions of land dates back to 1900. Under the Native Lands Acquisition Law enacted by the legislature of the Protectorate of Southern Nigeria, an alien was prohibited from acquiring an interest in land from a native or from a fellow alien except under an instrument, which has been previously approved by the Governor. This method of control was not applicable to the colony of Lagos. The Lagos State Government by an edict in 1971 (the Acquisition of Land by Aliens Edict) introduced similar policy.

The statutes on reform of customary law included the Kola Tenancy Act of 1935[11] and the Communal Land Rights Vesting in Trustee Law of Western Nigeria.[12] The Kola Tenancy Act, 1935 tried to reform the customary law with regard to kola tenancies prevalent in Onitsha and its environs. The Communal Land Rights Vesting in Trustee law had the aim of reconciling the customary law relating to the management of communal land with the realities of modern times in order to curb the abuses by traditional rulers who were building empires for themselves out of dispositions of communal land.

In Northern Nigeria, the shaping of land policy was a result of a number of historical events. Firstly, the activities of the Royal Niger Company ruled the Northern Nigeria before 1900 under a Charter. This company had during the period of its hegemony acquired vast areas of land along both sides of the River Niger and River Benue. On the declaration of the protectorate in 1900, the Government decided to take

---

[7] Sections 16 to 42 of the Ordinance.

[8] This was known as the Nigeria Town and Country Planning Ordinance of 1946

[9] See Section 4 of the ordinance. In each of the regions, the powers of the Governor-General were exercised on his behalf by the Minster responsible for planning matters.

[10] Raimi, *op. cit.*, at p82

[11] Cap. 98, Laws of Nigeria 1948. The Government of Eastern Nigeria adopted the same legislation in Cap.69, Laws of Eastern Nigeria, 1963.

[12] Cap.24, Laws of Western Nigeria, 1959.

over the land and thus became Crown land.[13] Secondly, British jurisdiction was extended over most areas ruled by the Fulani Emirs by conquest. The Government claimed as successors to the conquered or deposed rulers the land rights which the latter claimed. The land thus taken over from the Emirs was classified as public land while the Crown Land was vested in the Governor in trust for Her Majesty, public land was vested in the Governor in trust for the people.

In 1908, the Land and Native Rights Proclamation was enacted and later re-enacted with amendment as the land and Native Rights Ordinance of 1916. This Ordinance vested the whole land in the Northern Protectorate in the Government in trust for the natives. The Land Tenure Law of 1962 re-enacted the Land and Native Rights Ordinance of 1916. The interest, which an individual could hold under the 1962 law, was a right of occupancy, statutory or customary.

Background to the Land Use Act[14]

The difficulties associated with land acquisition for development project and individual ownership of land coupled with speculation in urban land were highlighted by the Military Administration of Murtala or Obasanjo in the third National Development Plan 1975-1980.[15] In urban areas, acquisition of land both for government projects and non-government building purposes became virtually impossible. In addition, there was the problem of insecurity of title under customary law. The poor performance of the economy, the inability of the country to feed itself, inability of both the public and the private sectors to provide sufficient shelter for the people and even the inflationary trends in the economy were blamed largely on the system of land tenure.

It was against the above background that in 1977, the Federal Military Government set up an eleven-man land Use Panel with the following terms of reference:

- To undertake an in-depth study of the various land tenure, land use, and land conservation practices in the country and recommend steps to be taken to streamline them;
- To study and analyse all the implications of a uniform land policy for the country;

---

[13] Similar steps were taken in the case of Southern Nigeria under the Niger Lands Transfer ordinance (later law) No.2 of 1916.

[14] Raimi, *op. cit.*, at p. 84

[15] See the Third National Development Plan 1975-1980, Volume 1 p.398.

- To examine the feasibility of a uniform land policy for the entire country, make necessary recommendations, and propose guidelines for implementation; and
- To examine steps necessary for controlling future land use and also opening and developing new land for the needs of Government and Nigeria growing population in both urban and rural areas and make appropriate recommendations.[16]

In its 300-page report, the panel recommended against nationalization of land in Nigeria. Only one member of panel, Prof. R.K. Udo, supported nationalization of land. All these development above culminated in the promulgation of the Land Use Act, 1978.[17]

The Act is based on the Land Tenure Law which had been in operation in the Northern States of Nigeria since 1962 and which nationalized practically all lands in that part of the country.[18]

The effect of the Land Use Act on land holding

The effect of the Act was to nationalize all the land within a state and turn all landowners into tenants.[19] This was emphasized in *Nkwocha v. Governor of Anambra State & Ors* [20] where Kayode Eso JSC who delivered the lead judgment held, *inter alia,* that:

> "The tenor of the Act as a single piece of legislation is the nationalization of all lands, in the country by vesting of its ownership in the state leaving the individual with an interest in land which is a mere right of occupancy, and which is the only right protected in his favour by law after the promulgation of the Act."[21]

It is clear from the provision of Section 1 of the Act that the Governor of each state is the legal owner of all land comprised in his state except those vested in the Federal Government. He however, holds such land in trust for the use and benefit of all Nigerians.

---

[16] See the Federal Government White Paper on the Report and Recommendations of the Land Use Panel published by the Federal Ministry of Information, Lagos, p.1.

[17] Raimi, *op. cit.*, at p.86

[18] See Sections 48 and 49 of the Law.

[19] S.A. Oretuyi "Title to Land in Nigeria: Past and Present" Inaugural Lecture Series 100(Ile-Ife: O.A.U. Press Ltd., 1996) P15 (The Lecture was actually delivered on June 11, 1991).

[20] (1984) I.S.C.N.L.R. 634

[21] Ibid., at 652.

The legal status of the Act

The Land Use Act was one of the four Acts incorporated into the 1979 Constitution and subsequently into the 1999 Constitution by the military administration.[22] The Act was very unpopular at its inception and there were threats by politicians during the 1978 political campaigns to abrogate it. This was the major rationale for its entrenchment in the Constitution.[23]

Section 315(5) of the 1999 Constitution provides:

> "Nothing in this Constitution shall invalidate the following enactments that is to say:
>
> The National Youth Service Corps Decree 1993;
> The Public Complaints Commission Act;
> The Land Use Act and the provisions of those enactments have full effect in accordance with their tenor and to the like extent as any other provisions forming part of this Constitution and shall not be altered or repealed except in accordance with the provisions of Section 9(2) of this Constitution".

The Supreme Court had held in *Nkwocha* v. *Governor of Anambra State & ors*[24] that the Land Use Act is not an integral part of the Constitution and that it is subject to Section 1(3) of the Constitution.

An appraisal of the Land Use Act, 1978

The Land Use Act was enacted as "a Decree" and came into effect on the 29th of March 1978. By the Adaptation of Law (Re-Designation of Decrees, etc) Order 1980, it assumed the appellation of an Act. The title suggests land use and thus a planning statute. This is generally misleading. The Act is basically a land law Statute which de-emphasizes private powers over, and interest in land in favour of the State.[25]

When the Act was promulgated in 1978, it looked good and promising. It was like the dawn of a new era, an epoch in the history of land law in Nigeria. The preamble to the Act eloquently expresses this sentiment. However, it has been observed that the objectives of the Land Use Act have remained largely unfulfilled and title to land appears to be more insecure now than it ever was.[26] This disappointment is attributable more to the implementation of the Act than its structure and

---

[22] See Section 274(5) of the 1999 Constitution and Section 315(5) of the 1999 Constitution.
[23] S.A. Oretunyi, *op. cit.*, pp.15-16.
[24] *Supra*
[25] See A.A. Utuama, *Nigerian Law of Real Property*, (Ibadan, Shaneson C.I. Ltd, 1989), p.145
[26] See Raimi, *op. cit.,* at p. 88

intendment. The position today is that land is less available to the ordinary Nigerian than it was prior to the Act thus holding most citizens to the unenviable state of perpetual tenants. According to Hon. Justice Augustine Nnamani, who as the Attorney-General, was responsible for the drafting of the Act and its incorporation into the Constitution:

> The lofty hope in the second stanza of the preamble – that the rights of all Nigerians to use and enjoy land in Nigeria and the natural fruits thereof in sufficient quantity to enable them provide for the sustenance of themselves and their families be assured, protected and preserved or in Section 1 of the Act that all land be held in trust and administered for the use and common benefit of all Nigerians – has been nothing but a forlorn hope, a pipe dream.[27]

The followings are some of the gray areas of the Land Use Act, 1978 that needs urgent review: The limit of the land allowed by Section 34(5) and (6)o of the Act has been totally ignored. The allocation polices of the various governments (both military and civilian) have been scandalous. The Land Use and Allocation Committees, which are supposed to make recommendations on these matters, are no more than appendages of the Governors and merely endorse lists approved by them. The Committees have been rendered impotent and their functions taken over by the Governors. Allocation of land has largely been to friends, relatives and party faithfuls. Indeed, land has become an item of patronage. Allocation is hardly made to low-income earners. Most State Governments have not earmarked a percentage of land available for allocation to this category of Nigerians as a deliberate policy. The combination of factors arising from the zeal attending the generation of internal revenue by State governments has put land beyond the reach of the ordinary Nigerian.

Similarly, the implementation of the Act has brought untold hardship on Nigerians. Examples are provisions relating to the issue of certificate of occupancy and grant of consent to alienate. Both can take years and an applicant is subjected to the vagaries of bureaucratic action with demands for survey plans, interminable fees, documents, etc. The import of section 22 of the Act is that the consent of the Governor is required before any legal transaction in land can be consummated. This is perhaps a major impediment created by the Act. In practical terms, it is nearly impossible to comply with the provisions of this clause. Consent is quite expensive to obtain. Also, it takes a long time to obtain. The entire process of obtaining Governor's consent is very frustrating.

---

[27] See "Land Use Act – 11 Years After" being an address presented to the N.B.A. Ikeja Branch by Hon. Justice Augustine Nnamani on 3rd of March 1989.

Similarly, it is generally believed that the consent provision in Section 22 of the Act is a clog in the wheel of economic progress and also a veritable avenue for corruption. Against this background, Obaseki JSC in *Savannah Bank Ltd* v. *Ajilo*,[28] *inter alia* declared that:

> It (consent clauses in the Act) is bound to have a suffocating effect on the commercial life of the land and house owing class of the society who use their properties to raise loans and advances from banks. I have no doubt that it will take the working hour of a State Governor to sign consent papers without going half way if these clauses are to be implemented. These areas of the Land Use Act need urgent review to remove their problem nature.[29]

Another problem of the Act is the misuse or abuse of Section 28 of the Act, which deals with the power of Governor to revoke rights of occupancy. For instance, commercial banks are uncertain as to the value of certificate of occupancy, which they are being asked to take as security for loans bearing in mind that these certificates can be revoked at the whims and caprices of the Governors. Similarly, the Act appears to hinder economic progress because of the unwillingness of and inability of banks and other financial institutions to give out loans on mortgage. This is because if a right of occupancy is revoked, a mortgagee has no right to the compensation payable, as the definition of "holder" or "occupier" in Section 51 of the Act does not include a mortgagee.

Again, certain provisions of the Act contradict the provisions of the 1999 Constitution. For example, the Act purports to exclude payment of compensation for empty undeveloped land. While the Act recognizes existing right in land including rights in undeveloped land, it limits the compensation for such land when compulsorily acquired.[30]

It is posited that the provisions of Sections 28 and 29 of the Land Use Act, 1978 do not conform to the doctrine of compensation provided for in Section 44 of the 1999 Constitution. They also do not recognize the interest of third parties in government allocated land. The importance of land and the injustice associated with taking over undeveloped land without compensation has been highlighted by Adedapo Adeniran as follows:

> It seems unfair that Government should take over without compensation capital invested in land ownership when capital invested in other fields for example government loans, bonds,

---

[28] (1989) I.S.C.N.J. 169; (1989 1 NWLR (pt.97) 305

[29] Ibid.

[30] See generally Sections 28 and 29 of the Land Use Act,1978.

companies, shares, industries or commercial businesses are left untouched.[31]

The compensation provided for in Section 29 and 35 of the Act is grossly inadequate, and concerned persons are never enthusiastic about yielding to the process. The method of assessing the compensation payable to the holders or occupiers for the value at the date of revocation of their unexhausted improvements lacks of peoples' confidence as government appointees under Section 2(2)(c), who cannot afford to be neutral, are the assessors. The abuses relating to the revocation of rights of occupancy would have been considerably minimized if the Act had provided an effective procedure for the payment of adequate compensation in the event of revocation of rights of occupancy. The Act further complicated the matter by excluding the courts from entertaining cases relating to compensations under the Act.[32] Section 4(8) of the 1999 Constitution provides that the legislature "shall not enact any law that ousts or purports to oust the jurisdiction of a court of law or of a judicial tribunal established by law."

Another area of contradiction is the provision of Section 41 of the Land Use Act, which deals with the jurisdiction of Area or Customary Courts in respect of proceedings in respect of a customary right of occupancy granted by Local Government under the Act. Section 41 of the Act confers on Customary or Area Court jurisdiction in respect of the proceeding in respect of any land the subject of customary right of occupancy granted by Local Government. The question is can the High Court of a State equally entertain similar proceedings apart from the ones mentioned in Section 39 of the Act over which it has exclusive original jurisdiction? In the case of *Alhaji Abubakar Sadikwu* v. *Alhaji Abba Dalori*,[33] the Supreme Court held that the Maiduguri High Court lacked original jurisdiction to entertain the suit or proceedings in respect of land subject of a customary right of occupancy. Similar decision was reached by the Supreme Court in *Abraham Oyeniran & Others* v. *James Egbetola & Another*.[34]

It must be noted that *Sadikwu* case was filed before the 1979 Constitution came into force while Egbetola's case was decided after the commencement of the 1979 Constitution. The latter judgment was given in contravention of the provision of Section 236 of the 1979 Constitution

---

[31] See Adedapo Adeniran "The Futility of the Land Use Decree, 1978," cited by S.A. Oretuyi in his Inaugural Lecture titled "Title to Land in Nigeria: Past and Present".

[32] See Section 47(2) of the Land Use Act.

[33] (1996) 4 SCNJ 20; (1996) 5 NWLR (pt.447) 151.

[34] (1997) 50 LRCN 1376.

(now S.272 of the 1999 Constitution), which gave unlimited jurisdiction to the State High Court in respect of civil and criminal proceedings.

In 2000, the Supreme Court in *Alhaji Karimu Adisa* v. *Emmanuel Oyinwola*[35] overruled itself by holding that its judgment in *Egbetola* case was given *per incuriam* as it was delivered in contravention of Section 236 of the 1979 Constitution (Section 272 of the 1999 Constitution). In 2004, the Supreme Court re-affirmed its judgment in *Oyinwola* case in the case of *Ezukwu* v. *Peter Ukachukwu.*[36]

The military regime of General Obasanjo, which enacted the Land Use Decree, complicated the matter from inception by entrenching the Act into the 1979 Constitution, and subsequently into the 1999 Constitution by yet another military regime of General Abdulsalami Abubakar, without any debate or approval by the Constituent Assembly.[37] However, in *Nkwocha* v. *Governor of Anambra State and Others,*[38] the Supreme Court held that the Land Use Act is not an integral part of the Constitution. It is an ordinary statute, which became extra-ordinary by virtue of its entrenchment in the Constitution. The provisions of the Act are therefore to be construed subject to the Constitution.

Another problem associated with the Act is that its administration has been chocked by bureaucratic bottlenecks and obstacles. Layouts are very limited and the process of applying and securing land in the government layouts has become a Herculean task. To even apply for certificate of occupancy for land already in one's possession is not easy.[39] The "Nigerian factor" has reared its head again. Land touts are fully back, making a lot of money "pushing" applications through the system. In the same vein, the Land Use Act has not had any appreciable impact on access to land. Most applications for certificates of occupancy are in respect of land acquired through private sale. Nigerians still fine it extremely difficult to acquire land through the official channels particularly in states other than their own state of origin. In fact, if one is not an indigene of a state it is futile to make a demand for the allocation of land.[40] It is, therefore, suggested that land should be vested in the Federal Government rather than in the State Governors. It is ironical that

---

[35] (2000) FWLR (pt.8) p.1349.

[36] (2004) 121, LRCN, 4880.

[37] See B.O. Okere, "The Constitutionality of Incorporating Certain Decrees into the 1979 Nigeria Constitution" *Nigeria Bar Journal,* 1980 Vol.16 p.44.

[38] (1984) 4 NWLR (pt.35) 361.

[39] For an account of the procedure, See U.J. Osimiri "Application for Certificate of Occupancy – Practice and Procedure" (1991) *Justice,* Vol.2, No.4 P.11.

[40] Ikechukwu O. Odeomelam "Governor's Consent under the Land Use Act: 20 Years After" *Modus International Law and Business Quarterly,* March 1999, Vol.4, No.1, p.49 at p.51.

the land is not always available even to government because it is not every land that the government can acquire.[41] Equitable distribution of land, which was one of the main reasons for the enactment of the Act, is yet to be achieved.

The Act also failed to specify how development made on land would be treated when the land reverts to the state. The life of a right of occupancy in most cases in 99 years. The effect of this is that every allottee of state land or indeed owner of a property covered by a certificate of occupancy is deemed to be a tenant of the state.

Also, the Act enacts in its Section 6(1) that Local Government can grant Customary Right of Occupancy even though title is never vested in that authority by the Act or any other enactment. This is wrong in law except it can be shown that this is an exception to the common law rule of *nemo dat quod non habet*. This lacuna has resulted in the inability of various land advisory committees to discharge their functions creditably.[42]

Apart from the above, the Land Use Act has abolished freehold title to land. Before the Act came into force there were holders of freehold titles to land in Nigeria. The Act has now limited the title that can be granted under it to leasehold interests not exceeding ninety-nine years. As said above, every allottee of State land or indeed owner of a property covered by a certificate of occupancy is deemed to be a tenant of the State.[43] Section 34(2) and (5a) of the Act requires separate mention here. Section 34(2) states *inter alia*:

> "Where the land is developed, the land shall continue to be held by the person in whom it was vested immediately before the commencement of this Decree as if the holder of the land was the holder of a statutory right of occupancy issued by the Military Governor under this Decree."

Section 34(5a) states:

> "Where on commencement of this Decree the land is undeveloped, the one plot or portion of land not exceeding half hectare in area shall subject to subsection (6) below, continue to be held by the person in whom the land was so vested as if the holder of the land was the

[41] P.A. Oluyede "A Decade of a Statutory Monster: The Land Use Act" in M. A. Ajomo (ed.), *New Dimension in Nigeria Law* (Lagos: 1989), pp.134-135.

[42] See G.A. Okpara "Land Ownership: which way Nigeria?" *Modern Practice Journal of Finance and Investment Law,* January/April 2004, Vol.8. No.1-2, pp.231-247.

[43] See Emeka D. Eleh, "The Land Use Act: A Time for Review", Vol.6 of *The Economy* of June 2001 at p.31.

> holder of a statutory right of occupancy granted by the Military Governor in respect of the plot or portion as aforesaid..."

The import of the above provisions is to confer something akin to a freehold title under English land law to the beneficiaries. This is however not achieved because of the following reasons.

First, the holders were supposed to pay ground rent to the Government, which should not be the case with a freehold title.

Secondly, the only current evidence of title that a holder could have is that upon application, the government will grant him a statutory right of occupancy which of cause amounts to a conversion of freehold title into a leasehold title provided for by the Decree.

Thirdly, if a holder desires to do any transaction on the land, he will be required to obtain the consent of the Governor for the transaction to be legally binding which in effect defeats the presumed freehold title, which he is supposed to hold.

The issue of Federal and State control over the land is not properly addressed by the Act. Section 1 of the Act clearly vests all land within the territory of each State in the State Governor. The import of this provision is that the Federal Government is also a tenant in each state where it has properties. It also means that the Federal Government must ask the state for land if it wants land for development purposes. This provision was grossly abused during the third republic when some State Governments refused to release land for political reasons. An attempt by the Babangida's administration to backdate a decree to acquire properties like the Obsorne layout in Lagos State was pronounced illegal by the court of law.

The amendment of the Act is made complex by its entrenchment in the Constitution. The provision of Section 315(5) of the 1999 Constitution makes it a near impossibility to expect a reform of the Act from a civilian government. This is due to the rigorous procedure for the amendment of the Constitution under Section 9(2) of the same Constitution. Against this background, Professor Omotola found his lamentation on the Act irresistible when he declared:

> "...This is a rather strange procedure for amending a statute that touches on the daily life of all citizens, a statute that was hurriedly prepared and containing a host of absurd provisions which appear unworkable. Meanwhile, the society is faced with an impasse and only God knows when it will end."[44]

---

[44] See. Omotola, J.A., "Compensation Provisions of the Land Use Decree," Nigeria Bar Journal, 1980, Vol. xvi, p. 37.

The courts have tried to water down some of the excesses committed under the Act. Judicial action is however not enough. The courts can only insist that revoking authorities comply strictly with procedure for the revocation of a right of occupancy. Once the revoking authority has complied with the procedural requirements under the Act, the courts are powerless. The helpless land occupier is left with no remedy save the token compensation payable under the Act.[45]

In view of the foregoing, the following reforms among others are recommended in respect of the Act.

First, there is the need to remove the Act from the Constitution so that amendments to it can easily be effected.

Secondly, the courts should be conferred with unfettered jurisdiction to inquire into the questions pertaining to the amount or adequacy of compensation in order to protect the ordinary citizens from arbitrary, punitive and capricious use of power by the government or its agencies, officials or representatives. Section 47 of the Act, which purports to oust the jurisdiction of the court, should be repealed as this section is inconsistent with Sections 1(1) 8(3), and 6(6) (b) of the 1999 Constitution.

Thirdly, the consent clauses in Section 21 and 22 of the Act should be amended. Only grants actually made by the Governor or the Local Government should require prior consent before alienation. Owners of deemed grants should be able to alienate without consent and such alienation should be notified to the Governor's office or the appropriate Local Government for information and record purposes only.[46]

The Land Use Act, which attempts to revolutionise title to land in Nigeria, is no doubt a complex legislation. It is in the interest of stability of Nigeria and security of title to land that some land reforms similar to the ones embodied in the Act should be introduced in the country. Nevertheless, it seems that the uncertainty regarding title to land is still with us, the Act notwithstanding. The expropriatory and confiscatory nature of the Act cannot be denied. The Act has divested individuals, families and communities of their ownership of land and has left them with a bare right of occupancy. This can only be justifiable if the generality of the people have practicable benefits in return.

---

[45] See A.A. Oba "The Land Use Act and Economic Development" in Modus International Law & Business Quarterly. December 2001, Vol. 6 No.4, pp. 36-47.

[46] See *Nigerian Tribune* of Monday, 15th of August 2005 at p.26.

Chapter 13

Ways of declaration of title to land

The *Black's Law Dictionary*[1] defines title as the union of all elements as ownership, possession and custody constituting the legal right to control and dispose of property; the legal link between a person who owns property and the property itself. No doubt it has always been an onerous task before the law courts to establish the link between the person and the property because of its growing importance.

No wonder then that Alubo[2] feels there is no doubt that one of the most seminal areas of land law in Nigeria is the issue of declaration of title to land. Given the spate, the panjandrum or coterie of land disputes in Nigeria today, the study of declaration of title to land in Nigeria becomes a worthy course.

The Supreme Court[3] posited that a party claiming a declaration of title to statutory or customary right of occupancy does not need to plead and prove any more than one of the five methods of proving title. Where the claimant pleads and/or relies on more than one method to prove his title, he merely does so *ex abundate cautela* as proof of one single root is sufficient to sustain the claim. This is because proof of one of the five is sufficient to establishing title to land it is the minimum that the law requires.

The Supreme Court in *Usung* v. *Nyong*[4] posited that there are five ways of establishing title to land. They are: (a) by traditional evidence; (b) by production of documents of title which are duly authenticated; (c) by acts of selling leasing, renting out all or part of the land or farming on it or a portion of it; (d) by acts of possession and enjoyment of land; and

---

[1] Byran, A., *Blacks Law Dictionary*,7th edition (London: West Group, St Paul,1999) at p1493

[2] Alubo,A,O., *Contemporary Nigerian Land Law* (Jos: Abeson Publishers,2005) at p 103

[3] See *Olagunju* v. *Adesoye* (2009) 9 NWLR at 229.In *Yele Oyeneyin* v. *Dr. Akinkugbe* (2010) 41NSCQR at 421, the Supreme Court held that when the issue as to which of the two claimants has a better right to possession or occupation of a piece or parcel of land in dispute, the law will ascribe such possession and / or occupation to the person who proves a better title. In *Okonkwo* v. *Okonkwo* (2010) All FWLR(Pt.535) p.252, the court held that the duty to prove identity of disputed land is on the plaintiff.

[4] (2010) 2 NWLR at 90. f.

(e) by proof of possession of connected or adjacent land and prove of a better title to the land and (f) oath taking.

By traditional evidence

The Supreme Court in the case of *Osu* v. *Nwadialo*,[5] was emphatic that a plea of "first occupation" or "original settlement" or "first settlement" is a plea of traditional history or evidence which must be properly pleaded and proved. The plaintiff must plead and prove: (a) who founded the land; (b) in what manner the land was founded and the circumstances leading to it; (c) the successive persons to whom the land thereafter devolved through and unbroken claim or in such a way that there is no gap which cannot be explained. Traditional evidence, by concept therefore deals with an event beyond human memory or is ancient through recollection beyond records or is what happened at a time out of mind and therefore qualifies to be immemorial.[6]

---

[5] (2009) 12 NWLR at 289, the facts of which were that at the Anambra State High Court at Onitsha the respondents/cross appellants in Suit No.0/23/81 claimed against the appellants/cross-respondents the following reliefs: an order of forfeiture of customary tenancy of Aguasi and Anisise parcels of land, damages for trespass and an order of injunction. The respondents claimed that they are the owners of a large parcel of land situate at Ossomala which land includes portions of land known as and called Aguasi, Anisise Otiegede, Agbode and Obulumani. The respondents alleged that their ancestors migrated from Igala river over 500 years ago and settled on the land in dispute. At the time of the settlement, the land was virgin forest. By settling on the land, the respondents' ancestors became the owners of the said land. As owners in possession, they farmed on the parcel of land and fished the pools and ponds thereon, hunted for animals on the land, cut trees and let portions of the land to tenants for farming under customary tenancy. They claimed that the appellant' ancestors migrated from the hinterland and the respondents family granted them portions of land for residential purposes and for farming. According to them, the appellants' ancestors were paying yearly tributes to the respondents' ancestors for the occupation and use of the said portion granted to them.
At the conclusion of trial, the trial court found in favour of the respondents/cross-appellants and granted the reliefs claimed except the one for damages for trespass. The appellants/cross respondents were aggrieved by the judgment and they appealed to the Court of Appeal, contending that the respondents/cross appellants did not establish their title to the land in dispute.
On their part, the respondents/cross-appellants cross appealed on the ground that the trial court was wrong in refusing to award them damages for trespass. The Court of Appeal unanimously allowed the appeal.

[6] In *Oko* v. *Okenwa* (2010) 3 NWLR at 408, the Court held that it was not sufficient in proving traditional history to say that the land in dispute belonged exclusively to his family from time immemorial and stop there. He must show how the family got the land either from some other persons or authority in succession or that the family found it a virgin land and deforested it. See also *Nwokidu* v. *Okanu* (2010) ALL FWLR (Pt.522) P. 1633.

In *Fatoyinbo* v. *Osadeyi*,[7] the Supreme Court held that a party to a suit for title to land who relies on traditional history must plead the root of his title and the names and history of his ancestors. He has a duty to trace his title to the original owner and to show how his predecessors acquired title to the land. The customs which recognizes the founding of the land and the incidents of that custom must be identified, specified and proved. In other words, the pleader has an onerous duty. A party is not only required to plead his historical connection with the land but to also plead how the land devolved on him through any of his ancestors. The line of succession must be traced without leaving gaps or creating mysterious linkages or allowing the link to break down.

Where there is a conflict of traditional history, one side or the other must be mistaken, yet, both may be honest in their belief. In such a case, demeanour is little guide to the truth. The best way is to test the traditional history by reference to the facts in recent years as established by evidence and by seeing which of the two competing histories is more probable.[8] More so, in such a claim, the plaintiff must prove his title by satisfactory clear cogent and uncontradicted evidence.[9]

The Supreme Court held in *Ukaegbu* v. *Nwololo*,[10] that the weight to be attached to traditional evidence is a matter which is left to the experience and wisdom of the trial Judge. Ogbuagu (JSC) held that:

> In the case of *Alade* v. *Awo* (1975) 4 SC 215 at 229, it was held that where evidence of traditional history is not satisfactory, the need then arises for a plaintiff to prove numerous acts of ownership. It is my respectful and firm view that *Kojo* v. *Bonsie* will apply where the land in dispute between the parties is in respect of one and the same piece or portion of land. In that case, the identity of the said land in dispute may be well known to the parties and by the court from the oral and/or documentary evidence such as a survey plan before it. It cannot be otherwise. In the instant case leading to this appeal, the evidence of the respondent as PW1 and his late brother PW2 and as

---

[7] (2009) 16 NWLR at 611. See also *Dim* v. *Enemou* (2009) 4-5 S.C. (pt.111) at 52 where the court held that in a claim for declaration of title to land based on traditional evidence, the duty is on the claimant to plead copiously the historical basis of this claim and succeed on the strength of his own case and not on the weakness of the defence. In *Alikor* v. *Ogwo* (2010)5NWLR at285, the court held that where a claimant to a right of occupancy (statutory or customary) based his claim on traditional history and he successfully discharged the onus of proof of that root of title, there is no need for him to lead evidence proving or showing acts of possession or any mode of proving title to land.

[8] See *Ukaegbu* v. *Nwololo* (2009) All FWLR at 1857-1888. See also *Chukwu* v. *Amadi* (2009) (pt.472) All FWLR 1189.

[9] See *Osuji* v. *Ekeocha* (2009) All FWLR (pt.490) at 614.

[10] *Supra*

> found as a fact and held by the trial court is that the land claimed by the respondent's family and the one claimed by the appellants, are different, separate and distinct. The evidence of the parties is as it was parallel. In other words, there is no conflict strictly speaking, in the instant case.

Indeed, in the case of *Obasi Ibenye & 3 Ors* v. *Abraham Agwu & Anor* (1988) 9 SCNJ 1 at 30-31 per Ogundare JSC, stated inter alia, as follows:

> The dictum of lord Denning in *Kojo* v. *Bonsie* does not mean that demeanour of witnesses is irrelevant in the resolution of conflicts in evidence in traditional history. What the noble and learned lord was saying was that where witnesses honestly testify as to what has been handed down to them by word of mouth, acts in recent times should be aid to resolve the conflict in the evidence of traditional history given.

The Supreme Court per Ogbuegu continued that:

> But a witness may not be honestly telling what he heard from his ancestors. A trial court that sees and hears him, must be in a position to determine whether or not he is honest about what he is narrating. This cannot be in the province of an appellant court. Where there is a conflict of evidence which the trial court failed to resolve, as in the case at hand, an appellant court cannot make a finding in such situation – *Okoye* v. *Kpajie* (1972) 6 SC 176 at 187. The proper course is to order a retrial before another judge.

Can it be honestly said that there was/is conflict in the evidence of the parties where it is fond as a fact that the land said to be in dispute is separate and distinct from that claimed by the appellant? I repeat that I think not. I have demonstrated that fact earlier above in this subject. So, by no stretch of imagination, can the said principle in *Kojo* v. *Bonsie* relied upon by the court below be applicable to the instant case now on appeal to this court.

The court in *Nwokorobia* v. *Nwogu*,[11] held that the law is settled that where evidence of the traditional history is relied on in proof of declaration of title to land, the plaintiff in the case must plead and establish such facts as who founded the land, how he founded the land and the particulars of the intervening owners through whom he claims and that was a leading principle of law that a party who seeks of an order of declaration of title to land and is predicated on traditional history he must plead and prove his case with cogent, credible, consistent and

[11] (2009) Vol. 172 LCRN.

uncontradicted evidence. Evidence that are not consistent but have discrepancies cannot sustain an act of useful declaration of title to land.

Documents of title[12]

The production of documents of title is one of the recognized methods of proving title to land but such a document of title must be admissible in evidence and be such a character as to be capable of conferring valid title on the party relying on it. It does not mean that once a claimant produces what he claims to be an instrument of grant, he is automatically entitled to a declaration that the property which such an instrument purports to grant is his own.

The Court of Appeal in *Usung* v. *Nyong*,[13] held that the failure to file a survey plan in a claim for declaration of title is not fatal if both parties give sufficient particulars of the land in dispute. Where, however, parties are disputing the boundaries of the land in dispute, a survey plan is absolutely necessary. According to per Omokri JCA at pp.113 Pers E.G. held that:

> Furthermore, exhibit "F" is an inchoate judgment without the plan ordered to be drawn by a surveyor in order to ascertain the boundaries of the land in dispute in my respectful view without ascertaining the borders of the land in dispute how can that be trespass.

Thus, the omission in evidence of a survey plan without objection will not entitle a court to ascribe to the survey plan a probative value which the survey plan does not otherwise possess when the survey plan itself is bereft of features which can give the boundaries in it the character of certainty.

The Supreme Court in *Oyeneyin* v. *Akinkugbe*,[14] held that mere production of a valid instrument of grant does not necessarily carry with it an automatic grant of the relief of declaration. The production of an

---

[12] Cf Alubo, *op. cit.*, at p.130. In Egute M.,A., *Essentials of Nigerian Land Law* (Makurdi: Onaivi Publishing Co. Ltd ,2002) at p.109 describes the production of documents to mean that the person claiming title shall produce documentary evidence to confirm and support his ownership of the property. For instance, he must show a certificate of occupancy, certificate of purchase, certificate of registration, conveyance or any similar document.

[13] (2010) 2 NWLR at 92.In *Monkom* v. *Odili* (2010)2NWLR, the court held that once a document qualifies as an instrument under section 15 of the land instrument registration law, non registration of such document makes it *prima facie* inadmissible. However, such unregistered document is admissible as an acknowledgement of payment of money.

[14] (2010) 41 NSCQR at 422.

instrument of grant of title carries with it the need for the court to inquire into a number of questions including (a) whether the document is genuine and valid (b) whether it has been duly executed, stamped and registered (c) whether the grantor had the authority and capacity to make the grant (d) whether the grantor had in fact what he purported to grant (e) whether it had the effect claimed by the holder of the instrument.

The production of documents of title as one of the recognized methods of proving title to land but such a document of title must be admissible in evidence and be such a character as to be capable of conferring valid title on the party relying on it. It does not mean that once a claimant produces what he claims to be an instrument of grant, he is automatically entitled to a declaration that the property which such an instrument purports to grant is his own. Rather, production and reliance on such an instrument inevitably carries with it the need for the court to inquire into some or all of a number of questions including (a) whether the document is genuine and valid; (b) whether it has been duly executed, stamped and registered; (c) whether the grantor has the authority and capacity to make the grant; (d) whether the grantor had in fact what he purported to grant; and (e) whether it has the effect claimed by the holder of the instrument.[15]

For 50 years, two communities in Dikenafai in Ideato south local government area of Imo State namely, Umuchoko and Umuabor locked horns over parcels of land. The tug of war in respect of the ownership of the fixed asset dragged for long until June 4, 2010, when the Supreme Court made a final pronouncement on the matter.

It was the Umuchoke community that ran to court for intervention when in 1961 all entreaties by elders to resolve the dispute allegedly failed. The community filed an action at the State High Court Orlu, claiming Customary Right of Occupancy to three parcels of land namely Ala Isiobi, Akusobi, Ala Isiobi ,Amaechi and Ala Migbola Onyewuluchi. The litigants asked the court to restrain the Umuabor community from further trespass into the said parcels of land. The Umuabor community filed a statement of defence and a counter affidavit claiming ownership of the lands in dispute in addition, the respondents asked for an order of forfeiture of the rights of the plaintiff (Umuchoke community) to the disputed parcels of land as well as an order of perpetual injunction

---

[15] See *Dabo* v. *Abdullahi* (2005) 7 NWLR (pt.923) 181 SC and *Ayorinde* v. *Kuforiji* (2007) 4 NWLR (pt.7024) 341 CA. In *Oyeneyin* v. *Akinkugbe* (2010) 4 NWLR, the Supreme Court recognized the production of document of title as one of the five ways in which ownership of title to land may be proved.

restraining the plaintiffs from further trespass into the parcels of land in dispute.

Both parcels canvassed arguments during the trial of the case with the plaintiffs relying heavily on the 1952 judgment, wherein the court ruled in their favour to establish their title to the parcels of land in dispute.

In support of claim to the disputed parcels of land, the plaintiffs who called other witnesses also subpoenaed the State Surveyor-General who testified as prosecution witness II (PWII) and tendered a full plan which verified and confirmed that the disputed land was indeed part of the larger area of land litigated between 1947 and 1952. The court in its judgment of August 14 1996 dismissed the case and entered judgment in favour of the Umuabor community. Not satisfied, the Umuchoke community filed an appeal before the Court of Appeal Port Harcourt Division. The Appeal Court in July 8, 2003 allowed the appeal and set aside the decision of the trial court. It was the position of the Court of Appeal that the title of the parcels of land in dispute had already been decided by the 1952 judgment of the Governors Court of Appeal Enugu, in favour of the Umuchoke community.

Dissatisfied with the judgment of the Enugu Division of the Court of Appeal, the Umuabor community went to the Supreme Court with a prayer to set aside the judgment. But, in its judgment declared June 4, 2010.[16] The Supreme Court upheld the decision of the appellant court and entered judgment in favour of the Umuchoke community.

In doing this, the apex court in a unanimous decision dismissed the appeal brought at by the Umuabor community as lacking in merit and also awarded a cost of ₦50,000 to the respondents. Judge Adekaye Oyelola Olatunlola who delivered the lead judgment of the Supreme Court said that the Port Harcourt division of the Court of Appeal was right to allow the appeal and set aside the judgment of the Imo State High Court, other justices penal were justices Niki Tobi, Walter Onnogle, Ikechi Ogbuagu and John Afabiyi. They all assumed that where the evidence of tradition is inconclusive, the case must rest on a question of fact.

The apex court said any loophole in the evidence of the respondents be based on traditional history were given necessary cogency and ownership of connected and adjacent land as established by the Governors Court judgment.

---

[16] The *Sun* newspaper of 28/6/2010titled "How Supreme Court finally settled a 50 year old land dispute".

The Supreme Court agreed with submissions of some to the Umuchoke community that the Umuabor community had before the trial failed to properly puncture the pleading of the respondents that their title to the disputed parcels of land was established by the judgment, in their favour. According to the court "in view of the fact that the appellants only pleaded that the judgment of the 1952 was irrelevant and nothing more, they are not in any position to law any evidence in rebuttal of their contention. It is trite that facts not pledged go to no issue".

It was also the position of the apex court that the appellants had failed to join issues on the facts of substance raised by the respondents regarding the 1952 judgment in their favour adding that it was satisfied that with the evidence of the PWII the Surveyor-General of Imo State that the parcels of land in dispute form part of the larger area of land in dispute in the 1952, case as shown by the composite plans tendered by the Surveyor-General.

The Court of Appeal in *Oseni Ladotun* v. *Lasis Oyewomi*,[17] held that it is not in all cases that the plaintiff seeking declaration of title to land must file a survey plan in respect of the land in dispute and over which he seeks declaration from the court. Where the land in dispute its extent and boundaries are facts in respect of which parties did not join issues with one asserting and the other denying these facts an enduring declaration of title can be decreed on the basis of parties knowledge of the land's identity. A survey plan classifying the land in dispute ceases to be a necessity. It is not always that a plan is fatal to the plaintiff's claim, if proper description of the land is available in the proceedings.

In other words, a survey plan is not a *sine qua non* to prove the clarity of a disputed land, the most important requirement the court ensures is met is the ascertainment of the identity of the land in dispute with definite certainty.

The Court of Appeal in *Lekwauwa* v. *Ukaegbe*,[18] held that where a registrable instrument has not been registered, it cannot be pleaded or given in evidence as affecting the land in dispute. Where an unregistered instrument is inadvertently tendered and received in evidence, it should be discountenanced and ignored even where no objection is taken as to its admissibility.

A registrable but unregistered instrument can be tendered and admitted in evidence to establish evidence of a transaction and to prove payment and receipt of money. Where a document evidences sale of land,

---

17 (2010) All FLWLR at 1560-1561.

18 (2009) All FWLR at 541.

but from the proceedings the said document is tendered in evidence not as an evidence of title, but simply to establish a fact which one of the parties has pleaded, then such document does not qualify as an instrument as defined in the land instruments registration law and is therefore admissible in evidence without being registered.[19]

Acts of ownership

The Supreme Court in *Jinadu* v. *Esuvombi-Aro*,[20] held that proof of acts of ownership is normally provided by acts of persons or persons claiming the land such as selling, leasing, renting out all or part of the land or farming on it or on a portion of it or otherwise utilizing the land beneficially; all evidence of ownership provided they extended over a sufficient length of time and are numerous and positive enough to warrant the inference that he is the true owner.

It is only after a party's root of title is established that consequential acts flowing therefrom can then properly qualify as acts of ownership. Consequently, where the title pleaded is not proved, it will be totally unnecessary to consider acts of ownership because such acts are no longer acts of ownership but acts of trespass.[21] Invariably therefore, the act of the plaintiff must be positive and numerous. An isolated act which fails to go on for a sufficient period of time or which is negative will not give rise to an inference that the plaintiff is the owner. The defendant, in order to defeat the claim of the plaintiff would need to prove better title.[22]

---

[19] *Supra.* See also *Oloworlarewo* v. *Umechewu* (2003) FWLR (pt.182) 109. In *Lekwarawa* v. *Ukeagbe* (*supra*) the respondent filed an action against the appellants at the High Court of Justice sitting at Owerri, seeking a declaration that he is entitled to the statutory right of occupancy over a parcel of land known as Uzoata, ₦500,000 (five hundred thousand naira) general and exempting or punitive damages for trespass and perpetual injunction restraining the appellants and their agents from further acts of trespass on the disputed land. At trial, the respondent sought to tender a deed of conveyance exhibit C, which the appellants raised an objection to on the grounds that the document was not prepared by a legal practitioner contrary to with the provisions of the Land Instruments Preparation Law, Laws of Eastern Nigeria 1963 applicable to Imo State and that the document was not registered in accordance with Section 15 of the land instrument registration law, Laws of Eastern Nigeria, 1963. The trial court in its ruling, overruled the objection raised on the document, admitting same in evidence. Dissatisfied the appellant appealed to the Court of Appeal, where the appellants appeal was allowed.

[20] (2009) 4 M.J.S.C. (pt.111) at 6.

[21] See *Usong* v. *Nyong* (2010) 2 NWLR at p.91.

[22] Alubo, *op. cit.*, at p.134.

Acts of long possession and enjoyment of the land

The *Black's Law Dictionary*,[23] defining possession as the right under which one may exercise control over something to the exclusion of all others, the continuing exercise of a claim to the exclusive use of a material object in or as regards land. Whilst the Evidence Act[24] provides that when the question is whether any person is owner of anything of which he is shown to be in possession the burden is on the person who asserts that he is not the owner.

It follows therefore that a plaintiff's acts of long possession and enjoyment of land may be prima facie evidence of ownership of the particular piece or quantity of land with reference to which such acts are done. In *Olagunju* v. *Adesoye*,[25] at the High Court of Kwara State, holding in Offa, the 1st respondent sued the appellant claiming a declaration that the certificate of occupancy No. KW 5676 dated 4th August, 1986 registered as No.248 in volume XVI at the laws Registry Ilorin, and subsequently extended by certificate of occupancy No. KW 5676 and registered as No.230 at page 230 in volume XVII was validly issued; a declaration that the 1st respondent was entitled to the grant of certificate of occupancy No.KW5676 and entitled to quiet enjoyment; a declaration for improvements and economic trees, was entitled to undisturbed possession; and perpetual injunction.

The appellant also file an action at the High Court against the respondents claiming that the appellant family was the exclusive owner of a large parcel of land situate and being along Igosun Road, Offa covering an area of 222,500 square metres and covered by an alienation permit and that the appellant's family was exclusively entitled to a certificate of occupancy thereon; an order setting aside and declaring as irregular, wrongful and void the purported certificate of occupancy No. KW5676 of 23rd April 1988 or any other certificate or title document(s) whatsoever unlawfully obtained by the 1st respondent over the appellant's family land; an order of perpetual injunction; and special and general damages. Both suits were consolidated.

---

23 Bryan A.G. *Black's Law Dictioinary,* 7th edition, (London: West Group St. Paul Minn, 1999) at p.1183.

24 Cap C5, Laws of the Federation of Nigeria, 2004

25 (2009) 9 NWLR at 229. In *Eresia-Eke* v. *Orikoha* (2010)8NWLR, as to whether long possession can confer title to land, the court held that by the provisions of section 146 of the evidence act, gives only a rebuttable presumption of ownership in favour of the person in possession. It does no more than that. It cannot stand when the true owner proves his ownership.

At the trial, the 1st respondent gave evidence that he applied for land in the G.R.A. and that after approval, the Government of Kwara State gave him the comprehensive list of all those entitled to compensation for the unexhausted development on the land and he paid all of them including the members of the appellant's family. After the initial grant, he applied for an extension which was also granted and he was asked to pay compensation for the unexhausted development which he did. He stated that at the time he was put in possession, neither the appellant nor any other person was in possession. PW2 a principal land officer in the Ministry of Lands testified that the respondent was allocated plots of land at the Government Reserved Area (G.R.A.) Offa for the construction of a secondary school, subject to the payment of compensation on any unexhausted improvement on the land. The Government carried out an assessment of the compensation payable on the unexhausted improvement on the land which the 1st respondent paid to all the beneficiaries and there was no complaint. After the payment of the compensation, the Government issued a certificate of occupancy to the 1st respondent. The 1st respondent therefore applied for an extension of the initial grant which was granted subject to the same conditions and the 1st respondent again effected payment of compensation for unexhausted developments on the land. The 1st respondent was issued a new certificate of occupancy, exhibit 1, covering the whole land. He stated that the land granted to the 1st respondent had been under the control of the government as far back as 1956; thereby exhibit 4, the land was designated as urban area since 1998; that all the processes for the issuance of certificate of occupancy were followed; and that some members of the appellant's family collected compensation.

The appellant gave evidence to the effect that the land in dispute belonged to his forefather; that his ancestral father, Bashorun came from Oyo and was friendly to Olofa Olotoni the founder of Offa. That Bashorun was put in control of the piece of land at Oke-Agba and the land in dispute is part of the land which Olofa gave to him with authority to control.

At the conclusion of trial, the trial court held that the appellant failed to sustain his claim for a declaration of title to the land in dispute but that the 1st respondent amply established his case on the preponderance of evidence. Consequently, the trial court granted the 1st respondent's claim and dismissed the appellant's claim.

The appellant's appeal to the Court of Appeal was dismissed and the Court of Appeal affirmed the judgment of the trial court.

Dissatisfied, the appellant appealed to the Supreme Court. The 1st respondent cross-appealed against the part of the judgment of the Court of Appeal which held that "there is evidence before the court to show how the land in dispute devolved from Bashorun to the appellant.

In determining the appeal, the Supreme Court considered the provisions of Section 5(1)(a) of the Land Use Act which states thus: "5(1) It shall be lawful for the Governor in respect of land, whether or not in an urban area – (a) to grant statutory rights of occupancy to any person for all purposes."

Unanimously dismissing the appeal and allowing the cross-appeal, the Supreme Court held that a plaintiff claiming a declaration of title to land who succeeds in establishing such acts that extend over a sufficient length of time and are numerous and positive enough to warrant the inference of exclusive ownership of such land is and will be entitled to the declaration. It would be safe and imperative to conclude that the party exercising such acts is the exclusive owner of the land.

Proof of possession of connected or adjacent land

Possession of connected or adjacent land in certain circumstances renders it probable that the owner of such connected or adjacent land would be the owner of the land in dispute.[26] Alubo,[27] opines that such a mode should rarely be used for it might be recognized with extreme condition that the ownership of properties belonging to others may in the absence of documents lost in a fire or inferno or flood, death of key witnesses be handed over, by default to a trespasser.

In *Jinadu* v. *Esurombi Aro*,[28] the Supreme Court of Nigeria held that in a claim for the ownership of land, the fact that the law dispute is contiguous with other lands belonging to the plaintiff is enough to raise a probability (though not presumptuous) that the land in dispute also belongs to the plaintiff.

---

26 Alubo, *op. cit.*, at p.136.

27 Ibid.

28 (2009) 4. M.J.S.C. (pt.111) at 5.

The taking of oath and juju

The taking of oath and juju in Nigeria has of recent been recognized as one of the ways of proving title to land. The Supreme Court gave imprimatur to this in the case of *Onyenoge & Ors* v. *Ebere,*[29] where the plaintiffs commenced an action at the Ukwa Customary Court in Abia State claiming that they were entitled to a customary right of occupancy over the piece of land called "Eubelu Ulogor" general damages and perpetual injunction. The plaintiffs agreed to take the oath and juju from Okija shrine in Anambra State, which was placed on the land in dispute. The plaintiffs took the oath and thereafter survived the customary one-year-oath taking. They then became entitled to the exclusive possession of the land in accordance with the custom of the parties. The refusal of the defendants to leave the land in dispute resulted in the action.

The Supreme Court held that: where a foreign juju was brought into a disputed land for the purpose of customary arbitration, it is the custom of the place where the land is located that should prevail in the determination of the outcome of the juju on the party who took the oath.[30]

Where two parties to a dispute voluntarily submit the case in customary before them to an arbitration according to customary law and agree expressly or by implication that the decision of such arbitration would be acceptable as final and binding, then once the arbitrators reach a decision, it would no longer be open to either party to subsequently back out or resile from the decision so pronounced.[31]

---

29 (2004) All FWLR (pt.210) 981-1001.

30 *Supra.*

31 Ibid.

Chapter 14

Legal mortgage: problems and controversies

Legal mortgage is the transfer of ownership of the assets by way of security upon the express or implied condition that ownership will be re-transferred to the debtor on discharge of his obligation. *The Black's Law Dictionary* defines the term as "an interest in land created by a written instrument providing security for the performance of a debt." This is a legal document that gives the lender a security interest in a property. If a borrower fails to meet its obligations under the loan, the lender can, after giving notice and following the procedures set down by law, take steps to sell the mortgaged property to recover the loan and unpaid interest plus any associated costs.[1]

Pennington J. enunciated the judicial definition of mortgage in *Seidu Olowu* v. *Miller Brothers (of L'pool) Ltd*,[2] when he said that mortgage is "a security created by contract for the payment of a debt already due to become one. It must be stressed right from the beginning that all mortgage transactions must be in writing. Section 4 of the Statute of Fraud 1677, which is applicable to all states of the Federation, provides that transactions in respect of answerable debts must be in writing.[3] Section 3(1) states that:

> No action shall be brought whereby to charge the defendant upon any special promise to answer for the debt, default or miscarriage of another person unless the agreement upon which such action is brought or some memorandum or note thereof is in writing and signed by the part to be charged therewith or some persons there onto by him lawfully authorized.[4]

---

[1] See Osaloni, D.O.,"Legal Mortgage: Problems and Controversies," *Modern Practice Journal of Finance & Investment Law* Vol. 10, Nos.3-4, 2006 at p. 542

[2] (1922) 3 NLR 110 at 111

[3] Osaloni, *op. cit.*, at p542

[4] See Law Reform (Contract) Law Cap. 25 of Lagos State

It is therefore important to know that a legal mortgage must have the following attributes:

a. There must be a covenant to pay the principal and interest on a given date;
b. A covenant to pay interest in the event of default in payment of the principal on the day named;
c. The demise or sub-demise of or the charge by way of legal mortgage on the mortgaged property;
d. The proviso for cesser; and
e. Such variations of the statutory provisions with regards to mortgages, as the arrangement between the parties requires.[5]

In a mortgage, delivery of possession is not necessary since the title resides in the mortgagee subject to the equity of redemption. This is the transfer of the deeds to a property as security for the repayment of a debt. The most potent power conferred by the mortgage is that of the unbridled right of sale upon default. Cootes stated that:

> The only obligation incumbent on a selling mortgagee under a power of sale in his mortgage is that he should act in good faith whether selling under an express or statutory power, he may generally conduct the sale in such manner as he think "most conducive to his own benefit, unless the deed contains any" restrictions as to the mode of exercising the power, provided he 'acts bona fide and observes reasonable precautions to obtain not the 'best price' but 'a proper price'.' The power of sale or foreclosure can therefore not be affected merely because the amount due under the mortgage is in dispute.[6]

Power of sale

Generally speaking, a mortgagee shall not exercise power of sale unless:

- Notice requiring repayment has been served on the mortgagor and payment has not been made and there is default;
- Some interests under the mortgage is in arrears and unpaid for two months after becoming due; and

---

[5] See *AIB Ltd* v. *Lee Ind. Ltd* (2003) 7 NWLR (Pt.819) at p398

[6] See Cootes on *Mortgages* Vol. 2, 9th edition at 927 and the case of *Sabbach & Anor* v. *The Bank of West Africa* (1962) All NLR 1153

- There has been breach of some provision contained in the mortgage deed other than a covenant for repayment of the mortgage money or interest.[7]

In *B.O.N. Ltd* v. *Aliyu*,[8] it was reiterated that the requirement of the law is that notice of intention to sell a mortgage property must be sent to the mortgagor as the words 'shall not' are mandatory and not advisory. Any sale therefore without the requisite notice is invalid *ab initio* and cannot convey any title to a subsequent purchaser. It is however noteworthy that a mortgagee without notice of fraud is entitled to claim his benefits under the mortgage deed. In *Davies* v. *Davies & G.B. Ollivant Ltd*,[9] it was held that the plaintiff was entitled to a declaration that the property in question belonged to him solely but subject to the encumbrances of the second defendant's indenture of mortgage since the plaintiff of the two innocent parties was the one who, by a little ordinary discreet care of his interest in the property, would have made the first defendant's fraud impossible.

In the *Davies* case, the plaintiff claimed declaration that the property in question belonged to him solely, and to set aside a deed of conveyance made in favour of the 1st defendant and the indenture of mortgage made by the 1st defendant to the 2nd defendant. The 1st defendant bought the property for the plaintiff with the plaintiff's money and so obtained the title deeds from the vendor. The plaintiff allowed the 1st defendant to retain the title deeds in his possession for eight years without taking steps by way of conveyance or endorsement on the title deed or otherwise to publish and safeguard his right, title and interest in the property. Eight years after the sale, the 1st defendant had a conveyance of the property executed in his favour by the success of the deceased vendor. This conveyance was duly registered. Following on that conveyance, the 1st defendant granted an indenture of mortgage to the 2nd defendant. 79 pounds 14 shillings was due under the indenture of mortgage at the time of the suit. The 2nd defendant had no notice of any interest of the plaintiff in the property. The 1st defendant in granting the indenture of mortgage was acting in fraud of the plaintiff.

It is therefore most usually advisable for the title deed of the property to remain in the custody of the mortgagee as long as the debt remains unpaid and the mortgage undischarged. A notice for foreclosure once

[7] See section 125(i)-(iii) of the Property & Conveyancing Law Cap1001959 of Western Nigeria
[8] (1999) 7 NWLR, p. 612.
[9] (1963)13 NLR, 39

given and received remains valid and in force until the exercise of the mortgagee's power of sale.[10]

The Supreme Court in *S.O.N. Okafor & Sons Ltd* v. *Nigeria Housing Dev. Society Ltd. & Anor,*[11] said that where under the terms of a mortgage deed the mortgage money is to be advanced not as a lump sum but in instalments, the mortgagee has a right to exercise his statutory power of sale under Section 19 of the Conveyancy Act 1881 if the mortgagor is in default as to the payment of interest, even if the principal sum has not been advanced in full, the mortgagee may, without agreement, set-off the unpaid balance of the mortgage money against the outstanding balance.

Sale at undervalue or low pricing had generated a lot of controversy but the law seems to be that sale at undervalue in itself will not vitiate a sale of mortgage property. In *M.J. Eka-Eteh* v. *Nig. Housing Dev. Soc. Ltd. & J.A. Adewumi,*[12] it was held that a sale at undervalue alone is not enough to vitiate the exercise of a mortgagee's power of sale and that it must be shown that the sale was made at a fraudulent or gross undervalue. If there is therefore no evidence of any mala fide the sale will stand. If a mortgagee selling under a power of sale takes pain in exercising that power, to act in good faith, his conduct in regards to that sale cannot be impeached.

This was well articulated in the case of *Okonkwo* v. *C.C.B & Ors,*[13] where the court posited that:

> "The acts which will affect the proper conduct of an auction sale are (a) improper or fraudulent acts which are likely to prevent the property put up from realizing its fair value...(b) any act which is likely to chill the sale for example, the solicitor in a cause in which property is sold bidding for it."

This was a case where the court considered the propriety or otherwise of the purchase of a mortgaged property by the mother of the chairman of the mortgage bank.

It is the law that a mortgagee is not a trustee of the power of sale for the mortgagor and where there is a conflict of interest, he is entitled to give preference to his own over those of the mortgagor. Salmon LJ stated that:

---

[10] See *Chief Ojikutu* v. *Agbonmagbe Bank* (1966) All NLR,533.
[11] (1972)All NLR 400.
[12] (1973) NSCC 373
[13] (2003) 6 MJSC 122.

> I accordingly conclude, both on principle and authority, that a mortgagee in exercising his power of sale does owe a duty to take reasonable precaution to obtain a true market value of the mortgaged property at the date on which he decides to sell it. No doubt, in deciding whether he has fallen short of that duty, the fact must be looked at broadly, and he will not be adjudged to be in default unless he is plainly on the wrong side of the line.[14]

The important thing here is that the mortgagee in exercising the right of sale is under a duty to take reasonable care to obtain the true value of the property.

A mortgagee who delays in the exercise of its right under the deed such as for the transaction to be statute barred shall be restrained from taking advantage of the covenant of sale in the said mortgage. Hence in *Lewis* v. *Plunket,*[15] it was decided that where 'the owner of a legal estate in fee simple in land executes a mortgage and hands over the mortgage and other title deeds to the mortgagee, but fails to pay interest on the mortgage or give any acknowledgement of the mortgage debt for more than twelve years, the mortgagee loses all title to the land and the mortgagor can recover possession of the mortgage and other title deeds'.

It is therefore necessary that the other party must be aware of the pending suit. A sale during the pendency of a suit by somebody not a party to the suit will not be vitiated.[16] It should be noted that *lis pendis* does not affect the acquisition of rights in land by parties to a dispute but restrains transfer of the disputed land. It is worthy to note that in sale of land under a writ of fifa the purchaser of mortgagor's interest takes subject to the existing encumbrances and the power of sale by writ of fifa under a mortgage can be effectively exercised.

Equity of redemption

Barring all principles and legalities of the laws of mortgages, the mortgagor's right to the equity of redemption is unimpeachable. The equity of redemption of the mortgaged property is particularly restricted,[17] as provided that:

> A power, when the mortgage money has become due, to sell or concur with any other person in selling, the mortgaged property, or any part thereof, either subject to prior charges or not, and either together or in lots, by public auction or private contract, subject to

[14] See *Cuckmere Bricks Co Ltd* v. *Mutual Finance Ltd* (1971) Ch. 949
[15] (1937) Ch. 306
[16] See *Clay Ind. Ltd* v. *Aina* (1997) 8 NWLR (pt. 516) p.208.
[17] See section 123(1)(i) of the Property & Conveyancing Law,1959

> such conditions respecting title, or evidence of title or other matter as the mortgagee thinks fit, with power to vary any contract for sale, and to buy it at any auction or to rescind any contract for sale and to resell, without being answerable for any loss occasioned thereby.

The Supreme Court extensively discussed the issue of equity of redemption in the case of *Usen Fewokan* v. *Idowu & Anor,*[18] the Plaintiff in this case claimed in the High Court a declaration that he is the owner in equity of the property at 47, Idumagbo Avenue Lagos and an order directing the defendants to convey the said property to him. The facts which both sides admitted are as follows: the property was mortgaged by one Onashile, the original owner, to the Barclays Bank before 1961 as security for an overdraft of 10,000 pounds with interest. Onashile deposited his title deeds with Barclays Bank thus creating an equitable mortgage. In 1962, the plaintiff knew of the equitable mortgage but nevertheless agreed to purchase the property from Onashile for 10,000 pounds; receipts issued for the instalmental payment of the purchase price between 1962 and 1964 were tendered in evidence. Barclays Bank sued Onashile for the repayment of his overdraft and by consent got judgment of 12000 pounds entered against Onashile. The Barclays Bank obtained leave of court for the sale of the property. The defendants purchased the property from the court and obtained purchase certificate from the court for the right, title and interest of Onashile. The defendants registered their title to the property under the Registration of Titles Act 1935 Cap 181.

On appeal, the plaintiff/appellant contended that the right, title and interest of Onashile, which the defendants/respondents bought was subject to the equitable interest which the plaintiff obtained when he purported to have purchased the property from Onashile in 1962. The defendants contended, however that at the time Onashile sold the property to the defendants, the plaintiff was aware that there was an equitable mortgage in favour of the Barclays Bank. The lower court gave judgment in favour of the defendants declaring them as the registered title owner of the property as claimed in their counterclaim and dismissed the plaintiff's claim on the ground that Onashile had no property to sell in 1962. It was therefore held:

That Onashile had only an equity of redemption since the equitable mortgage by way of deposit of the title deed remained with the Barclays Bank in 1962. When the defendants purchased the property from Barclays Bank (judgment creditor) they obtained the interest of the

---

[18] (1975) NSCC 175

Barclays Bank in the equitable mortgage as well as the equity of redemption which was still vested in Onashile, and they thereby acquired good title to the property. When Onashile purported to sell his property to the plaintiff, all he had sold but did not in fact sell to the plaintiff is the equity of redemption which had been extinguished by the court order of sale of the property. In the result, in 1962, what the plaintiff purchased did not constitute any interest in the property under the receipts issued to him.

> "The only evidence led and which the courts below had accepted, and rightly too, is that a company known as B.B. Apugo & Sons Ltd was the corporate body that was granted the loan, and not the Respondent. If the Respondent did not take any loan from the Appellant and was not even found to be a customer of the Appellant, it must follow that he cannot be properly described as a person indebted to the Appellant."

In this case, the Respondent/Cross-Appellant was carrying on business under the name B.B. Apugo & Sons Ltd. He was not indebted to 1st Appellant bank who instructed the 3rd Appellant (Auctioneer) to sell by public auction certain leasehold and freehold properties belonging to him. When in accordance with the instruction of the 1st Appellant, the 3rd Appellant/Auctioneer advertised the auction of the properties in the *Nigerian Statesman* of 20/8/1983 and 21/8/1983, Mr. Apugo felt that it conveyed the erroneous impression that it was as a result of his indebtedness to the 1st Appellant that his properties were advertised for auction in the newspaper.

When a public notice of an auction sale of land is given, it must be allowed to last at least seven days before the sale takes place. Thus, no sale validly take place within less than seven days from the day the public notice is put out at the principal town of the district in which the land is situated and the very place the land intended to be sold is. It is to be noted that an earlier notice of an aborted auction sale of a property is inoperative to constitute the necessary notice of a subsequent auction sale of the same property.[19]

Private treaty

This is the sale of a mortgaged property without the involvement of a real estate agent/auctioneer. Statute law allows mortgagee to sell the property of a defaulting mortgagor either by private treaty or by auction. Where a covenant in the mortgage deed provides to the contrary the mode

---

[19] See *Ihekwoaba* v. *ACB Ltd* (1998) 10 NWLR (Pt.571)

specified in the deed must be adhered to. If the mortgage deed does not restrict sale by public auction, sale by private treaty could be affected. A breach of this principle is a valid ground for an application for an injunction restraining the sale of a mortgaged property. Where either mode of sale is permitted, a sale by private treaty, even without advertisement, is good, provided it is made bona fide and to a fair price. Where the sale is to be by private treaty, it is preferable to put the matter in the hands of a competent agent. If the sale is by the mortgagee himself, at least a proper valuation should be obtained.[20]

Statutory mortgage corporations

The status of statutory mortgage corporations has not been very clear in term of when title passes to determine liquidation of the indebtedness. When a corporation, like a Building Society, builds a house and sells it to an interested party, they have created a mortgage and interest in the property will only pass upon full liquidation of the cost. The power of sale resides in the mortgagee until indebtedness is fully satisfied.[21]

In the above case, as a result of an advertisement published in the dailies by the plaintiff, Anambra State Housing Development Corporation, for the sale of houses being built by it in Onitsha, the defendant JCO Emekwue applied in December 1978 for the sale of one of the houses to him. In response to the defendant's application, the plaintiff made an offer to him for the sale of one of such houses to wit: Plot 125 Niger Bridge Head Estate Phase II, at the cost of ₦40,000. As stipulated in the offer by the plaintiff, the defendant paid the 1st instalment of ₦10,000. Subsequent to payment, plaintiff wrote a letter allocating Plot 125 to the defendant, which he has accepted would pay ₦5,000 as part payment of the 2nd instalment in a week's time. The defendant did not honour this arrangement, but later paid the ₦5,000.00 upon request.

Having completed the 50% payment of the selling price, the plaintiff executed a deed of sub-lease of the property in favour of the defendant as agreed. The defendant refused to pay the balance of the purchase price. By a letter of 11th November 1981, the plaintiff demanded payment of the balance within the next three weeks or the plaintiff:

---

[20] See Osaloni, *op. cit.*, at p.554

[21] See *Anambra State Housing Development Corporation* v. *JCO Emekwue* (1996)34LRCN. See also Osaloni, *op. cit.*, m at p. 554.

> Will assume that you are no longer keen on the purchase of this house and will therefore re-allocate it to a purchaser who will fully pay for the house and collect the keys from us."

By another letter dated 20th April 1982, when the defendant did not respond to the earlier one, the plaintiff informed him that Plot 125 had been re-allocated to another purchaser on full cash payment. He should therefore apply for refund of the earlier deposit of ₦20,000. The defendant refused to execute the release of the sub-lease hence this action.

On when interest will pass to a mortgagor in this type of transaction, Wali JSC (as he then was) held at p.125 that:

> "It is clear from the oral evidence presented by the appellant; Exhibit O was executed and registered by the parties subject to the payment in full of the purchase price of the property in dispute by the respondent... The respondent was not put into possession of the property, nor did the legal estate in it vest in him. His conduct of accepting and cashing the cheque of ₦20,000.00 being refund of the money deposited by him as part payment for the purchase of the house, is a clear manifestation of accepting the rescission of the provisional offer to him in Exhibit G."

Effect of wrong sale

Irregularity in the conduct of the sale of a mortgaged property will not invalidate it. According to Section 21(1) of the Conveyancing Act 1881 England:

> "Where a conveyance is made in professed exercise of the power of sale conferred by this Act, the title of the purchase shall not be impeached on the ground that no case has arisen to authorize the sale or that due notice was not given or that the power was otherwise improperly or irregularly exercised, but any person damnified by an unauthorized or improper or irregular exercise of the power shall have his remedy in damages against the person exercising the powers".

Jibowu Ag. FCJ (as he then was) in *Sanusi* v. *Daniels*[22] said:

> The appellant's complaint is against an irregular exercise of the power of sale on the ground that there was a contravention of Section 19(1) of the Sale by Auction Ordinance. It seems to me that the title of the 2nd Respondent cannot be impeached since the property was conveyed to him, and that the appellant's remedy is in damages

[22] (1956) SCNLR 288

against the 1st Respondent as provided by Section 21 (2) of the Conveyance Act 1881.

The case of sale occasioning fraud was well articulated in the case of *Viatonu* v. *Odutayo and Kuyoro,*[23] in this case, Viatonu (plaintiff in the first suit) had mortgaged his property to Odutayo, which Odutayo, exercising power of sale, sold by private treaty to Kuyoro. Viatonu sued to set aside the sale, and Kuyoro to recover possession of the premises, which Viatonu was still occupying plus sum for the use of them. The mortgage debt was 250 pounds, the market value of the premises 1,500 pounds

Upon receiving notice of foreclosure, Viatonu (the mortgagor) went to Odutayo (the mortgagee) and Odutayo agreed to grant an extension of two months. Within that period, Viatonu tendered the debt in full but Odutayo said it was too late. The property was sold for 600 pounds by private treaty on the day the debt was tendered. The mortgagee, auctioneer and purchaser, were members of the firm of auctioneers that sold the property.

The Supreme Court judgment of Ademola J. (as he then was) distinguished between improper or irregular sale, which can only entitle the mortgagor to damages, and a fraudulent sale, which is a nullity. He revealed at page 120 that the sinister aspect of the transaction is that the mortgagee (first defendant), one Odulaja, the auctioneer, and the purchaser (second defendant) who bought by private treaty are all partners in the firm of Odulaja & Co which sold the property as auctioneers. The mortgagee (first defendant) is a money lender, and a wife to the second partner Odulaja who actually transacted the sale, and the purchaser (second defendant) a friend of the second partner is the third partner in the firm.

The judgment referred to *Hudson* v. *Deans,*[24] where the plaintiff mortgaged certain property to the trustees of a friendly society to secure an advance, the society sold by public auction under their power of sale, and an officer of the society bought the property for himself. It was held that the sale was invalid and the plaintiff was still entitled to redeem the mortgage.

The duty of a mortgagee to obtain the true market value when exercising power of sale was considered in the case of *TseKwong Lam* v. *Wong Chit Sen,*[25] here the mortgaged property was sold by auction to the

23 (1950) 19 NLR 119
24 (1903) 2 Ch.
25 (1983) 1 WLR1394

only bid received and that happened to be from the mortgagee's wife, at the reserved price. Lord Templeman opined that while a sale at auction does not in itself show that a true market value had not been obtained, the mortgagee has not in this circumstance consulted estate agent, allowed only fifteen days between first advertisement and sale, the reserved price fixed by the mortgagee, who as a property investor knew all about the property unlike if it were an independent bidder.

An attempt to challenge the mortgagee's right of sale on ground of undue influence was unsuccessful.

If however the purchaser has notice, actual or constructive, of any irregularity in the sale, the mortgagor can have it set-aside provided he acted timeously. In the case of *Nutt* v. *Easton,*[26] it was decided that, by reason of his laches, the plaintiff could not maintain the action. In this case, the mortgagee of a reversionary interest sold it under the power of sale in January 1888. The reversioner had notice of the sale and he then took legal advice to his rights, but he took no steps to impeach the sale until December 1897, when he commenced an action to set aside. The reversioner had fallen into possession in April 1897.

What is apparent from the plethora of authorities examined above is that where sale is evidently and manifestly not seen to have been conducted bona fide it will be declared invalid and therefore set aside. A borrower would equally not be allowed to avoid liability from a patently genuine transaction under the guise of invalid mortgage or sale.

The golden thread that runs through the entire law of mortgages in Nigeria is that both mortgagor and mortgagee are adequately protected. While a sincere Bank with an upright lending motive, and in fulfilment of existing statutory provisions that regulate both its operations and procedure, seek to have a fallback position so that it is not left in the cold in an event of default, a prudent and frugal businessman whose property is applied to secure a loan is equally insulated from acts of 'oppression' by not allowing the mortgagee take advantage of his weakness.[27]

---

[26] (1900)1 Ch.29

[27] Osaloni, *op. cit.*, at pp. 554-558

Chapter 15

The position of landlord and tenant under the Land Use Act, 1978

A Search through the provisions of the Land Use Act,[1] 1978 as it relate to a customary tenancy with a view to finding out whether and to what extent if any, the Act has affected it and the legal implication of Section 1 and 36 of the Act as well as the judicial position on the landlord and tenant relationship under the Act will equally be considered

Implications of Section 1 and 36(2) of the Act

Since the Act came into operation in March 1978, there have been a lot of misgivings from the interpretation of Section 1 of the Act that in so far as land in each state of the federation is vested in the governor of the state to be held in trust for the use and benefit of all Nigerians, the Act has expropriated all proprietary rights of Nigerians in land benefit of all Nigerians, the Act has expropriated all proprietary rights of Nigerians in land and transferred same to the State. This trail of thought even received a judicial support in *Nkwocha* v. *Governor of Anambra State*,[2] where Kayode Eso JSC (as he then was) ruled that:

> The use of the word 'vested' in Section 1 of the Land Use Act, 1978 has the effect of transferring to the Governor of a state the ownership of all land in the State.

The learned justice went to emphasize the expropriatory effect of the Act when he said:

> The tenor of the Act as a piece of legislation is the nationalization of lands in the country by the besting of its ownership in the state

[1] Land Use Act (Decree No.6) of 1978 hereinafter referred to as the Act.
[2] (1983) 4 NJLR 719.

> leaving the private individual with an interest in land which is a mere right of occupancy.[3]

This interpretation if taken as gospel truth is fraught with obvious danger.[4] Much as it is indisputable that by the tenor of the Act, the concept of absolute ownership by a community, family or individual has given way to a right of occupancy which may be either statutory or customary, it is wrong to suppose that the Act vests ownership of lands comprised in a state in the Governor. The actual power which the Act confers on the Governor could be found in Section 2 which vests in him the control and management of all lands comprised in the urban areas of the State. The same section also vests in the Local Government in their areas of jurisdiction all land not designated "urban areas" by the Governor.[5] It is evident that the emphasis of the Act is on administrative control of land by the Governor and not of real ownership.[6]

The idea of the Governor acquiring ownership of land within his domain is ruled by these facts: first, if the general intendment of the Act is to confer absolute ownership of land on the Governor, there would have been no need for the inclusion of Section 29 of the Act which enjoins the Governor to pay compensation to a holder of a right of occupancy upon revocation of same. It is quite illogical for the owner of property whilst taking it over from their tenant or a licensee to pay compensation to a stranger who has no title to such property.[7] Secondly, it is the principle of property law down the ages that an owner of property is entitled to use it as he desires.[8] Based on this principle, to regard the Governor as the owner will be inappropriate regarding the intention of the legislature because the Governor is only empowered by the Act to administer land in the state for the use and benefit of all Nigerians in accordance with the provisions of the Act, not according to the dictate of his conscience. This point has received judicial acknowledgement that it is now beyond doubt, that the nature of the Governor's interest in land under the Act is no more than control and management,[9] an interest which is not much in contrast with that of the head of family or family property.

---

[3] *Nkwocha* v. *Gov. of Anambra State*, ibid.

[4] See Agbana J.,O.," An Overview of the Positions of Landlord & Tenant Under the Land Use Act, 1978" *Ikeja Bar Review*, Vol 2 Part2, Sept2007-Mar.2008 at p254

[5] *Salati* v. *Shehu* (1986) 1 NWLR (pt.15) p.189 at 210.

[6] J.F. Fekumo, "Does the Land Use Act Expropriate" a rejoinder (Oct. 1987-April 1988) 8-9 J.P.P.L.12.

[7] *Francis* v. *Ibitoye* (1930) 12 NLR 11.

[8] Lawson, *Law of Property*, p. 8.

[9] *Salami* v. *Oke* (1987) 4 NWLR (pt.63) 1.

Another relevant provision of the Act which has elicited seemingly irreconcilable controversies regarding the continued existence of customary tenant is Section 36. Section 36(1) and (2) provides that:

> (1) the following provisions of this section shall have effect in respect of land not in an urban area which was immediately before the commencement of the Decree held or occupied by any person;
>
> (2) any occupier or holder of such land, whether under customary rights or otherwise howsoever, shall if that land was on the commencement of this Decree being used for agricultural purposes continue to be entitled to possession of the land for use for agricultural purposes as if a customary right of occupancy had been granted to the occupier holder there or by the appropriate local government and the reference in this subsection to land being used for agricultural purposes include land which is, in accordance with the custom of the locality concerned, allowed to lie fallow for purposes of recuperation of the soil.

The crux of the controversy is whether as a result of long possession, the customary tenant should as against his overlord be entitled to the deemed customary right of occupancy under the above section, and thereby freed from his obligations to the overlord. Scholars in their attempts to interpret the above provisions of the Act have proffered conflicting solutions. Prof. J. A. Omotola (late), after a critical examination of the Section 36(2) of the Act said:

> "...the person who shall be entitled to possession of the land as if he held a customary right of occupancy granted by the Local Government shall be the person by whom the land was being used for agricultural purpose."[10]

The same author elsewhere, appeared to have shifted his position when he said:

> "In considering the effect of Section 36(2) of the Land Use Act, 1978, care should be taken to avoid giving the provision a literal interpretation...It seems correct to say that the principle of law that statutes should not be taken to expropriate vested rights except by plain language should be the rule in interpreting this provision."[11]

Agbosu, did not mince words in concluding that the Land Use Act has abolished the concept of customary tenancy. He argued that:

---

[10] J.A. Omotola, *Essays on the Land Use Act 1978*, University of Lagos Press Ltd, p.12.
[11] J.A. Omotola, *Cases on the Land Use Act 1978*, University of Lagos Press Ltd, p.163.

> "In examining the totality of its effects therefore, it can be concluded that the Land Use Act has caused the demise of customary scheme of tenure and with its customary tenancy."[12]

In his own contribution on the subject, James is of the opinion that the provision that until the tenant gets himself registered under Section 36(2) of the Act, he remains burdened by obligation to pay tribute to his overlord. In other words, on registration, the tenant is freed from his obligation.[13]

The pronouncements by some High Court Judges on the matter have been most contradictory as to offer practical solution to the controversy. For example, in *Akinloye* v. *Ogunde*,[14] the Oyo State High Court was asked to determine among other issues the operative effect of the provisions of Sections 1 and 36(2) of the Act on the plaintiff to bring an action for forfeiture. Sijuade J. after examining the provisions in the sections in relation to issues rose held that the court could not legally grant forfeiture of the land in dispute since the occupier of such land is enjoined to continue in such occupation as if a customary right of occupancy had been granted by the appropriate local government thereof. He further held that since the ownership of the land in dispute was vested in the State Government whose Local Government was authorized to issue customary rights of occupancy in respect of a land falling within Section 36(2) of the Act, it was only that authority which could properly and legally complain a breach that would warrant forfeiture (reversing the decision of the lower court).

The obvious implication of the above decision is that by virtue of Section 1 and 36(2) of the Act, the customary tenant has been disenfranchised from his obligation to pay tribute to his overlord as the radical title which was the basis of the relationship between them has been transferred to the Governor. This interpretation has been taken by some as meaning an extinction of customary tenancy.[15]

Another issue that also touched mainly on Section 1 and 36(2) of the Act came up again for determination in *Ogunola* v. *Elekoye*,[16] and once again, the High Court ruled that as the defendants were occupiers of the

---

[12] L.K. Agbosu, "Extinction of Customary Tenancy by the Land Use Act, *Akinloye* v. *Odunde* (1978-88) Vol. 3, *Nig. Juridical Review*, p.153.

[13] James, R.,W., *Nigeria Land Use Act; Policy and Principle*, Unife Press Ltd 1978 p.168.

[14] (1979) 2 LRW 282.

[15] Akintola, A. L., "The Dilemma of Customary Tenant under the Land Use Act," *University of Ibadan law Review*, Vol.4 No.1 JANLFAB.1989, p.47, at 50.

[16] J.A. Omotola, *Cases on the Land Use Act*, 1978 p.15.

disputed land immediately before the commencement of the Act, they were therefore entitled to a customary right of occupancy.

However, in contrast with the judgments in the two cases above, Adeloye J. (as he then was), after reviewing the provisions of the same Sections 1 and 36(2) of the Act in *Owoeye* v. *Adedara*,[17] held that nothing in the sections extinguish the right of the overlord to take tribute or rent from the tenant just as much as the tenant was not affected in his obligation to continue to pay same to the overlord.

It is easy to support the decision of his lordship in the above case on these grounds; the Act has not abolished the existing state land laws including customary land law.[18] It also recognize the right of revocation,[19] the Act also recognizes the devolution of property right of a person upon death to be administered in accordance with the customary law prevailing in eh area where the property is situated.[20] It logically follows that with the recognition of all the aforementioned customary institutions under the Act, there is no express provision in the Act kicking against customary tenancy with all its incidents.[21]

The foregoing has revealed the divergent positions of some High Court Judges and the views of some scholars on the probable effect of the Act on customary tenancy.

The interpretation of Sections 1 and 36 of the Land Use Act as they affect the relationship of the landlord and tenant was settled by Supreme Court in a number of cases.[22] It will be examined from decided cases whether the Court has finally defined their rightful positions under the Act so as to free their minds from any misgiving regarding the correct interpretation of Section 36(2) of the Act.

In *Salami* v. *Oke*,[23] the Supreme Court had to consider among other issues the effect of Section 36(2) of the Act on the title of owners of land who held freehold title prior to the coming into force of the Land Use Act. For the purpose of clarity, the facts of the case are as follows.

In 1973, the plaintiff/respondent sued the defendant/appellant for a declaration of title, forfeiture of customary tenancy, arrears of Isakole and an injunction. The defendants were customary tenants to the

---

[17] J.A. Omotola, ibid. p.143.
[18] S.4 and 48 of the Act.
[19] S.29 of the Act.
[20] S.24 of the Act.
[21] Oke, G.,D., "Customary Tenancy in Nigeria – A Critical Examination of the Contradiction in the Status of the Landlord and his Tenant under the Land Use Act, 1978," JUSA Vol. 2 No. 6, p.133 at 135.
[22] For example: *Salami* v. *Oke* (*supra*), *Ogunleye* v. *Oni* (1990) 2 NWLR 745.
[23] *Salami* v. *Oke, supra.*

plaintiffs and were paying Isakole to the respondents' family as their ancestors had done. They however, stopped paying the Isakole claiming that the land in dispute belonged to them. The High Court gave judgment in favour of the plaintiffs in accordance with Section 40 of the Act and in addition awarded forfeiture and injunction against the defendants who appealed unsuccessfully to the Court of Appeal. On a further appeal to the Supreme Court, the court held that the Land Use Act was not intended to transfer the possession of the land from the owner to the tenant by whom the tenant is in possession. The Court further held that the Act did not abolish the remedies of forfeiture and injunction whenever a tenant committed any of the gross acts of misconduct that would have been visited by forfeiture under the native law.

A much controversial issue in those cases was the interpretation to be given to the words "occupier" and "holder" as used in the Act. The question was whether it is the customary tenant by reason of long possession or the overlord in whom the title was vested immediately before the Act came into force is to be entitled to the deemed right of occupancy. In an attempt to determine the meaning of the words, the court had recourse to Section 50 of the Act which provides that:

> "Holder in relation to a right of occupancy means a person entitled to a right of occupancy and includes any person to whom a right of occupancy has been validly assigned or has validly passed on the death of a holder but does not include any person to whom a right of occupancy has been sold or transferred without a valid assignment, nor a mortgage, subleasee or sub-underlessee; and an "occupier" means any person lawfully occupying land under customary law and a person using or occupying land in accordance with customary law and includes the sub-underlessee of a holder."

It was the submission of the counsel for the appellant that being tenants under customary law, the appellants were qualified as "holders" and "occupiers" by virtue of Section 36(2). The Supreme Court however not only rejected this submission but strangely refrained from giving any definite meaning to the words. The question as to who between the landlord and tenant is an "occupier" or "holder" under Section 36(2) was then left unanswered and the controversy rages on.

As the Supreme Court refrained in *Salami* v. *Oke*,[24] from making a definite pronouncement on whether or not a customary tenant is a

[24] *Supra*

"holder" or "occupier", two years after, in *Onwuka* v. *Ediala*,[25] the same apex court faced the problem of defining the relationship between the landlord and tenant under the Act and the proper interpretation of "holder" and "occupier". In delivering its judgment in that case, the court held that:

> Section 36 does not enlarge the right of customary tenant to any piece of land in non-urban area which at the commencement of the Act is in his possession and occupation. A customary tenant remains so and is subject to the conditions attached to the tenancy ...the word "holder" or "occupier" means person entitled to a customary right of occupancy, that is, the customary landowner other than a customary tenant."[26]

By this pronouncement, it would appear that all have been said on the matter, especially when no other authority than the Supreme Court had declared that the overlord is the "holder" or "occupier", which follows that he is entitled to the customary right of occupancy. This decision remains the Supreme Court's position on the landlord-tenant relationship until the celebrated case of *Abioye* v. *Yakubu*.[27]

In that case, which essentially involved a refusal by the respondents to pay tributes to the appellants as their ancestors had done and challenge of the appellants' title, being customary tenants of the appellants, the Court was asked to determine whether the Land Use Act, 1978 particularly Section 1 and 36 and the definition of "holder" and "occupier" under Section 50, read together with other provisions of the Act has abolished the rights of customary owners vis-a-vis customary tenants of land used for agricultural purpose. The Supreme Court realizing that the case raised an important question of law of public interest invited all the Attorneys-General in all the states of the Federation and five Senior Advocates of Nigeria to appear and address the courts as *amicus curiae* on the issue and they all did. After an exhaustive deliberation on the issues raised in the appeal, the Court, in unanimously upholding the appeal, held among others that the Act never set out to curb the relationship of customary overlord and his tenant other than vesting the land in the Governor. The landlord still retains his right to payment of tribute from the tenant under the Act.

In what will adequately serve as the final words on the controversy for the proper construction of "holder" or "occupier" for the purpose of

---

[25] (1989) 1 NWLR (pt. 96) 182.
[26] (1991) 5 NWLR (pt. 190) 130.
[27] At p. 204.

settlement of customary right of occupancy, Bello C.J.N (as he then was) said:

> "...I do not need to invoke any cannon of interpretation to hold that a customary tenant was deemed to have been granted a customary right of occupancy while the customary owner was also deemed to have been granted a customary right of occupancy in respect of all his land which was not subject to any customary tenancy at the commencement of the Act. By no stretch of any rule of interpretation could the deemed right in the dissected sub-section (2) be said to have been granted to the customary owner.[28]

It is pertinent to note that in holding that the customary tenant as against his overlord is entitled under Section 36(2) to a deemed right of occupancy, the court strongly emphasized that the grant is subject to the existing right of and obligation to his overlord. The overlord can still legally impugn the tenant's right of occupancy if he commits acts which would have amounted to misbehaviours under the native law according to the original terms of the grant. The court further held that where certificate of occupancy granted a customary tenant by the appropriate authority is revoked for any reason, the overlord may as a person entitled to the reversion under the terms of the tenancy apply for a certificate of occupancy to be granted to him.[29]

The judgment of the Supreme Court in the above cases has been reaffirmed in a long line of subsequent cases of similar facts.[30] It is therefore incontrovertible that the Land Use Act has not radically affected the concept of customary tenancy, the relationship of the tenant and his overlord remains even with the promulgation of the Act.[30]

---

[28] Per Nnaemeka-Agu J.S.C. p. 251.

[29] Ibid.

[30] *E.G. Akinola* v. *Oyelade* (1993) 3 NWLR (pt. 285) p. 379; *Odunsi* v. *Bamgbala* (1995) 1 NWLR (pt. 373) p. 641.

[30] Agbana, *op. cit.*, at p. 260

Chapter 16

The procedure for recovery of premises under the recovery of premises law

The recovery of premises more than ever is on the increase especially with the rapid growth in commercial-cum-residential buildings, just as both landlords and tenants are increasingly recognizing the import of solicitors to so act on their behalf. Recovery of premises in modern times become more topical to regulate the relationship between the landlords and tenants, a coterie of laws have been promulgated across the length and breath of the country dealing with matters such as the need to prevent arbitrary increment in rents, unlawful ejection of tenants and illegal holding over the tenants.[1]

Virtually all states in the Federation of Nigeria have one or two laws dealing with recovery of premises. In 1958,[2] there was the Recovery of Premise Act Cap 176. In Lagos there is the Rent Control and Recovery of Residential Premises Law, 1978.

The issue of jurisdiction

Jurisdiction in legal parlance is more than not the wheel upon which any legal cause can ride. It is of so immense import that a court without it is apparently seized of powers to pronounce or make any decision on the subject matter. Its fundamental importance is buttressed by the fact that it can be raised at any stage of the proceedings, either in the court of first instance or in the Appeal Court. It can be raised by any of the parties or the court can *suo motu* raise it. The court therefore, has a duty to raise

---

[1] See Olong M. A., The Procedure for the Recovery of Premises under the Recovery of Premises Law: An Appraisal. *Solicitors Law Journal*, Ministry of Justice, Ado-Ekiti, 2006 at p25

[2] Originally, the main Statutes providing for the Recovery of Premises Pursuant to a terminated tenancy were the Recovery of Premises Ordinance Cap.193 Vol.1 of the 1948 Laws of Nigeria. With the coming into force of the Lyttleton Constitution of 1954, a Federal Structure was adopted for the country, consequent upon which the various regions had their own legislature. Each region then reproduced the original ordinance.

the issue of jurisdiction on the facts presented if the court's competence appears to be in question.[3]

In *Yusuf* v. *Obasanjo*,[4] the court held that jurisdiction is the authority which a court has to decide matters which are litigated before it or to take cognizance of matters presented in a formal way for its decision. The limits of this authority are imposed by the Constitution, Statute, Charter or Commission under which the court is constituted and may be extended or restricted by similar means. If no restriction or limits is imposed, the court's jurisdiction is said to be unlimited. So, generally, Magistrates Courts and High Courts have jurisdiction to entertain recovery of premises cases. However, in Lagos State, like in many other states in Nigeria, Magistrate Courts or Customary Courts are divested of jurisdiction with respect to residential premises.[5] Jurisdiction lies in the various Rent Tribunals.[6] High Courts have jurisdiction by virtue of Section 272,[7] which provides that:

> Subject to the provisions of Section 251 and other provisions of this Constitution, the High Court of a state shall have jurisdiction to hear and determine any civil proceedings in the existence or extent of legal

---

[3] See *Oloba* v. *Akereja* (1988) 7. S.C.N.J. (pt.56), *Ijebu-Ode Local Government* v. *Adedeji Balogun & Co Ltd* (1991) 1 NWLR (pt.166) 0.136, *Materi* v. *Dangaladima* (1993) 1 LRCN 335, *Pertojessica Enterprises Ltd* v. *Leventis Technical Co Ltd* (1992) 5 NWLR (pt.224) p.675.

[4] (2004) All FWLR (pt.213) p.1884 at 1901, in *Nuhu* v. *Ogele* (2004) Vol.1 M.J.S.C., the Supreme Court held that the issue of jurisdiction is fundamental to the existence of the writ or claim. The form, nature or procedure of how it is raised is not strictly material. Where a challenge to the decision of a court is founded on lack of jurisdiction, the court is bound to consider such challenge. A party to litigation cannot be shut out and court inhibited from entertaining a matter on technical ground particularly where the issue of jurisdiction is concerned. See also *Galadima* v. *Tomboi* (2000) 11, NWLR (pt.677) p.76, *Nonye* v. *Anyichie* (2005) 1 SCM 133, *Usiobaifo* v. *Usiobaifo* (2005) 1 SCM, 193.

[5] In *Nebedum* v. *Labisi* (2001) 1 NWLR (pt.693) p.87, the Court of Appeal Lagos Division, held on whether error in assumption of jurisdiction deprives a Magistrate's Court of jurisdiction in all cases, that a Magistrate Court lacks jurisdiction in cases of arrears of rent and possession. In the instant appeal, the fact that the Magistrate in his ruling assumed jurisdiction in cases of arrears or rent and possession does not lead to a conclusion that in all cases a Magistrate Court has no jurisdiction in cases of arrears of rent and possession. The Court, Per Ogundare said that with respect to the objection as to the jurisdiction of the lower court in respect to his ruling, the worst that can be said of the ruling is that the learned magistrate might have erred in his decision that he had jurisdiction in claims of arrears and possession. Although it was the objection of the appellant that title was involved in the matter, the fact that he assumed jurisdiction in his ruling does not lead to the conclusion that in all cases a Magistrate Court has no jurisdiction in cases of rent and possession. This was not therefore a case in which cetioriari or prohibition could issue on the grounds that a magistrate sat over a matter in which it had no jurisdiction. If the learned trial Magistrate had erroneously decided on the objection as to the jurisdiction, that only gave to the appellant the right of his election to bring an appeal against the ruling

[6] See, for instance, Section 7 of the Rent Control and Recovery of Residential Premises Edit of Lagos State Edict, 1997.

[7] Constitution of the Federal Republic of Nigeria, 1999.

right, power, duty, liability, privilege, interest, obligation or claim is in issue.

Subsection 2,[8] provides that the reference to civil proceedings includes a reference to the proceedings which originate in the High Court of a state and those which are brought before the High Court to be dealt with by the court in the exercise of its appellant or supervisory jurisdiction. The Court of Appeal in *Edet* v. *Mattias*,[9] held that by the provisions of Section 6(4)(a) and (k) of the Constitution of the Federal Republic of Nigeria, 1999, landlord and tenant matters are adjudicated upon by Rent Tribunals in States of Nigeria.

Recovery of premises procedure[10]

In *Okutade* v. *Adewunmi*,[11] the court held that a landlord has unfettered legal right to terminate a tenancy upon giving adequate notice this is because the property is his and he can at any time terminate subject to the conditions of the tenancy agreement once he abides by the provisions of the tenancy agreement the tenant has no choice than to vacate possession.

The procedure for recovery of premises remains a highly technical and very strict procedure. As such, strict adherence to the step by step

---

[8] Ibid.

[9] (2009) All FWLR at 1549, the facts of which were that the plaintiff prayed the High Court of Justice, Delta State for a declaration that the quit notices issued and served on her by the defendants was invalid to vacate the apartment situate at the Senior/Ministers Quarters, low's Kingdom society, was unlawful, null and void and of no effect and an order of two bedroom, perpetual injunction restraining the defendants, for further issuing quit notices to her. The defendants appealed to the Court to dismiss or strike out the suit on grounds that the court lacks jurisdiction. Aggrieved, the plaintiff appealed to the Court of Appeal. The Court of Appeal held that by the provisions of Section 27(1) of the Constitution of the Federal Republic of Nigeria, 1999, the State High Court possess very wide powers as regard civil or criminal matters. Section 257 of the Constitution of the Federal Republic of Nigeria, 1999 spills out the jurisdiction of the Federal High Court which is exercisable to the exclusion of an other courts in civil cases and matters. It curtails the powers of State High Court and robs the court of part of the powers enjoyed.

[10] Osimiri U.J., *Modern Law of Landlord and Tenant in Nigeria* (Nigeria: Pam Unique Publishers, 1994) at p.203 sums up the procedure stipulated by the statutes as follows; firstly, the landlord or his agent must serve the prescribed notice to quit determining the tenancy and thereafter serves seven days notice of intention to apply to court to recover possession. Secondly, the landlord or his solicitor would file a claim in eh court of competent jurisdiction and summons shall be issued by the court and served by the bailiffs from the deputy sheriff's office. Thirdly, a hearing date would be fixed and in absence of admission of evidence to prove all the ingredients required by the statute or common law where the tenancy is regulated by the latter. Fourthly, if the landlord proved his case order of possession arrears of rent and mesne profit could be made in form of judgment by the court. Fifthly, the victorious landlord can enforce the judgment on application to the Deputy Sheriff who would issue a warrant of possession directing the bailiff to forcibly eject the tenant therefrom. The procedure is only applicable where there is a relationship between the parties; else ordinary action for possession can be maintained.

[11] (2010) 8 NWLR

procedure is a prerequisite if the entire proceeding is not to be declared null and void. Displacement of any of the steps would render nugatory the entire proceedings.

Section 7[12] provides that when and so soon as the term of interest of the tenant of any premises held by him at will or for any term either with or without being liable to the payment of any rent ends or is duly determined by a written notice to quit as in form B,[13] C[1415] or D,[16] whichever is applicable to the case or is otherwise duly determined and the tenant or if the tenant does not occupy the premises or only occupies a part thereof, a person by whom the premises or any part thereof, is actually occupied neglects or refuses to quit and deliver up possession of the premises or of such part thereof respectively, the landlord of the premises or his agent may cause the person so neglecting or refusing to quit and deliver up possession to be served in the manner mentioned with a written notice as in form E[17] signed by the landlord or his agent, of the landlord's intention to proceed to recover possession on a date, not less than seven days from the date of the service of the notice.

A landlord is empowered to personally issue notices to the tenant to quit and deliver up premises occupied by him.[18] If the landlord however, has a caretaker or a solicitor, the landlord must authorize such a caretaker or solicitor to issue notices on his behalf.[19]

Service of notice or process

Service of process of notices under the various provisions of the premises laws shall or must be effected by personal service[20] on the tenant or where it is impracticable to so do, a copy of the process shall be posted on some conspicuous part of the premises sought to be recovered and it shall be deemed good service on the defendant.[21]

The bailiff is required in the proof of service to sign however, that service was by posting.[22] Section 28[23] provides that:

---

[12] Abuja Act Cap.544 Laws of the Federation of Nigeria, 1990 (now 2004).
[13] Form B is ordinarily signed by the Landlord himself.
[14] Whoever is the agent of the landlord signs this form.
[15] Osimiri, *op. cit.,* stated that though the use of Forms in the various schedules of the rent Act are not mandatory but counsels are advised to get acquainted with them.
[16] This form ordinarily relates to a lodger.
[17] This is owner's intention to recover possession.
[18] See Alubo A.O., *Contemporary Nigerian Land Law* (Jos: Abeson Publishers Ltd, 2006) p.491
[19] See *Wemabod Estate ltd* v. *C.O. Kotun* (1997) 10 ICCHCJ 13319 at 2332, *Balogun* v. *CEDB* (1973) 2 All NLR, 80.
[20] See Section 28 Abuja Act.
[21] See Alubo, *op. cit.,* at p.191.
[22] See Section 28 Recovery of Premises Act 1958. See also *Chiwete* v. *Amissah* (1958) LCR 1.

> Service of any notice under the provisions of the edict or any summons or warrant or other process shall be effected in accordance with the provisions of the law for the time being in force, relating to the service of the civil process of Magistrate Court i.e. personal service and if the defendant shall either not be known on admission thereto cannot be obtained for serving any such process personally, a copy of the process shall be posted on some conspicuous part of the premise sought to be recovered and such posting shall be deemed good service on the defendant.[24]

The issue of service touches on the jurisdiction of the court.[25] In *Auto Import* v. *Adebayo*,[26] it was held that service of process is a condition precedent to the exercise of jurisdiction by the court out of whose registry, the writ or process was issued, unless, the processes are duly followed, the jurisdiction of the court to look into the matter is ousted.

Service of notice by the agent or solicitor

A landlord's agent, be him a solicitor or a layman, is empowered to serve the two statutory notices which must be served on the tenant; the notice to quit and the notice of owner's intention to recover possession. A solicitor unless specially authorized in writing cannot give a statutory notice to quit.[27] But the court in *Olusi* v. *Solana*[28] and *Labadedi* v. *James*[29] held that the requirement of a written authority applies only to the notice of intention to recover possession. However, the Court of Appeal in *Coker* v. *Adetayo*[30] held that the requirement of written authority applies to both notice to quit and of intention to recover possession. In other words, for an agent or a solicitor, to validly serve statutory notices, he must be authorized in writing by the landlord.[31]

---

[23] Abuja Act, *op. cit.*

[24] See *Summonu* v. *Onayemi* (1955) 21 NLR 45. In *Adubiara* v. *Etti* (1962) 4 R 104, it was held that notice on the premises was not good service unless: (a) the tenant could not be found; (b) his place of dwelling was earlier not known or admission thereto could not be obtained for giving the notice.

[25] See Alubo, *op. cit.* at p.192.

[26] (2002) 103 LRCN 2397. See also *Onuorah* v. *Kaduna Refining Ltd* (2002) 21 NSCPR 130 *Dangote* v. *Civil Service Commission* (2001) 86 LRCN 1204 and *Teno Construction ltd* v. *Yusuf* v. *Adisa* (2005) 21 NSCQR 562.

[27] See Section 707 of the Recovery of Premises Ordinance, *op. cit.*

[28] (1956) LLR 18.

[29] (1972) NRNLR

[30] (1992) 6 NWLR (pt.249) p.612.

[31] The court's decision in *Coker* v. *Adetayo* (*supra*) is in all forms wrong in law in view of the provision of Section 7 and Section 3 of both the Abuja Act and the Lagos Edict which clearly state that only a written authority is required in respect of a notice of intention to recover possession.

Notice to quit and owner's intention to recover possession

The Recovery of Premises laws in Nigeria recognize the fact that parties to a tenant agreement may agree on the length of notice to determine the relationship.[32] In the absence of such a stipulation, the law prescribes various lengths of notices from the weekly tenant to the yearly tenant[33] and these are:

- in the case of a tenant at will or a weekly tenancy, a week's notice;
- in the case of a monthly tenancy, a month's notice;
- in the case of a quarterly tenancy, a quarter's notice; and
- in the case of a yearly tenancy, half a year's notice.

The notices to quit shall state whether it is the landlord that is giving it or as agent or solicitor of the landlord and should as contents, contain that:

- the tenant should quit and deliver up possession of the premises, houses, flat or room with the appurtenances;
- the situation of the premises, the town or district and number of the street;
- the kind of tenancy, whether it is weekly, monthly or a tenancy at will;
- the date of commencement and expiration of the tenancy; and
- the date the notice to quit is to expire, the notice is then dated and signed by the person giving the notice.

By the rules of legal practice, if no notice is given until the expiration of the tenancy, the tenant is only entitled to a seven days notice after which the other notice of owner's intention to recover possession is issued. A notice to quit may be given at anytime before the date of expiration of the current term of tenancy but such notice shall not be effective if the time between the giving of the notice and the time when the tenancy is to be determined is less than those respectively set out in the various recovery laws. For instance, a yearly tenancy due to end on 31st December 2006, a quit notice to be effective, must be for duration of six month; six calendar months in line with the Gregorian calendar, meaning the six calendar months notice to terminate exactly on the 31st

[32] See Ntephe E.C., Termination of Tenancy by Notices to Quit. The Plateau State Experience, Vol.1 No.1 JJPL (1996) p.80.

[33] See Section 8(3) Abuja, Section 14(2) Lagos, Section 8(1) Recovery of Premises Law Cap.155, Laws of Northern Nigeria,(1963) and Section 16(1) Rent Control and Recovery of Premises Edict, 1994.

December 2006. It could have more days extending to 2007 but not less than 31st December 2006.[34]

The notice to quit is followed by what is popularly referred to as the seven days notice otherwise known as notice of owner's intention to apply to recover possession.[35] This is only given if tenant still fails to quit in response to the notice to quit[36] and refuses to deliver possession of the premises. The Form E is ordinarily signed by the owner or his agent or his solicitor. In *Chiwete* v. *Amisah,*[37] the court held that at this point the landlord is referred to as the owner because the relationship of landlord and tenant had been severed at the expiry of the notice.[38]

Writ of summons or plaint against a person refusing to deliver up possession

Where at the expiration of the seven days notice stated in the owner's intention to apply to recover possession and the tenant or any person holding or claiming by through or order proceeds or fails, or neglects to quit, an application in form of a plaint, or a writ is made to the court known as Form F. the Form F shall contain the fact that:

---

[34] See *Oyekoya* v. *GBO Nig. Ltd* (1989) 6 WSCC, *Lateef Aminu* v. *Amade* (1977) 10 IHJP, *Amoniyi & Ors* v. *Igbakuye Brothers* (1965) 4 WSCC 123, *Osewaru* v. *Ezeiruka* (1978) p.52 SC 125, In *African Petroleum* v. *Owochunmi* (1991) 11 SCNJ p.81, the Supreme Court stated that it is settled that a notice to quit in order to be effective ought to determine the tenancy at the end of the current term of tenancy. See also *U.I.C* v. *Harmond Nig. Ltd* (1998) 7 NWLR (pt.565) p.340. The nature of a tenancy may be determined by evidence. In its absence, it is ascertained by reference to the time when the rent is paid or demanded. This was the observation of the court in *NCHCv. Oyewole* (1998) 4 NWLR (pt.90) p. 588 at 590, where the court also held that in determining the nature of a tenancy between a landlord and a tenant especially where the agreement is oral, the intention of the parties is a paramount consideration and this is discovered from the circumstances surrounding the particular transaction. In *Pan Asian African Co.* v. *NICON* (1982) NSCC Vol.13, p.293, the Supreme Court restated that mandatory statutory provisions as to notices to quit and intention to recover possession must be given effect to. It held that the absence of service of initiating notice is fatal to a residential matter. In *Tinuola* v. *Okon* (1966) 2 ANLR 188, the court held that where the agreement of the parties is for a fixed term, landlord may proceed with the seven days notice. Obi Okoye, *Essays on Civil Proceedings* (Nigeria: Fourth Dimension Publishing Co, 1981) at p.27 noted that the aim of a notice to quit is to terminate the tenancy, so possession of premises may revert to the landlord, where the tenancy has come to an end by effluxion of time, service of any notice to quit is a surplusage.

[35] See, Form F. See also Alubo, *op. cit.*, p.193.

[36] See Form C.

[37] *Supra.*

[38] In *Udih* v. *Izedonmwen* (1990) 2 NWLR (pt.32) p.257, the court held that once a valid notice to quit at proper length has been served on the court in accordance with the law, the tenancy is automatically determined at the expiration of the notice. See also Woodfall, *Landlord and Tenant* 27th edn. P.952, Male J.M. *Landlord and Tenant* (Great Britain: Pearson Professional Ltd 1955) at p.81-86. See the cases of *Contemploy* v. *Met Lodge Ltd* (1973) 12 All ER and 1074) *Shi Prudential Assurance Co. Ltd* v. *London Residuary Bory* (1992) 2 AC 386; *Sidebotham* v. *Holland* (1995) QB 378. See Osimiri, *op. cit.*, at p.39.

- The plaintiff is entitled to the possession of the premises which were let by the plaintiff to the defendant.
- Brief and accurate description of the said premises.
- The period of tenancy and the rent attached.
- The date of the expiration of the tenancy and notice to quit.
- The fact of the notice in writing of the plaintiff to apply to recover possession of the premises. A duplicate of this notice and form E must be attached.
- A description of how the service of this notice in Form E was effected.
- That in spite of the notice in Form E the defendant has refused or neglected to and still retains the same.
- Claim for possession, arrears of rent or mesne profit.

If at the expiration of the notice to quit the tenant owes rents, they are called arrears of rent. Whilst from that date until possession is given up, the rents which have accrued are known as mesne profit.[39]

What the plaintiff should prove at the trial or hearing

The burden of proof is on the plaintiff and the standard is one of the preponderance of evidence or on the balance of probabilities. Where however issues have been joined, the trail will proceed.[40] The plaintiff would be expected to tender all the notices served on the defendant and prove other claims such as arrears of rent and mesne profits. Where the landlord is entitled to possession, the court may issue a warrant of possession.

The recovery of premises by a landlord can only be obtained by order of court in compliance with the various laws, otherwise the landlord may be liable in trespass for forcible ejection of the tenant.[41]

Role of a solicitor and the power of attorney

The role of a solicitor is subsumed in the interest of the landlord who chooses not to file the claim himself, before or even at the expiration of the seven days notice given to the tenant. The solicitor may act for the

---

[39] See *Coswanu* v. *Ezeriruka* (1978) 687 SC, *Oyelatun* v. *Shomonye* (1960) WNLR, 126. See also Nwadialo F., *Civil Procedure in Nigeria*, 2nd edn. (Nigeria: University Press, 2000) p.401.

[40] See *Rjuefemi* v. *Olaiye* (2001) LRCN, *Adeokev. Iyande* (2001) 88 LRCN, 2162.

[41] See *Iheanecho* v. *Ume Uzochukwu* (1997) 2 NWLR (pt.487) p. 257 where possession was obtained through an affidavit sworn to by the landlord and endorsed for possession by the Magistrate without service of statutory notice or issuance of a writ. The landlord was held liable in trespass for the ejection of the tenant on the basis of the said affidavit.

landlord in court or after being given a power of attorney to represent him.

The solicitor must bear in mind the following as regards the power of attorney:

(a) The suit may be prosecuted by the donee/attorney as if it is by the donor or landlord.[42] Since it is customary for the attorney to let out the premises for and on behalf of the landlord,[43] he cannot sue in his own name as no cause of action is vested on him personally but on his principal's name.[44] in *Boyejoh* v. *Alonge*,[45] it was held that if the plaintiff holds a power of attorney to act for the owner of the premises, that will not only permit him to sue in the name of the owner but will confer authority on him to sue in his own name.

The use of forms in filing claims in the court is permissive and not obligatory.[46]

The position of subtenants/statutory tenants and the recovery of premises law

By the provisions of Section 2[47] of the recovery law to apply, there must exist relation of landlord and tenant. A tenant includes a subtenant or any person occupying any premises whether on payment of rent or otherwise but does not include a person occupying premises under a bona fide claim to be the owner of the premises; the term tenant does not include a licensee but a statutory tenant.

The Rent Control and Recovery of Premises Edicts makes it clear for residential premises, the term tenant includes a subtenant. The provision of the Law makes it imperative that service of a notice to quit must be complied with before ejecting him. In this wise statute protects the employee or servant of a company of statutory corporation occupying the official quarters allocated to him by the employers. In *Sule* v. *Nigerian Cotton Board*,[48] the court held that a Landlord is not entitled to go into the premises and physically throw out the tenant who was an employee but must be given statutory notices to the person in possession. In *Oduye*

[42] See Osimiri, *op. cit.*, at p.396.
[43] See *Boyejoh* v. *Alonge* (1976) 3 OYSHC.
[44] See *Blundell Formaglaze* v. *Olorunde* (1981) 10 YSHC 78.
[45] *Supra.*
[46] See *Adejumo* v. *David Hughes & Co. Ltd* (1989) 5 NWLR (pt.120), p. 146.
[47] Abuja Act. See also Section 36 of the Lagos Act.
[48] (1985) 2 NWLR (pt. 5) p.17. See also *Eliochun* v. *Mbadiwe* (1981) 1 SC p.99.

v. *Nigerian Airways*,[49] the Supreme Court regarded Oduye as a statutory tenant of her official quarters even after the determination of her employment. As far as official quarters of employees are concerned, the law requires that such employees be served with notices to quit even if they are licensed.

What then is essential is lawful occupation. The law protects public servants as well as parastatals domestic servants and people paying commercial rent.[50]

A statutory tenancy remains a compendious expression to describe the rights of a tenant of protected premises to remain in possession of those premises, notwithstanding the determination of his contractual interest until such time as either he voluntarily gives up possession or the court on cause shown makes an order against him to deliver up possession.[51] A statutory tenant is a tenant whose tenancy has expires under the ordinary rules of law but who has rights by statute to pay rent by the control or other emergency legislation.[52]

At common law, a statutory tenant is known in English parlance as a tenant at sufferance and has little or no right. This is because after the valid termination of the tenancy, a tenant who holds over becomes a trespasser and a landlord is given the right to re-enter premises.[53] Where the landlord exercises his right, the tenant who holds over cannot maintain an action for trespass in tort against him except where the landlord has used force more than reasonably necessary to eject him.[54]

The Supreme Court in a coterie of cases[55] has assented to the fact that statutory tenants even though not necessarily wanted by landlords, have some basic rights such as:

---

[49] (1987) SC, See *Chukwuma* v. *Shell Petroleum Development Co. (Nig) Ltd* (1993) 5 SCNJ and *FCDA* v. *Emeka* (1998) 4 NWLR (pt. 554), p. 73.

[50] See Ntephe, *op. cit.*, at p. 83. See also *Ben Chukwu* v. *Shell PDC* (1993) SSCNJ.91.

[51] See Blundell and Wellings MA, Woodfall *Landlord and Tenant, op. cit.*, at p.296; Chianu E., *Law of Landlord and Tenant* (Nigeria: Qliz Publishers, 2001) p.85 Lush J. in *Keeves* v. *Decan* (1924) 1 KB 685 at 685 at 682 described statutory tenant as state of irrevocability. Nnaemeka-Agu JSC in *African Petroleum Ltd* v. *Owolumni* (*supra*) at p.94 defined statutory tenancy as security of tenure to a tenant after his contractual tenancy has expired.

[52] See Ijaiya H., The Rights of Statutory Tenants in Nigeria (2003) 2 UNADLJ at p.207. See Section 44(1) Housing Repairs and Rents Act 1954. Blundell, *op. cit.*, at p.1553 defined a statutory tenant as a tenant whose protected tenancy has come to an end but continued to occupy the dwelling house as his residence or a tenant whose holds over by virtue of his statutory rights after the expiration of a notice to quit.

[53] Ijaiya, *op. cit.*, p. 206.

[54] Ibid.

[55] See *Oduye* v. *Nigerian Airways* (supra), *Chukwuma* v. *Shell P.D.C.* (*supra*).

- Right to peaceable and quite enjoyment of the premises without let or hindrance by the landlord or his agent during the subsistence of the tenancy.[56]
- Right to institute legal action in the court of law against his landlord for trespass, where the landlord arbitrarily enters the premises to disturb the tenant's quiet enjoyment of the premises.[57]
- Right to apply to court to fix or determine a reasonable rent payable on premises where the landlord arbitrarily increases same.[58]

Appraising the recovery of premises laws

It is puzzling to note that the various recovery of premises laws in Nigeria may be due to oversight on the part of the lawmakers did not make any specific provisions as to the length and nature of notice necessary for the determination of a statutory tenancy.[59] As we emphasized in *Oduya case*,[60] the length and nature of notice required depends upon the relevant length of notice that would have been necessary to determine the original tenancy. However, the courts in their efforts to determine the length and nature of the notice for statutory tenancy in Nigeria have been resorted to the period of notice required to determine the period tenancy. To have, therefore, a statutory tenant six months in the case where a yearly tenancy is implied, seems too long having in mind the fact that a statutory tenant still remains a tenant that his landlord does not want.

Again, the overwhelming view of majority of landlords in that the recovery of premises law operative in Nigeria are heavily biased against the landlords is according to them, the laws have made it difficult, if not impossible or impracticable to recover premises with ease. The landlords alluded to the fact that the laws have introduced all sorts of technical details, the fulfilment of which, on the part of the landlord or solicitor have very stringent. Some of the technicalities referred to by concerned landlords are: the technicalities that end the notices, the timing, calendar month, the giving of another notice to recover possession before the tenant to vacate the premises, even after judgment and the due regard

[56] See *Dawodu* v. *Ijale* (1946) 12 WACA, see also *Pan Asian African Co. Ltd* v. *National Insurance Corp* (1982) 1 All NCR 229, where the court held that a statutory tenant is occupier, who when his contractual tenancy expires holds over and continues in possession by vote of special statutory provision. See also *Yurner* v. *Watts* (1928) 97 LJC at 92.

[57] See *Sobamowo* v. *The Federal Public Trustee* (1970) All NCR, 261.

[58] See Falose S. "Tenant Rights in a Tenancy Agreement", *The Punch*, Monday January 27, 2003 p.59.

[59] See Ijaiya, *op. cit.*, at p.213.

[60] *Supra*

given to the convenience of the tenant. In *Nnodi* v. *Princewill*,[61] the appellant, through his agent appointed by power of attorney entered into a lease agreement with one G and M Company Limited of No.6, Sumbo Jibowa Street, South West Ikoyi, Lagos in respect of the property of the appellant of No.8, Alhaji Bashorun Street, South West Ikoyi, Lagos r one year but with an option to renew same further term of two years.

The lease was entered into on 1st October, 1997. at the expiration of the term, the leasee renewed same for a term of two years and which term was to expire on 21st October, 2000. After the renewal, G & M Co. Ltd unilaterally proceeded to sublet the premises to other persons without the consent of the Appellant contrary to the terms and condition of the lease agreement. Having completed the sublease, the G & M Co. Ltd then dropped off the scene completely without a trace, leaving persons unknown to the Appellant in possession and the subject property. The original leasee also changed its contact addresses. The sub-leasees then started massive reconstruction and alteration of the premises without the authority and consent of the Appellant who after the expiration of the further term of two years, issued an originating commons for recovery of possession. The trial court granted the relief sought. The respondent then filed a motion for an order that the judgment in default of appearance entered against them be set aside and that the suit be heard on the merit.

The trial court in a considered ruling set aside its earlier judgment and reinstated the respondents to the property in issue, meanwhile, the appellant sold the property to the interviewer/respondent after the judgment who then brought a motion to arrest the ruling. The court however went ahead to deliver the judgment. Not satisfied, the appellant appealed. On the issues for determination, it was formulated as follows:

Can it rightly be said that the solemn judgment of the court delivered on 1/12/2000 had been set aside by the court or that a valid order had been made reinstated the defendant/respondents to the subject property when the court order specifically referred to a judgment delivered on 4/12/2000 and the enrolment order stated that the judgment was delivered on 14/12/2000 when both in the court order nothing was said about reinstating the defendants/respondents.

Whether an unlawful subtenant executing premises though a tenant expressly forbidden to let, assign or part with possession without the express written consent of the plaintiff/appellant can become a tenant of the land and or if the holding of the defendants/respondents in the subject property was at best tenancy at sufferance, was the court below

---

61 (2006) 2 CWLR at 366.

right in supposedly making an order reinstating the defendant/respondents to the subject property?

Was the court below right after setting aside its judgment to December 7, 2000 supposedly to have made a final order reinstating the defendants/respondents to the subject property?

The court unanimously allowing the appeal held on:

when a court is permitted to set aside its own judgment –

> it is trite that a court lacks jurisdiction to set aside its own decision except as permitted by the common law such as when the decision is a nullity by reason of a breach of procedure or has occasioned a miscarriage of justice or as provided for by the rules such as when judgment is given in default or the court is given the power to discharge an order it had made.

On the purpose of the procedure in Order 59 of the Lagos State High Court Civil Procedure Rules for recovery of possession of land that –

> The procedure under Order 59 offers an applicant a summary procedure for recovery of possession of land wrongfully occupied by a trespasser or trespassers whose or some of whose names the applicant or plaintiff does not know. This is contrary to an ordinary or normal action for recovery of possession of land in which the person in possession should be made a defendant so that he would be bound by the order for possession when made by the court. In a case where the landlord does not know the names of the illegal occupiers of his land or cannot even physically identify all of them, the requirement that the person be made defendants of the action would result n great injustice and hardship to the landlord or landowner, thus giving rise to the procedure under Order 59.

When a plaintiff may resort to the procedure under Order 59 of the Lagos State High Court (Civil Procedure) Rule –

> A plaintiff may resort to the procedure where he claims possession of land which he allege is occupied solely by a person (not being a tenant or a tenant holding over after the termination of the tenancy) who entered into and remained in occupation without his license or consent or that of predecessor in title of his.

How landlord and tenancy relationship is created –

> Generally speaking, the relation of landlord and tenant was originally one of contract only, but from early times the contract has conferred on the tenant an estate in land without losing all its contractually characteristics. The relation arise as a rule by an agreement by which one party the right to the exclusive possession of that land for an ascertainable period of time less than that of the grantor's interest.

> The landlord and tenant are thus parties to a contract and parties to the grant of an estate.

Effect of breach of express covenant prohibiting subletting –

> A sub-tenancy granted in breach of an absolute prohibition against subletting is not binding on the landlord.

The court per Onnoghe (JCA)[62] held on whether the respondents were tenants that:

> Respondents contend that they were known persons to the appellant and as such they could not be said to be persons unknown so as to invoke the provisions of Order 59. I do not agree with the respondents in that submission. The question is not whether the appellant knew the respondents, particularly the 2nd respondent but whether he knew then in relation to their legal status in the property vis-à-vis the appellant as the landlord of that property. There is no evidence before the court that the respondents were tenants of the appellant in respect of the property and I hold the view that the lower court was wrong in invoking that there was a subsisting tenancy between the parties. That being the case, it is my considered view that the possession of the property by the respondents under the circumstances without license or consent of the Appellant is wrongful occupation and is without any right or interest thereto.
>
> The respondents cannot legally be said to be tenants holding over after determination of their tenancy as argued by learned counsel for the respondents because their initial occupation of the property is wrongful, unlawful and their acts amounts in law to trespass since they entered the property without the license or consent, or any right title or interest in the property in question.
>
> I hold the view that the question whether the respondents were tenants at sufferance or holding over tenants is very irrelevant to the facts of this case particularly since for the two forms of presumed tenancies to exist and be entitled to the incidence of such tenancies the pre-condition necessary is that the tenant must have initially come upon the land or premises lawfully.
>
> The tenancies concerned depend upon the law and not on the agreement of the parties; they are in effect presumed by law. In the present case however, there is no tenancy at all between the parties and the initial occupation of the property by the Respondents not being lawful, the Respondents cannot be presumed in law to be either tenants at sufferance or holding over tenants. I therefore hold the

---

[62] *Nnodi* v. *Princewill* (*supra*) pp.391-392.

view that the procedure adopted in recovering possession under Order 59 is proper under the circumstances of the case.

Landlord and tenant relationship should be that of reciprocity and the unwholesome practices going on in real property investments should at all times be frowned at. The writer's view is in line with per Onnoghe's observations in *Nnodi* v. *Princewill*[63] as he reiterated that:

> I have observed that this case once more demonstrates the unwholesome practices going on in real property investments. Here is a landlord who leased his property to a tenant with expressed condition not to sub-let or part with possession thereof without the written consent of the landlord but the tenant, for whatever reason not known to the landlord, decided to do the very opposite. Having granted a sublease to the respondents contrary to the conditions of the lease, the landlord made efforts within the 'time granted the tenant and after its expiration to get the "sub-tenants" to atone tenancy to the landlord without success. The subtenant snubbed landlord'. There is evidence that the originating processes were served on the property by substituted means yet the sub-tenant did not react. Judgment was duly obtained and execution carried out only for the subtenant to go to court to claim that he is a subsisting tenant etc. and prayed the court to set aside its judgment. Incidentally, there is no single document exhibited to the application which confirm the existence of any tenancy between the appellant/landlord and the respondents/subtenants neither is there any to show that the sublease was with the written consent of the appellant so as to establish a landlord/tenant relationship between the parties, yet the court not only set aside its judgment but ordered reinstatement of the respondent to the property. Certain questions then become relevant:
>
> (a) Whose tenants are the reinstated respondents?
> (b) What are the terms and conditions of their tenancy? Or
> (c) Are the respondents to occupy the property rent free? etc.

In *R.C.C. (Nig.) Ltd* v. *R.P.C. Ltd*,[64] the respondent owned an estate consisting of several buildings in Enugu. It leased several of these buildings to the appellant a foreign construction company. Dispute arose from the landlord-tenant relationship so created and the respondent sued the appellant at the High Court in Enugu, then in Anambra State. It claimed arrears of rent and mesne profit in respect of properties it leased to the appellant. The respondent also claimed interest on the arrears of

---

[63] *Supra*, 2006.

[64] (2005) 10 NWLR (pt. 934) at 615-618.

rent and sought an order of the trial court directing the appellant to restore the properties to their pre-tenancy condition.

The appellant on the other hand, admitted that its tenancy was determined in 1984. It however, averred and deduced evidence that it restore the demised premise to their pre-tenancy condition; that the respondent refused to accept its surrender of the restored premises notwithstanding the appellant's offer to pay the sum of ₦100,000 to the respondent as additional compensation.

In its judgment, the trial court held that the respondent did not prove its claim and that even if it did, it would not have been entitled to the claims sought because it failed to mitigate its damages. Consequently, the trail court dismissed the respondent's suit in its entirety. Dissatisfied at the trial court, the respondent appealed to the Court of Appeal. The appellant was also dissatisfied with the judgment of the trial court and it filed a cross appeal.

In its judgment, the Court of Appeal held that the trial court erred when it based its decision on the issue of mitigation of damages because the issue did not arise from the pleadings of the parties. Consequently, without considering the merit of the respondent's claims the Court of Appeal allowed the appeal and cross appeal. It set aside the judgment of the trial court, and awarded the arrears of rent and mesne profit – claimed by the respondent.

Dissatisfied, the appellant appealed to the Supreme Court. The Supreme Court unanimously allowing the appeal held:

> A landlord's remedies for breach of a tenant of his covenant to repair are: (a) forfeiture and/or (b) damages; or (c) entry to carry out the repairs and recovery of the cost of doing so if the terms of the lease so provides. Specific performance of a tenant's covenant to repair will not ordinarily be granted.

In the twenty-first century Nigeria, with the increasing wave of commercial activities, the issue of landlord and tenant relationship becomes even more appropriate, the more reason the author lucidly examine the procedure for the recovery of premises law in Nigeria. It is apposite therefore, to make some recommendations; a uniform period of not more than three month be given to determine statutory tenancy in Nigeria, the rights of statutory tenants to protect their interests in the premises against their landlords by appropriate action in courts should be preserved and protected. Laws should therefore be made to cater for the rights of statutory tenant's to retain possession of the property until tenancy is determined in the law courts.

It should be borne in mind that any major amendment of existing legislation in favour of the landlord would certainly be grossly abused and would also, most probably, open floodgate to cases of ejection of tenants even when the reasons for embarking on this are far from genuine. The defendant should continue to have a right upon recovering a plaint to counterclaim for expenses and the court may otherwise grant him judgment upon successful proof.

An appraisal of the Plateau State Rent Control and Recovery of Premises Law[66a]

The Plateau State Rent Control and Recovery of Premises Law, No.1, 1998, is a fine piece of responsive, timely, and pro-active legislation to emanate from the Government of Plateau State in a very long while. The law recognizes the central character of the tenant in his relationship with his landlord. Before the enactment of the law, the landlord rode roughshod over the tenant by exploiting to his advantage the limitations in the existing recovery enactments. Not anymore! No wonder, most, if not all landlords, especially those in the capital city of Jos have called for the repeal of the law.

The rest of the chapter examines the desirability of the law, its application, and impact on landlord/tenant relationships.

Who is a tenant?

A tenant, in the broadest sense, is one who holds or possesses lands or tenements by any kind of right or title, whether in fee, for life, for years, at will, or otherwise.[65]

In a more restricted sense, a tenant could refer to one who holds land of another; one who has the temporary use and occupation of real property owned by another person, (called the landlord), the duration and terms of his tenancy being usually fixed by an instrument called a lease.[66]

The Plateau State Rent Control and Recovery of Premises Law, No.1, 1998, defines a tenant in Section 1 including a subtenant or any person occupying premises whether on payment of rent or otherwise, but does

---

[65] Black, H.C., *Black's Law Dictionary* (6th ed.), (St. Paul Minn., West Publishing Co., 1990) p.466.
[66] Ibid.

not include a person occupying a premises under a bona fide claim of right as the owner of the premises.[67]

To qualify as a tenant according to Kenneth N. Nwoye,[68] you must have some kind of legal relationship with the landlord. This can be achieved by entering a tenancy agreement with the landlord on paying rent to him. Thus he opines that, where three people are living in a house, it is the one who pays the rent or signs an agreement with the landlord that is the tenant. He is the only one who is in lawful occupation or lawfully living in the premises.[69]

Nwoye's conclusion, it would appear, does not take into cognizance the statutory and judicial definition of a tenant. It would also appear not to recognize one who is in lawful occupation of premises as a sub-tenant of the tenant. Furthermore, his analysis of a tenant places too much premium on payment of rent to the landlord.

A sub-tenant, it is opined, may pay rent to the tenant, who is his landlord and not to the main landlord. As a matter of fact, tenancy may exist even where there is no payment of rent. Thus, in *Registered Trustees of Missions* v. *All States Trust Bank PLC*,[70] the court whilst conceding that the definition of the word "tenant" is very wide, held that it includes all persons who occupy premises lawfully, whether that persons pays rent, subsidized rent or indeed no rent at all. The qualification for becoming a tenant, the court further held, is lawful occupation. Whenever the initial entry is lawful, such occupier becomes a tenant qua the landlord.[71]

A sub-tenant, (that is someone put into possession by a tenant to complete or continue with the tenancy), is a tenant, and indeed a tenant of the landlord. This means that where the landlord does not forbid the subletting in writing, a tenant can bring in someone else to complete or continue with his tenancy. This can happen, for instance, where a tenant does not need the premises or apartment any more and has a friend or relation who needs it. Where subletting is not prohibited, the tenant can give out the demised premises. Where the subletting of the premises or apartment is done, the sub-tenant, as he is now called, has equal rights and privileges of a former tenant.

---

[67] This definition of a tenant is similar to the definition in other Laws to landlords and tenants in the country. See for instance S.2(1) of the Recovery of Premises Law, Cap.115, Laws of Northern Nigeria, 1963.

[68] Nwoye, K.N., *The Landlord and the Tenant: Basic Principle of Tenancy Law in Nigeria*, (Jos: Matchers Publishers Limited, 1999) p.13.

[69] Ibid.

[70] (2003) FWLR (pt.172) 1804.

[71] See also *African Petroleum Limited* v. *Owodunni* (1991) 8 NWLR (pt. 210) 419 and *Marine and General Assurance* v. *Rossek* (1986) 2 NWLR (pt. 25) 750.

A landlord who does not want subletting is required by law to give notice in eh tenancy agreement or the receipt to the tenant that the premises or apartment should not be sublet without his prior consent. Where he gives such notice, any person the tenant puts in the premises or apartment cannot be the landlord's tenant. Such a person does not qualify to be called or treated as a tenant, as he did not get into possession of the premises lawfully. The person is seen as a trespasser or a squatter and has no protection of a tenant under the law.

The implication of the depictment of a tenant in S.1 of the law is that unlike in the past, where landlords could insist that a tenancy subsists against the person whom they put into possession alone, the law envisages other persons who come into possession of the property not by the landlord's grace but through the tenant(s) as subtenant(s), who now have equal right and privileges of the tenant or former tenant. Thus, the protection accorded the tenant in relation to rent payable, security of tenancy and the tenant's access to court recognized by the Law are now also applicable to the subtenant.

The need for the protection of the tenant

The need to protect the tenant has been restated in *Oduye* v. *Nigeria Airways Ltd.*[72] as being paramount. The court held that to protect the tenant against presumed avarice and heartlessness of the landlord, who, relying upon strict principle of contractual relationship, would not scruple at throwing the tenant, possibly together with his family, out of his lodgings for them to face adverse circumstances in the street. There is therefore the need to guard against the social and economic evils generated by the shortage of housing and the greed and rapacity of some landlords who increase rents and try to evict tenants who refuse or are unable to pay the higher rent.

Types of protection accorded the tenant under the law

Although the law contains several novel provisions, all aimed at protecting the tenant in his relationship with the landlord, our interest is limited to those provisions relating to the protection of the tenant's security of tenancy, access to court, the protection accorded the tenant by the court, and also the criminalization of certain acts and actions of the landlord.

---

[72] (1987) 2 NWLR (pt. 55) 126.

Protection relating to jurisdiction

The laws confers jurisdiction on the district court to hear and determine all matters arising from the provision of the law.[73] Furthermore, in so far as jurisdiction is conferred on the district court in respect of causes or matters mentioned in the provisions of the law, the High Court or any other court or tribunal of the state shall, to the extent that jurisdiction is so conferred on the district court, cease to have jurisdiction in relation to such matters.[74] This provision is gratifying in the sense that it will put a stop to the antics of some landlords and their collaborator judges, mostly of the area court cadre, who are in the habit of hiding behind different legal headings, such as abatement of nuisance, etc., to recover possession from unsuspecting tenants.

It is however doubtful whether the provisions in question will serve to limit the jurisdiction of the High Court of the State, given the fact that its jurisdiction is derived from the Constitution, making the Law to the extent of that inconsistency, void.[75]

It may however be argued in the light of *Faloye* v. *Omoseni*,[76] and other such authorities, where the court held that the provision of Section 236 of the Constitution of the Federal Republic of Nigeria, 1979,[77] which provide for the jurisdiction of the High Court of a State, is not an open gate for all High Courts to assume jurisdiction. Thus, where a court has no jurisdiction to hear and determine a matter before it, any step taken in relation to the matter is a nullity and is consequently void.[78]

It must however be cautioned that the limit to the jurisdiction of the High Court envisaged in Section 13(1) of the Plateau State Rent Control and Recovery of Premises Law, does not extent to prerogative writs, such as mandamus, certiorari, etc. In *Nebedum* v. *Labisis*,[79] the Court of Appeal relying on the Supreme Court case of *Head of the Federal Military Government and Commander-in-Chief* v. *The Military Governor, Mid Western State of Nigeria and Anor*,[80] Ex parte Ambrose I. Obiyan held that certiorari extends to all authorities and bodies exercising judicial and quasi-judicial control.

---

[73] SS.7&9 of the Plateau State Rent Control and Recovery of Premises Law, No.1, 1998.
[74] S.13(1) of the Plateau State Rent Control and Recovery of Premises Law, No.1, 1998.
[75] See S.1(3) of the Constitution of the Federal Republic of Nigeria, 1999.
[76] (2001) 9 NWLR (pt.717) 190.
[77] Which is *in pari materia* with S.272 of the Constitution of the Federal Republic of Nigeria, 1999.
[78] *Faloye* v. *Omoseni* (supra). See also *Timitimi* v. *Amabebe* (1953) 14 WACA 374 and *Adesola* v. *Abioye* (1999) 14 NWLR (pt. 637) 28.
[79] (2001) 1 NWLR (pt. 693) 82.
[80] (1993) 12 S.C. 23.

Protection relating to rent chargeable

The Law for the purpose of rent chargeable divides Plateau State into zones i.e. A.B.C., with the Jos and Bukuru environs as Zone A. The law further delineates the state into low density, medium density and high density areas with the appropriate rent ceiling for each density fixed.

To ensure compliance with the provisions of the law and most especially with respect to rent chargeable as provided in S.4, the law requires the landlord from the commencement of the law to keep and maintain a Rent Book, in which book each payment shall be entered, and each entry shall be signed by the landlord and the tenant.[81]

Any landlord who fails to comply with the provisions relating to the keeping of a Rent Book shall be guilty of an offence and shall be liable on conviction to fine of ₦5,000.00 or to a term of imprisonment for two months or both.[82] Furthermore, the district court shall decline to hear or entertain any claim or action by a landlord if at the time of filing the action he has not complied with the provisions of subsection (1) and (2) of this Section.[83] However, the court may dispense with the strict adherence to this Section if the landlord pays a condonation fee of ₦2,000.00.[84]

Protection relating to the payment of rent

Closely related to the above is the method of payment of rent by the tenant to the landlord. The law gives the tenant the right to pay rent into Court or into any bank account of the landlord known to the tenant in fulfilment of his obligation to pay rent, where the landlord refuses to accept the same, either because of a disagreement with the tenant or for any other reason, if the rent is paid into Court, the Court will deduct 10% of the money as penalty when the landlord comes to collect it.[85] Thus, a tenant who pays a refused rent into court or into the landlord's account has paid rent for the period and cannot be ejected for non-payment of such rent. Furthermore, from the commencement of this Law, rents payable in advance by a private residential tenant shall not exceed a period of three months, six months and four months for high density, medium density and low density areas respectively.

[81] S.5(1) & (2) of the Plateau State Rent Control and Recovery of Premises Law, 1998.
[82] S.5(3) of the Plateau State Rent Control and Recovery of Premises Law, 1998.
[83] S.5(4) of the Plateau State Rent Control and Recovery of Premises Law, 1998.
[84] S.5(5) of the Plateau State Rent Control and Recovery of Premises Law, 1998.
[85] S.21 of the Plateau State Rent Control and Recovery of Premises Law, 1998.

The right of the tenant to sue

Another novel provision in the Law is the right of the tenant to initiate action against the landlord. Virtually every tenant, it has been argued, avoids taking the landlord to court for fear of being ejected by the landlord. This is even where the landlord's rent is excessive and is increased every year, or where the landlord collects water rate and light bills, but fails to pay them to the relevant utility agencies, thus leaving the tenant to suffer lack of water and light.

Under the law, a tenant has the right to sue his landlord to seek the court to resolve any dispute between the tenant and the landlord as to the amount of rent to be paid and for any other dispute between the landlord and the tenant relating to the payment of rents, repairs and bills.[86] A tenant, who exercises the option, is protected by the law from being ejected by the landlord.[87] In fact, the law provides that where a tenant has made an application to the court, any notice to quit issued by the landlord to the tenant shall be of no effect before the court determines the application of the tenant before it.[88] Notwithstanding the provisions of any law or enactment, a district court may declare as invalid and of no effect a notice to quit served on the tenant if it is satisfied that such a notice was not issued in good faith, and endorsement of the court to that effect on the purported notice to quit shall be sufficient evidence of such decision before any court of law.[89]

Protection relating to the issuance of notices to quit

The Law recognizes different types of tenancies and tenants, depending on the use of which the premises is put, the intervals at which the tenant pays rent and the duration the tenancy is to last.[90] Generally, there are two common types of tenancies, viz: commercial and residential tenancies. Commercial tenancy is where the premises let out is used for commercial purposes only. Thus, where a premise is used as a shop, market, clinic and such other purposes, the premises is generally referred to as commercial premises.

However, by the provision of S.3(1) of the Plateau State Rent Control and Recovery of Premises Law, the law is made applicable to only residential accommodation. Residential tenancy refers to a tenancy where

---

[86] S.9(1)(b) of the Plateau State Rent Control and Recovery of Premises Law, 1998.
[87] S.14 of the Plateau State Rent Control and Recovery of Premises Law, 1998.
[88] S.15(1) of the Plateau State Rent Control and Recovery of Premises Law, 1998.
[89] S.15(2) of the Plateau State Rent Control and Recovery of Premises Law, 1998.
[90] Nwoye, *op. cit.*, p.17.

the premises are used for residential purposes only.[91] The types of residential tenancies recognized by the law are weekly tenancy,[92] monthly tenancy,[93] quarterly tenancy,[94] yearly tenancy,[95] tenant at will,[96] and lease.[97]

By virtue of S.17 of the law, where there is no express stipulation as to the notice to be given by either party to determine the tenancy, the following period of time shall be given,[98] in the case of a tenancy at will or weekly tenancy, a week's notice; in the case of a monthly tenancy, a monthly notice; in the case of quarterly tenancy, a quarter's notice and in the case of a yearly tenancy, half a year's notice. Provided that in the case of a monthly tenancy, where a tenant is in arrears of rent for three months after the commencement of this law, the tenancy shall determine and the court shall on application of the landlord make an order for possession and arrears of rent. The nature of a tenancy shall, in the absence of any evidence to the contrary, be determined by reference to the time when the rent is paid or demanded.[99]

By a weekly, monthly, quarterly or yearly tenancy is meant a tenancy, which is not for that period only, but one that is meant to run from week to week, month to month, quarter to quarter or year to year.[100] In the absence of an express provision in writing, the nature of the tenancy is a matter for evidence, and in the absence of any direct evidence to the contrary, it shall be determined by reference to the time when the rent is

---

[91] Ibid.

[92] This simply means that the tenancy runs from week to week as the tenant pays or is expected to pay his rent weekly.

[93] This is a common type of tenancy which simply means the tenancy runs from month to month as the tenant pays or is expected to pay his rent monthly.

[94] This is a tenancy where the tenant pays rent every three months.

[95] This is a tenancy which runs from year to year and in which the rent is paid yearly.

[96] This is a tenancy where the landlord and the tenant intend and have agreed that the tenancy is for no definite period and could be terminated by any of them at any time, with or without notice usually, short notices, like a week's notice are required for the determination of this type of tenancy.

[97] This is a tenancy for a period not less than three years and not usually more than ninety nine years. This type of tenancy is common among large companies, factories, manufacturers, foreigners and top civil servants who can afford to pay rent for a long period in advance.

[98] This section is *in pari materia* with S.8(1) Recovery of Premises Law, Cap.186 Laws of Northern Nigeria, 1963, applicable in Plateau State.

[99] S.17(2) of the Plateau State Rent Control and Recovery of Premises Law, 1998. and S.8(2), Recovery of Premises Cap.186, Laws of Northern Nigeria, 1963, applicable in Plateau State.

[100] Obi-Okoye, A., *Essays on Civil Proceedings* (Vol. 1), (Enugu: Fourth Dimension Publishing Company limited, 1986) p. 27.

paid or demanded.[101] Thus, where a tenancy for a fixed time is followed by a monthly tenancy, the tenancy becomes a monthly tenancy.[102]

The plateau State Rent Control and Recovery of Premises Law, like most other laws in respect to recovery of premises, does not make provision for the length of notice needed for the determination of a tenancy of a "tenant at sufferance",[103] such a tenant, it is submitted, is therefore not entitled to any notice,[104] except the statutory notice to the tenant of the landlord's intention to apply to recover possession of the premises.[105]

For the purpose of issuance and service of notices, the notice to quit must be made to expire on the last day of a current term of the tenancy.[106] That is to say, a tenancy expires at the midnight of the day preceding the anniversary of tenancy.[107]

From the foregoing, we can summarize the procedure for obtaining possession as thus; a landlord desiring to recover possession of the premises let to his tenant shall firstly, unless the tenancy has already ended, determine the tenancy by service on the defendant of a notice to quit in the requisite form. On the determination of the tenancy the landlord shall serve the tenant with a statutory notice of his intention to apply to the court to recover possession. This is commonly referred to as seven days notice.[108] Thereafter, the landlord shall file his claim in the proper form in a court of competent jurisdiction. The summons will be issued and served by the court. At the hearing the landlord shall, unless the claim is admitted, lead sufficient evidence to establish his entitlement to possession having regard to the provisions of the Recovery of Premises Law and Rent Control legislation. If the court makes an order for possession and the tenant disobeys it, the court may, on the application of the plaintiff, issue a warrant directing the bailiffs to forcibly eject the

---

[101] Ibid.

[102] *Otegbade* v. *Adekoya* (1962) 2 All NLR 52. See also *International Polymera System Limited* v. *Globver* (2002) 7 NWLR (pt.765) 124.

[103] "Tenant at Sufferance" is a common law concept used to describe a tenant who holds over and detains the premises from the landlord after the determination of the tenancy.

[104] See *Begho* v. *Cole* (1957) WNLR 5.

[105] *International Polymera Systems Limited* v. *Glover* (*supra*)

[106] *Ugochukwu & Sons* v. *Buraimoh* (1963) 2 All NLR 123, *Awobiyi & Sons* v. *Igbalaiye Bros.* (1965) 1 All NLR 163: (1965) NMLR 306.

[107] See Obi-Okoye, *op. cit.*, p.27. See also *Nigerian Joint Agency Limited* v. *J. Arrow Engineering & General Transport Company Limited* (1970) 1 All NLR 325.

[108] In *International Polymera Systems Limited* v. *Glover* (*supra*) the court held that these notices must first be served on the tenant in addition to the Notice of owner's intention to apply and recover possession, popularly called the seven days notice, for the court.

tenant from the premises and deliver possession thereof to the landlord.[109]

Right against forceful and illegal ejection under the Plateau State Rent Control and Recovery of Premises Law

Perhaps of all the provisions of the Plateau State Rent Control and Recovery of Premises Law, the most novel and one capable of having impact on landlord/tenant relationship is the provisions of S.30 of the Law. By its provisions, any person who fails to comply with an order of the district court shall be guilty of an offence, and liable on conviction to a fine not exceeding ten thousand naira or to imprisonment for a term not exceeding three months or to both such fine and imprisonment.[110]

This reference in the subsection to the district court, it would seem to suggest, include orders of the court in civil trials. This conclusion is reached based on the fact that the district court, whilst entertaining cases in its criminal jurisdiction, is referred to as a magistrate court. Thus, if the law had intended that the orders in question should be orders made by the magistrate court, the subsection would have explicitly referred to the magistrate court and not district court.

Furthermore, anybody who forcibly ejects or attempt to eject a tenant; or harasses, molests or annoys a tenant by words or action with a view of ejecting such tenant; or does anything contrary to any provision of this law; or wilfully damages any dwelling house; or does any act or thing whatsoever calculated or likely to stultify the provisions of this law, shall be guilty of an offence and liable on conviction to a fine not exceeding twenty thousand naira or to imprisonment for a term not exceeding three months or to both such fine and imprisonment.[111]

To ensure that the law is not one sided; the law also accords the landlords to measure of protection against the acts and antics of the tenant. The law provides in addition to the above that any person who harasses, molests or annoys a landlord by action or words in respect of accommodation let by him, or wilfully damages any dwelling house shall be guilty of an offence and liable on conviction to a fine not exceeding ten thousand naira or to imprisonment for a term not exceeding four months or to both such fine and imprisonment.[112]

---

[109] Obi-Okoye, *op. cit.*, pp. 25-26.
[110] S.30(1) of Plateau State Rent Control and Recovery of Premises Law, 1998.
[111] S.30(2) of Plateau State Rent Control and Recovery of Premises Law, 1998.
[112] S.30(3) of Plateau State Rent Control and Recovery of Premises Law, 1998.

Furthermore, any person who demolishes alters or modifies a building to which this Edict applies with a view to ejecting a tenant without the approval of the court shall be guilty of an offence and liable on conviction to a fine of ten thousand naira or to three months imprisonment or both.[113]

The law further provides that; any person who resists, molests, assaults or in any way obstructs an officer or any other person engaged in the service of any process or in executing of a warrant of possession, in carrying out an order of a court shall be guilty of an offence and liable to a fine of twenty thousand naira or four months imprisonment or both.[114]

To check the antics of some petulant landlords who either misrepresent or conceal material facts from the court or collaborate with judges, especially of the area court cadre to fraudulently recover possession from an unsuspecting tenant, the law provides that; any landlord who obtains an order for possession of any accommodation under this edict by fraud, misrepresentation or concealment of any imprisonment or both.[115]

In addition to the above, where the landlord has obtained an order for possession of an application made by summons by the tenant, and the court is satisfied that such order was obtained by fraud, misrepresentation, or concealment of any material fact, the court shall order the landlord to pay reasonable compensation to the tenant.[116]

To protect the tenant against the exorbitant commission charged by agents, the law provides that; it shall be unlawful for any person or an agent to demand or receive more than 5% of the annual rent as commission. Any person who contravenes the provision of this subsection shall be guilty of an offence and liable to a fine of twenty thousand naira or four months imprisonment or both.[117]

Lastly, it shall be unlawful for a landlord to convert a residential accommodation for commercial purpose without approval from the approving authorities. Any person who contravenes the provisions of this subsection shall be guilty of an offence and shall be liable to a fine of twenty five thousand naira or five months imprisonment or both.[118]

It is improper and indeed unlawful for any landlord to pester the life of a tenant or disturb his tenancy under whatever guise. Consequently, it is in accord with the government's drive to guide against social and

---

[113] S.30(4) of Plateau State Rent Control and Recovery of Premises Law, 1998.
[114] S.30(5) of Plateau State Rent Control and Recovery of Premises Law, 1998.
[115] S.30(6) of Plateau State Rent Control and Recovery of Premises Law, 1998.
[116] S.30(7) of Plateau State Rent Control and Recovery of Premises Law, 1998.
[117] S.30(8) of Plateau State Rent Control and Recovery of Premises Law, 1998.
[118] S.30(9) of Plateau State Rent Control and Recovery of Premises Law, 1998.

economic evils generated by the shortages of housing and the greed and rapacity of some landlords who increase rents at will and try to evict tenants who refuse or are unable to pay the higher rent. Commenting on a similar enactment, the Supreme Court held that:

> The Edict therefore seeks to provide personal security to the tenant in actual residential occupation in respect of his accommodation. The Edict, therefore invalidates any agreement which by its terms or provisions, seek to preclude all tenants (to whom the Edict applies) from taking advantage of or exercising their rights under the Edict and enjoins the Courts to lean in favour of implementing the rights of tenant under the Edict.

Chapter 17

Classification of Right of Occupancy

Statutory right

This is defined in Section 50 of the Land Use Act. Statutory right can be expressly granted by the Governor under Section 5(1) of the Act subject to the stipulation, under section 8. Section 8 provides that a statutory right may be for a definite term and may also contain provision of a contract between the Governor and the holder in conformity with the act. Further, where land in an urban area was developed before the commencement of the Act, the land remains vested in that person as if the Governor had granted to that person a statutory right of occupancy.

The Governor has the power by Section 3 of the Act to say what areas of a state constitute urban areas. In effect, a statutory right of occupancy can manifest either as an actual grant under Section 5(1)(a) or as deemed grant under Section 34. In both instances, the Governor can issue a certificate in evidence of the right under Section 9 (1)(b). All other lands apart from those consisting urban areas are under the control and management of local government within whose jurisdiction the land is situated. Section 36(3) recognizes that where land was not in an urban area but such lands was held and occupied for agricultural purposes, the holder after 1978 became entitled to continue to hold the land as if the customary right of occupancy had been granted to him by the local government.[1]

In *Ogunleye* v. *Oni*,[2] Ogunleye claimed land based on document of grant made in early 1978 and a certificate of occupancy granted to him in 1983 by the Commissioner for Land. He asked for damages for trespass. The defendant on his point said he inherited the land from his father in 1936 for valuable consideration. The court applied Section 34 of the Act and held that the plaintiff was not the holder of the land in dispute before

[1] Both section 34 & 36 deal with transitional and related provision. Neither section 34 nor 36 has the word deemed.

[2] (1990) NWLR (Pt.135)

1978. The certificate of occupancy could therefore make him a holder of a statutory right from 1983.

Furthermore, since the defendant held the land before the LUA came into force, the defendant was deemed to be the holder of statutory right granted by the Governor. Since the Governor did not revoke the defendant's deemed right before making a grant to the plaintiff, the plaintiff's right was invalid and against the letter and spirit of the Act. The defendant had better title. The land was in a local government, a non-urban area but the appellant (Ogunleye) had obtained a certificate from the Governor and it is clear from Section 5 that a Governor can grant a statutory right in both urban and non-urban areas.

The effect of a grant of right of occupancy by government

Section 5(2) of the LUA says that upon the grant of statutory right, all existing rights to the use and occupation of the land in question stand extinguished. In interpreting this Section, the court had maintained that where it is shown by evidence that another person had a better right or grant, the court would have no alternative but to set aside the grant. In *Ogunleye* v. *Oni*[3] on the effect of Section 5(2) when read with Section 34 of the Act, the court held that section 5 must be read in conjunction with Section 34. Section 5 empowers the Governor of a state to grant land, Section 34 confirms the holding of land already held prior to 1978 as if it was granted by the Governor. Furthermore, Section 34 provides for the security and guarantee of land in an urban area already held and enjoyed by its pre-1978 holder and most essentially it guards against the arbitrary deprivation of a holder's right to own his property as enshrined in the 1979 Constitution. But in the final analysis, both the holder under Section 34 and subject to the Governor holds a better title to the land because the land was vested in him by virtue of Section 34(5) of the Act and in the absence of any improper motive by the Governor, the right of occupancy deemed granted cannot be extinguished under Section 5 of the Act by the act of the Governor in granting a certificate of occupancy to another person. Section 9(1)(b) specifically says that it shall be lawful for the governor when any person in the prescribed manner to issue a certificate under his hand in evidence of such right. This section failed to

[3] *Supra*

be interpreted in the case of *Titiloye* v. *Olubo*,[4] here the plaintiffs who were the appellant sued the defendant for several relief including a declaration that the plaintiffs were holders and occupiers of a piece of land before the LUA was enacted and were therefore entitled to be vested with a customary right of occupancy. Both parties based their cases on traditional evidence and claimed their respective ancestors were the first settlers on the land. The trial judge was of the opinion that the plaintiffs have failed to prove they were entitled to a grant of right of occupancy. He accordingly dismissed their claim. They appealed all the way to the Supreme Court and the Supreme Court in its judgment said that it was clear from Section 9(1)(b) that a Governor is empowered to issue a statutory right of occupancy to a person who is already in occupation of land, under a customary right of occupancy. The court went on to say that it was not the law that the customary right enjoyed by that person must first be revoked before the grant of a statutory right; the court then went ahead to dismiss the appeal.

But with respect, the Supreme Court decision can be faulted because it was not supported by the law. If you read Section 9(1), it states out the three instances when the governor may issue a certificate to any person in evidence of his right. It does not pertain to the Governor's power to grant. The power to grant the right is contained in Section 5.

Section 9 simply deals with the Governor's power to issue certificate of occupancy and on the question of issuing certificate, it is clear that the Governor can issue certificate evidencing both statutory and customary right of occupancy. Under section 5, the Governor can grant a statutory right of occupancy whether or not the land is in an urban area. The Supreme Court was therefore in error when it held that Section 9(1) (b) empowers the military Governor to issue a statutory right to a person who is already in occupation.

The conversion of a customary right of occupancy to a statutory right of occupancy is not within the contemplation of the Act. The position of the law is that a person who has been in occupation of land in a non-urban area by virtue of an actual grant by the local government under Section 6 or a deemed grant under Section 36 can apply to the Governor who can issue a certificate to such a person in evidence of his customary right. The Governor's power under Section 9(3) applies to a statutory right granted pursuant to Section 9(1)(a) in the exercise of the governor's limited power under Section 5(1)(a). The power is amplified by Section 28(5)(c). These sections clearly showed Governor's limited powers to

---

[4] (1991) NWLR (Pt.2005)

revoke in those instances since the existence of a customary right of occupancy is not affected by Section 9(3) or by Section 28(5) if a person to who certificate in evidence of a customary right of occupancy is granted refuses to accept and pay for the certificate and recover from the person the expenses incurred in preparing the certificate. Again, the deemed holder of a statutory rights of occupancy who has applied for a certificate in evidence of a right and therefore comes within section 9(1)(c), cannot as a result of his deemed right be revoked. However, the Governor has other powers under section 28 to revoke right of occupancy for the reasons set out in section 28(1)(2)(3) & (4) of the Act.

Certificate of occupancy[5a]

The certificate of occupancy is merely evidence that a grantee has a right of occupancy customary or statutory. In this way, the Supreme Court has noted that indeed a certificate of occupancy properly issued under of the Act is a reflection and an assurance that the grantee has occupation of the land where it is shown by evidence that another person has a better title or a better right, the court would have no alternative but to set aside the grant. So a certificate of occupancy cannot confer on a grantee any right or interest which he did not have before.[5] It is clear then that no right is to be granted by means of a certificate. A holder who accepts a certificate from the Governor is bound by all the terms and conditions in the certificate by virtue of the wide provision of Section 9(4). In addition the holder is bound by the deemed covenant in Section 10(a) & (b). And Section 10(a) binds the holder to pay to the Governor any amount accessed as being payable for unexhausted improvements existing on the land at the date of entry into occupation by the holder as he binds himself to pay rent to the Governor in accordance with Section 16. Unexhausted improvements are found in Section 50 of the Act.

Any improvement effected on the land pursuant to the terms and conditions in the certificate of occupancy can only be lawfully transferred, assigned or mortgaged with the Governor's prior consent.

Local governments are not empowered under the Act to issue certificate of occupancy. The local government powers are clearly stated or listed Section 6 Section 2(7)(b) of the Act. Regarding deemed grants

[5a] In *Orlu* v. *Gogo-Abite* (2010) 8 NWLR, the court held that a certificate of occupancy is never associated with title. A certificate of statutory or customary right of occupancy issued under the Land Use Act, 1978 cannot be said to be conclusive evidence of any right, interest or valid title to land in favour of the grantee. See also *Boye Ind. Ltd* v. *Sowemimo* (2010) AAL FWLR (Pt. 521) p. 1462.

[5] See *Ogunleye* v. *Oni, supra.*

under Section 36 if the local government is satisfied that the holder in case of developed land is entitled to the possession of the land. The local government shall register the holder in its records as one to whom a right to customary right of occupancy had been issued in respect of the land in question.

Consent requirement

Section 21 of the LUA makes it unlawful for a customary right of occupancy to be alienated in any manner without appropriate authorization. In cases where the property is to be sold in furtherance of a court judgment, the consent of the governor had to be obtained and in all other cases the approval of the local government must be obtained. Section 24 does not impose a duty on any particular person to obtain the consent or approval. It can be therefore being argued that any party to the alienation i.e. the grantor or the grantee can ensure that the provisions of the section are strictly complied with.

Regarding statutory right of occupancy, Section 22 makes it unlawful for any holder to alienate his right in any manner however without the consent of the Governor first heard and received. Exceptions exist where the holder had earlier obtained consent to equitably mortgage the property to the same person with whom the legal mortgage is contemplated. Again, an exception exists where the mortgagor has fully settled its obligations to the mortgagee. In these two instances, there is no need to seek fresh consent to mortgage transaction or to the deed reconveying the mortgagor's property to him. Thus in *Union Bank of Nigeria Plc* v. *Astra Builders,*[6] the court held that it was the duty of a holder of a certificate of occupancy to obtain Governors consent before transferring his title. Under Section 32 a sublease of a statutory right may with the prior consent of the holder of the right further sublease or under let. Governor's consent to the renewal of a sublease should be sought and obtained.

---

[6] (2010)5NWLR.See also *Monkom* v. *Odili* (2010)2NWLR.The law is that it is the owner of a statutory right of occupancy that is obliged to obtain the consent of the Governor of the State in respect of the land which he wishes to sell, transfer or mortgage, *et cetera* by virtue of section 22 of the Land Use Act, and the relevant provisions of the Land Tenure Law of Northern Nigeria. See also *B.N Plc* v. *Songonuga* (2007)3 NWLR (pt. 1021) 230 CA. Again, the law is that the person who seeks to alienate his property has the duty to seek and obtain the consent of the Governor to the transaction and can be compelled by the order of the court for specific performance to do so. See *Sosan* v. *HFP Eng. (Nig) Ltd* (2004) 3 NWLR (Pt. 861). In *Iragunima* v. *R.S.H.P.D.A.* (2003) 12 NWLR (Pt.834) , the court held that it is not correct to say that failure to obtain the prior consent of the Governor before a deed of assignment is executed means that the assignment is null and void. This is because, in practice, it is on the deed of assignment that the Governors consent is usually endorsed.

The effect of non-compliance with the provision for consent and approval[7]

First, under section 26 any transaction or instrument, which purports to confer or vest any right in any person other than the provision of the Act, is void.

Secondly, the Governor can revoke a right of occupancy for overriding public interest under Section 28(1). This phrase according to section 28(2)(a) means *inter alia:* alienation by the occupier of his right of occupancy contrary to the provisions of the Act in the case of a statutory right of occupancy. The Governor can also revoke a customary right for similar reasons under section 28(3)(d).

In both instances, the holder and the occupier shall not be entitled to compensation. Under 29, this power of revocation also cover deemed grant. This is clear from the provision of Section 38 of the Act.

Thirdly, by section 20, the Governor can impose a penal rent for each day the land, the subject of a statutory right, which was alienated without consent, remains in the possession, or control of any person other than the holder. This section applies to statutory rights. The acceptance of such penal rent does not constitute a waiver of a continuing breach. The power to impose penal rent is also recognized by section 5(1)(f).

Fourthly, under section 18 the Governor can take steps to have a right of occupancy forfeited. This section is applied subject to Section 19, 20 and 21.

Again under section 34(7) under develop plots in urban area held under deemed titles can only be transferred to another person with prior consent of the Governor under section 34(7). An instrument purporting to do so contrary to this subsection shall be void and any party there to shall be guilty of an offence and if convicted shall be liable to a fine of N5,000 or spend one year in prison. The importance of the requirement for consent or approval cannot be over emphasized and those provisions served to strengthen the wide powers given to the Governor under Section 1&1 and the local government under Section 2 of the Act.

Chapter 18

Match towards reform of the Land Use Act, 1978

When the then President Yar' Adua assumed office as the President of the Federal Republic of Nigeria on 29th May 2007, he made promises known as the Seven Point Agenda. One of the agendas was the reform of the Land Use Act which according to him, was ineffective and was not properly made. He took a laudable step to the amendment of the Land Use Act, following the presentation of the report of the committee on Land Use Reform, having forwarded a Bill to the National Assembly for some amendments to the Land Act, to be known as the Land Use (Amendment) Act 2009. The Bill seeks to score off seven sections of the existing Act, which was originally enacted in 1978. The main thrust according to Mr. Olusegun Adeniyi, special and publicity, "is to restrict the requirement for a governor's consent in land transactions to assignments only." The said Land Use Act was promulgated by the Federal Military Government under Gen. Olusegun Obasanjo on 29 March, 1978, the Land Use Act did not pass through the crucible of any parliamentary debate from which one could have discerned the objective of the legislators. However, from the preamble, the inalienable right of every Nigerian to partake of land, a major factor of production was deducible. That explains why not a few Nigerian military rejoiced at the promulgation of the Decree (now an Act) entrenched in the 1999 Constitution by virtue of Section 315 thereof.

The Land Use Act, except for a few of its provisions, is based, almost verbatim, on the 1962 Land Tenure Law of the defunct Northern Region. Mr. Segun Adeniyi said that the amendment is to restrict the requirement for Governor's consent in land transactions to assignment according to the provisions of section 1 of the Land Use Act that says all land conferred in the federation are hereby vested in the governor of that state and such land shall be held in trust and administered for the use and common benefit of all Nigerians in accordance to the provisions of this Act (Land Use Act). Also, Section 5 of the Act makes it lawful for a governor to grant statutory rights of occupancy in respect of land, whether or not in an urban area to any persons. This amendment put forward as proposed by President Umaru Musa Yar'Adua will enable the consent of governors in land matter to be unnecessary for mortgage, sublease and other land transfers in order to make transactions in land less cumbersome and facilitate economic growth. The presentation of the bill to the National Assembly marks the commencement of the implementation of the Yar'Adua administration strategic agenda to overcome some of the major legal and logistical constraints to capital accumulation in Nigeria. If it is passed into law, it will make land more easily convertible without hindrance in other to raise capital for venture. However, it will also facilitate and empower the mortgage industries.

Land Reform/Amendment

The amendment being proposed by the Presidency relates to sections 5,7,15,21,22,23 and 28, which is presented in the following manner.

Amendment of Section 5(1)(f), by deleting all words immediately after "sales" in the third line.

Amendment of Section 7 of the Act by (a) deleting word "or subletting" immediately after the word assignment in the second line (b) deleting the word "subletting immediately after the word "assignment" in the third line of paragraph (a) of the provision.

Amendment of Section1 5 by deleting the words "or mortgage immediately after the word "assign" in the first line.

Amendment of Section 21 by deleting the words immediately after "assignment", in the second line and making it a subsection.

Amendment of Section 23 by substituting the section with the following new sections.

Amending the provisions of Section 28 of the Land Use Act, when deals with the power of the Governor to revoke the statutory right of occupancy granted to a person.

However, some analysts were of the opinion that the amendment of the Land Use Act might not make any difference to Nigerians since the president do not know the particular area of the Land Use Act that bothers them. They pointed out that the new amendment of the Land Use Act did not consider the poor who are at the services of the rich.

The amendment of the Land Use Act is very vital to any meaningful development in the country, since development anywhere in the world is predicated on the development of land. Thus, amendment of the Act is a step in the right direction, as it will assist the overall development of the nation.

The amendment of Act will fast-track the process of development across the cities of the nation as developers would easily access land without the present cumbersome process foisted on the nation by the Act as presently operated.

In amending the Land Use Act, the poor masses should also be taken into consideration; the Act must not neglect the indigent and should make room for persons like welders, vulcanizers, cobblers, etc.

The old legal traditions contained in the Land Use Act i.e. the principle *quid quic plantatur solo solo cedit*, meaning whatever is attached to the land belong to land should be amended, this is perhaps that greatest impediment to property ownership in composite urban block and thus, a new form of split ownership can emerge after the amendment of the Act.

The Yar'Adua Seven Point Agenda with respect to land reform, will take Nigeria to a greater height when this amendment becomes a reality not just for our immediate interest or benefit, but for generation yet unborn. A major reform amongst others preceding the constitutional amendment by the Yar'Adua administration is the modification of the law of the Land Use Act on which a bill has been sent to the National Assembly by President Umaru Musa Yar'Adua.[1]

The Bill proposes to amend the Land Use Act by restricting the requirement of the governor's consent to assignment only.[2]

The president's proposed amendments relate to Section 5, 7, 15, 21, 22, 23 and 28 of the existing Land Use Act, which makes it a total of 14 amendments. They are as follows:

Amendment of Section 5

Subsection (1)(f) of Section 5 of the Act is amended by deleting all words immediately after sales in the third line, which reads that to impose a penal rent for a breach of any condition, express or implied, which precludes the holder of a statutory right of occupancy from alienating the right of occupancy from alienating the right of or any part thereof by sale, mortgage, transfer of possession, sublease ore request or otherwise however, without the prior consent of the governor.

Amendment of Section 7

This section is amended by:

---

[1] The *Guardian,* Sunday March 15, 2009.

[2] The *Guardian,* Sunday March 8, 2009.

(a) Deleting the words 'of subletting' immediately after the word 'assignment' in the third line of paragraph (a) of the provision.

Amendment of Section 15

This section is amended by deleting the words 'or mortgage' immediately after the word 'assign' in the first line.

Amendment of Section 21

This section is amended by:

Deleting all the words immediately after 'assignment' in the second line and making it subsection (1).

Creating a subsection (2) in the following words:

> (2) The right of a holder of a customary right of occupancy to alienate such right by mortgage is hereby required.

Amendment of Section 22

Section 22 is amended by:

Deleting from subsection (1) the words 'mortgage, transfer of possession, sublease or otherwise however', immediately after the word 'assignment' in the second line;

Deleting the proviso to subsection (1)

Deleting from subsection (2) the words mortgage or sublease immediately after the word 'assignment' in the first line.

Creating new subsection 3 in the following words:

> (3) The consent of the governor shall not be required for the creation of mortgage or sublease under this section.

Amendment of Section 23

This Section is amended by:

Substituting the second with the following new Section:

> 23, a sublease or the statutory right of occupancy, demise by way of sub-under lease to another person the land comprised in the sublease held by him or any other portion of the land.

(b) Deleting the provisions of subsection (2)

Amendment of Section 28

Subsection (2) of Section 28 is amended by substituting paragraphs (a) with the following new paragraph:

The alienation of the occupier by assignment or sublease contrary to the provisions of this Act or any regulations made thereunder.

Subsection (3) of Section 28 is amended by substituting paragraph (d) with the following new paragraph:

> (d) The alienation by the occupier by sale, assignment or sublease without the requisite consent or approval.

This Act may be cited as the Land Use Act (Amendment) Act, 2009 or the Constitution (first amendment) Act, 2009.[3]

The main thrust of the amendment is to restrict the requirement for governor's consent in land transactions to assignment only.

The assignment may render such consent unnecessary for mortgages, subleases and other land transfers in order to make transactions in land less cumbersome and facilitate economic growth.

The main thrust of the land reform is to change the existing land laws and ensure the emergence of land reforms that will optimize Nigeria's growth through the release of land for commercial farming and other large scale business by the private sector. The final result will ensure unhindered access to land to boost output and improve capacity for wealth creation.

[3] Ibid. at p. 6.

Appendix

THE LAND USE ACT, 1978

LAND USE ACT

An Act to vest all land comprised in the territory of each state (except land vested in the Federal Government or its agencies) solely in the Governor of the State, who would hold such land in trust for the people and would henceforth be responsible for allocation of land in all urban areas to individuals resident in the State and to organizations for residential, agricultural, commercial and other purposes while similar powers with respect to non-urban areas are conferred on Local Governments.

PART 1 – GENERAL

1. Subject to the provisions of this Act, all land comprised in the territory of each State in the Federation are hereby vested in the Governor of that State and such land shall be held in trust and administered for the use and common benefit of all Nigerians in accordance with the provisions of this Act.

2. (1) As from the commencement of this Act –

(a) all land in urban areas shall be under the control and management of the Governor of each State; and

(b) all other land shall, subject to this Act, be under the control and management of the Local Government within the area of jurisdiction of which the land is situated.

(2) There will be established in each state a body to be known as "the Land Use and Allocation Committee" which shall have responsibility for –

(a) advising the Governor on any matter connected with the management of land to which paragraph (a) of subsection (1) of this section relates;

(b) advising the Governor on any matter connected with the resettlement of persons affected by the revocation of rights of occupancy on the ground of overriding public interest under this Act; and

(c) determining disputes as to the amount of compensation payable under this Act for improvements on land.

(3) The Land Use and Allocation Committee shall consist of such number of persons as the Governor may determine and shall include in its membership –

(a) not less than two persons possessing qualifications approved for appointment to the civil service as estate surveyors or land officers and who have had such qualification for not less than five years; and

(b) a legal practitioner.

(4) The Land Use and Allocation Committee shall be presided over by such one of its members as may be designed by the Governor and subject to such directions as may be given in that regard by the Governor, shall have power to regulate its proceedings.

(5) There shall also be established for each Local Government a body to be known as "the Land Allocation Advisory Committee" which shall consist of such persons as may be determined by the Governor acting after consultation with the Local Government and shall have responsibility for advising the Local Government on any matter connected with the management of land to which paragraph (b) of section (1) of this section relates.

3. Subject to such General conditions as may be specified in that behalf by the National Council of States, the Governor may for the purposes of this Act by order published in the State Gazette designate the parts of the area of the territory of the state constituting land in an urban area.

4. Until other provisions are made in that behalf and, subject to the provisions of this Act, land under the control and management of the Governor under this Act shall be administered.

   (a) in the case of any State where the Land Tenure Law of the former Northern Nigerian applies, in accordance with the provisions of that Law; and

   (b) in every other case, in accordance with the provisions of the State Land Law applicable in respect of State land in the State, and the provisions of the Land Tenure Law or the State Land Law, as the case may be, shall have effect with such modifications as would bring those laws into conformity with this Act or its general intendment.

PART II – PRINCIPLES OF LAND TENURE, POWER OF GOVERNOR AND LOCAL GOVERNMENTS, AND RIGHTS OF OCCUPIERS

5. (1) It shall be lawful for the Governor in respect of land, whether or not in an urban area –

   (a) to grant statutory rights of occupancy to any person for all purposes;

   (b) to grant easements appurtenant to statutory rights of occupancy;

   (c) to demand rental for any such land granted to any person;

   (d) to revise the said rental –

   (i) at such intervals as may be specified in the certificate of occupancy, or

   (ii) where no intervals are specified in the certificate of occupancy at any time during the term of the statutory right of occupancy;

   (e) to improve a penal rent for a breach of any covenant in a certificate of occupancy requiring the holder to develop or effect improvements on the land, the subject of the certificate of occupancy, and to revise such penal rent as provided in section 19 of this Act;

   (f) to impose a penal rent for a breach of any condition, express or implied, which precludes the holder of a statutory right of occupancy from alienating the right of occupancy or any part thereof by sale, mortgage, transfer of possession, sub-lease or bequest or otherwise howsoever without the prior consent of the Governor;

   (g) to waive, wholly or partially, except as otherwise prescribed, all or any of the covenants is subject where, owing to special circumstances, compliance therewith would be impossible or great hardship would be imposed upon the holder;

   (h) to extend except as otherwise prescribed, the time to the holder of a statutory right of occupancy for performing any of the conditions of the right of occupancy upon such terms and conditions as he may think fit.

(2) Upon the grant of a statutory right of occupancy under the provisions of subsection (1) of this section, all existing rights to the use and occupation of the land which is the subject of the statutory right of occupancy shall be extinguished.

6. (1) It shall be lawful for a Local Government in respect of land not in an urban area –

(a) to grant customary rights of occupancy to any person or organization for the use of land in the local government area for agricultural, residential and other purposes;

(b) to grant customary rights of occupancy to any person or organization for the use of land for grazing purposes and such other purposes ancillary to agricultural purposes as may be customary in the Local Government Area concerned.

(2) No single customary right of occupancy shall be granted in respect of an area of land in excess of 500 hectares if granted for agricultural purposes, or 5,000 hectares if granted for grazing purposes, except with the consent of the Governor.

(3) It shall be lawful for a Local Government to enter upon, use and occupy for public purposes any land within the area of its jurisdiction which is not –

(a) land within an area declared to be an urban area pursuant to section 3 of this Act;

(b) the subject of a statutory right of occupancy;

(c) within any area compulsorily acquired by the Government of the Federation or of the State concerned;

(d) the subject of any laws relating to minerals or mineral oils, and for the purpose, to revoke any customary right of occupancy on any such land.

(4) The Local Government shall have exclusive rights to the lands so occupied against all persons except the Governor.

(5) The holder and the occupier according to their respective interests of any customary right of occupancy revoked under subsection (3) of this section shall be entitled to compensation, for the value at the date of revocation, of their unexhausted improvements.

(6) Where land in respect of which a customary right of occupancy is revoked under this Act was used for agricultural purposes by the holder, the Local Government shall allocate to such holder alternative land for use for the same purpose.

(7) If a Local Government refuses or neglects within a reasonable time to pay compensation to a holder and an occupier according to their respective interests under the provisions of subsection (5) of this section, the Governor may proceed to the assessment of compensation under section 29 of this Act and direct the Local Government to pay the amount of such compensation to the holder and occupier according to their respective interests.

7. It shall not be lawful for the Governor to grant a statutory right of occupancy or consent to the assignment or subletting of a statutory right of occupancy to a person under the age of twenty-one years;

Provided that –

(a) where a guardian or trustee for a person under the age of 21 years has been duly appointed for such purpose, the Governor may grant or consent to the assignment or subletting of a statutory right of occupancy to such guardian or trustee on behalf of such person under age;

(b) a person under the age of 21 years upon whom a statutory right of occupancy devolves on the death of the holder, shall have the same liabilities and obligations under and in respect of his right of occupancy as if he were of full age, notwithstanding the fact that no guardian or trustee has been appointed for him.

8. Statutory right of occupancy granted under the provisions of section 5 (1) (a) of this Act shall be for a definite term and may made by the Governor and the holder not being inconsistent with the provisions of this Act.

9. (1) It shall be lawful for the Governor –

(a) when granting a statutory right of occupancy to any persons; or

(b) when any person is in occupation of land under a customary right of occupancy and applied in the prescribed manner; or

(c) when any person is entitled to a statutory right of occupancy, to issue a certificate under his hand in evidence of such right of occupancy.

(2) Such certificate shall be termed a certificate of occupancy and there shall be paid therefor, by the person in whose name it is issued, such fee (if any) as may be prescribed.

(3) If the person in whose name a certificate of occupancy is issued, without lawful excuse, refuses or neglects to accept and pay for the certificate, the Governor may cancel the certificate and recover from such person any expenses incidental thereto, and in the case of a certificate evidencing a statutory right of occupancy to be granted under paragraph (a) of subsection (1) of this section, the Governor may revoke the statutory right of occupancy.

(4) The terms and conditions of a certificate of occupancy granted under this Act and which has been accepted by the holder shall be enforceable against the holder and his successors in title, notwithstanding that the acceptance of such terms and conditions is not evidenced by the signature only of some person purporting to accept on behalf of the corporation.

10. Every certificate of occupancy shall be deemed to contain provisions to the following effect –

(a) that the holder binds himself to pay to the Governor the amount found to be payable in respect of any unexhausted improvements existing on the land at the date of his entering into occupations;

(b) that the holder binds himself to pay to the Governor the rent fixed by the Governor and any rent which may be agreed or fixed on revision in accordance with the provisions of section 16 of this Act.

11. The Governor or any public officer duly authorized by the Governor in that behalf, shall have the power to enter upon and inspect the land comprised in any statutory right of occupancy or any improvements effected thereon, at any reasonable hours in the day time and the occupier shall permit and give free access to the Governor or any such officer to enter and inspect.

12. (1) It shall be lawful for the Governor to grant a licence to any person to enter upon any land which is not the subject of a statutory right of occupancy or of a

mining lease, mining right or exclusive prospecting licence granted under the Minerals Act or any other enactment, and remove or extract therefrom any stone, gravel, clay, sand or other similar substance (not being a mineral within the meaning assigned to that term in the Mineral Act) that may be required for building or for the manufacture of building materials.

(2) Any such licence may be granted for such period and subject to such conditions as the Governor may think proper or as may be prescribed.

(3) No such licence shall be granted in respect of an area exceeding 400 hectares.

(4) It shall not be lawful for any licensee to transfer his licence in any manner whatsoever without the consent of the Governor first had and obtained, and any such transfer effected without the consent of the Governor shall be null and void.

(5) The Governor may cancel any such licence if the licensee fails to comply with any of the conditions of the licence.

13. (1) The occupier of statutory right of occupancy shall at all times maintain in good and substantial repair to the satisfaction of the Governor, or of such public officer as the Governor may appoint in that behalf. All beacons or other land markets by which the boundaries of the land comprised in the statutory right of occupancy are defined and in default of his so doing the Governor or such public officer as aforesaid may by notice in writing require the occupier to define the boundaries in the manner and within the time specifies in such notice.

(2) If the occupier of a statutory right of occupancy fails to comply with a notice served under subsection (1) of this section he shall be liable to pay the expenses (if any) incurred by the Governor in defining the boundaries which the occupier has neglected to define.

14. Subject to the other provisions of this Act and of any laws relating to way leaves, to prospecting for minerals or mineral oils or to mining or to oil pipelines and subject to the terms and conditions of any contract made under section 8 of this Act, the occupier shall have exclusive rights to the land the subject of the statutory right of occupancy against all persons other than the Governor.

15. During the term of a statutory right of occupancy the holder –

(a) shall have the sole right to and absolute possession of all the improvements on the land;

(b) may, subject to the prior consent of the Governor, transfer, assign or mortgage any improvements on the land which have been effected pursuant to the terms and conditions of the certificate of occupancy relating to the land.

PART III – RENTS

16. In determining the amount of the original rent to be fixed for any particular land and the amount of the revised rent to be fixed on any subsequent revision of rent, the Governor –

(a) shall take into consideration the rent previously fixed in respect of any other like land in the immediate neighbourhood, and shall have regard to all the circumstances of the case;

(b) shall not take into consideration any value due to capital expended upon the land by the same or any previous occupier during his term or terms of occupancy, or any increase in the value of the land the rental of which is under consideration, due to the employment of such capital.

17. (1) The Governor may grant a statutory right of occupancy free of rent or at a reduced rent in any case in which he is satisfied that it would be in the public interest to do so.

(2) Where a statutory right of occupancy has been granted free of rent the Governor may, subject to the express provisions of the certificate of occupancy, nevertheless impose a rent in expect of the land the subject of the right of occupancy if and when he may thin fit.

18. Subject to the provisions of sections 20 and 21 of this Act, the acceptance by or on behalf of the Governor of any rent shall not operate as a waiver by the Governor of any forfeiture accruing by reason of the breach of any covenant or condition, express or implied, in any certificate of occupancy granted under this Act.

19. (1) When in any certificate of occupancy the holder has covenanted to develop or effect improvements on the land the subject of the certificate of occupancy and has committed a breach of such covenant the Governor may.

(a) at the time of such breach or at any time thereafter, so long as the breach remains un remedied, fix a penal rent which shall be payable for twelve months from the date of such breach; and

(b) on the expiration of twelve months from the date of such breach and on the expiration of every subsequent twelve months so long as the breach continues revise the penal rent to be paid.

(2) Such penal rent or any revision thereof shall be in addition to the rent reserved by the certificate of occupancy and shall be recoverable as rent:

Provided that the first penal rent fixed shall not exceed the rent so reserved and any revised penal rent shall not exceed double the penal rent payable in respect of the twelve months preceding the date of revision.

(3) If the Governor fixes or revises a penal rent he shall cause a notice in writing to be sent to the holder informing him of the amount thereof and the rent so fixed or revised shall commence to be payable one calendar month from the date of the receipt of such notice.

(4) If the breach for which a penal rent has been imposed is remedied before the expiration of the period for which such rent has been paid, the Governor may in his discretion refund cash portion of the penal rent paid for such period as he may think fit.

(5) The fact that a penal rent or a revised penal rent has been imposed shall not preclude the Governor, in lieu of fixing a subsequent penal rent, from revoking the statutory right of occupancy.

Provided that the statutory right of occupancy shall not be revoked during the period for which a penal rent has been paid.

20. (1) If there has been any breach of any of the provisions of section 22 or 23 of this Act the Governor may in lieu of revoking the statutory right of occupancy

concerned, demand that the holder shall pay an additional and penal rent for and in respect of each day during which the land the subject of the statutory right of occupancy or any portion thereof or any buildings or other works erected thereon shall be or remain in the possession, control or occupation of any person whomsoever other than the holder.

(2) Such additional and penal rent shall be payable upon demand and shall be recoverable a rent.

(3) The acceptance by or on behalf of the Governor of any such additional and penal rent shall not operate as a waiver by the Governor of any breach of section 22 or 23 of this Act which may continue after the date up to and in respect of which such additional and penal rent has been paid or is due and owing and the Governor shall accordingly be entitled to exercise in respect of any such continuing breach all or any of the powers conferred upon him by this Act.

PART IV – ALIENATION AND SURRENDER OF RIGHTS OF OCCUPANCY

21. It shall not be lawful for any customary right of occupancy or any part thereof to be alienated by assignment, mortgage, transfer of possession, sublease or otherwise however –
    (a) without the consent of the Governor in cases where the property is to be sold by or under the order of any court under the provisions of the applicable Sheriffs and Civil Process Law; or
    (b) in other cases without the approval of the appropriate Local Government.

22. (1) It shall not be lawful for the holder of a statutory right of occupancy granted by the Governor to alienate his right of occupancy or any part thereof by assignment, mortgage, transfer of possession, sublease or otherwise howsoever without the consent of the Governor first had and obtained:

Provided that the consent of the Governor –
    (a) shall not be required to the creation of a legal mortgage over a statutory right of occupancy in favour of a person in whose favour an equitable mortgage over the right of occupancy has already been created with the consent of the Governor;
    (b) Shall not be required to be reconveyance or release by a mortgage to a holder or occupier of a statutory right of occupancy which that holder or occupier has mortgaged to that mortgagee with the consent of the Governor;
    (c) To the renewal of a sub-lease shall not be presumed by reason only of his having consented to the grant of a sub-lease containing an option to renew the same.

(2) The Governor when giving his consent to an assignment, mortgage or sub-lease may require the holder of a statutory right of occupancy to submit an instrument executed in evidence of the assignment, mortgage or sub-lease and the holder shall when so required deliver the said instrument to the Governor in order that the consent given by the Governor under subsection (1) of this section may be signified by endorsement thereon.

23. (1) A sub-lease of a statutory right of occupancy may, with the prior consent of the Governor and with the approval of the holder of the statutory right of

occupancy, demise by way of sub-under lease to another person the land comprised in the sub-lease held by him or any portion of the land.

(2) The provisions of subsection (2) of section 22 of this Act shall apply mutatis mutandis to any transaction effected under subsection 91) of this section as if it were a sub-lease granted under section 22 of this Act.

24. The devolution of the rights of an occupier upon death shall –

(a) in the case of a customary right of occupancy, unless non-customary law or any other customary law applies, be regulated by the customary law existing in the locality in which the land is situated; and

(b) in the case of a statutory right of occupancy (unless any non-customary law or other customary law applied) be regulated by the customary law of the deceased occupier at the time of his death relating to the distribution of property of like nature to a right of occupancy:

Provided that –

(a) no customary law prohibiting, restricting or regulating the devolution on death to any particular class of persons or the right to occupy any land shall operate to deprive any person of any beneficial interest in such land (other than the right to occupy the same) or in the proceeds of sale thereof to which he may be entitled under the rules of inheritance of any other customary law;

(b) a statutory right of occupancy shall not be divided into two or more parts on devolution by the death of the occupier, except with the consent of the Governor.

25. In the case of the devolution or transfer of rights to which any non-customary law applied, no deed or will shall operate to create any proprietary right over land except that of a plain transfer of the whole of the rights of occupancy over the whole of the land.

26. Any transaction or any instrument which purports to confer on or vest in any person any interest or right over land other than in accordance with the provisions of this Act shall be null and void.

27. The Governor may accept on such terms and conditions as he may think proper the surrender of any statutory right of occupancy granted under this Act.

PART V – REVOCATION OF RIGHT OF OCCUPANCY AND COMPENSATION THEREFOR

28. (1) It shall be lawful for the Governor to revoke a right of occupancy for overriding public interest.

(2) Overriding public interest in the case of a statutory right of occupancy means –

(a) the alienation by the occupier by assignment, mortgage, transfer of possession, sub-lease, or otherwise of any right of occupancy or part thereof contrary to the provisions of this Act or of any regulations made thereunder;

(b) the requirement of the land by the Government of the state or by a Local Government in the State, in either case for public purposes within the state, or the requirement of the land by the Government of the Federation for public purposes of the Federation;

(c) the requirement of the land for mining purposes or oil pipelines or for any purpose connected therewith.
(3) Overriding public interest in the case of a customary right of occupancy means –
(a) the requirement of the land by the Government of the State or by a Local Government in the State, in either case for public purposes within the State, or the requirement of the land by the Government of the Federation for public purposes of the Federation;
(b) the requirement of the land for mining purposes or oil pipelines or for any purpose connected therewith;
(c) The requirement of the land for the extraction of building materials;
(d) the alienation by the occupier by sale, assignment, mortgage, transfer of possession, sub-lease, bequest or otherwise of the right of occupancy without the requisite consent or approval.
(4) The Governor shall revoke a right of occupancy in the event of the issue of a notice by or on behalf of the President if such notice declares such land to be required by the Government for public purposes.
(5) The Governor may revoke a statutory right of occupancy on the ground of –
(a) a breach of any of the provisions which a certificate of occupancy is by section 10 of this Act deemed to contain;
(b) a breach of any term contained in the certificate of occupancy or in any special contract made, under section 8 of this Act;
(c) a refusal or neglect to accept and pay for a certificate which was issued in evidence of a right of occupancy but has been cancelled by the Governor under subsection (3) of section 9 of this Act.
(6) The revocation of a right of occupancy shall be signified under the hand of a public officer duly authorized in that behalf by the Governor and notice thereof shall be given to the holder.
(7) The title of the holder of a right of occupancy shall be extinguished on receipt by him of a notice given under subsection (6) of this section or on such later date as may be stated in the notice.

29. (1) If a right of occupancy is revoked for the cause set out in paragraph (b) of subsection (2) of section 28 of this Act or in paragraph (a) or (c) of subsection (3) of the same section, the holder and the occupier shall be entitled to compensation for the value at the date of revocation of their unexhausted improvements.

(2) If a right of occupancy is revoked for the cause set out in paragraph (c) of subsection (2) of section 28 of this Act or in paragraph (b) of subsection (3) of the same section the holder and the occupier shall be entitled to compensation under the appropriate provisions of the Minerals Act or the Petroleum Act or any legislation replacing the same.
(3) If the holder or the occupier entitled to compensation under this section is a community the Governor may direct that any compensation payable to it shall be paid –
(a) to the community; or

(b) to the chief or leader of the community to be disposed of by him for the befit of the community in accordance with the applicable customary law; or
(c) into some fund specified by the Governor for the purpose of being utilized or applied for the benefit of the community.
(4) Compensation under subsection (1) of this section shall be, as respects –
(a) the land, for an amount equal to the rent, if any, paid by the occupier during the year in which the right of occupancy was revoked.
(b) buildings, installation or improvements thereon, for the amount of the replacement cost of the building, installation or improvement, that is to say, such cost as may be assessed on the basis of the prescribed method of assessment as determined by the appropriate officer less any depreciation, together with interest at the bank rate for delayed payment of compensation and in respect of any improvement in the nature of reclamation works, being such cost thereof as may be substantiated by documentary evidence and proof to the satisfaction of the appropriate officer;
(c) crops on land apart from any building, installation or improvement thereon, for an amount equal to the value as prescribed and determined by the appropriate officer.
(5) Where the land in respect of which a right of occupancy has been revoked forms part of a larger area, the compensation payable shall be computed as in subsection (4) (a) of this section less a proportionate amount calculated in relation to that part of the area not affected by the revocation, but of which the portion revoked forms a part and any interest payable shall be assessed and computed in the like manner.
(6) Where there is any building, installation or improvement or crops on the land to which subsection (5) of this section applies, then compensation shall be computed as specified hereunder, that is as respects –
(a) such land, on the basis specified in that subsection;
(b) any building, installation or improvement or crops thereon (or any combination of two or all of those things) on the basis specified in that subsection and subsection (4) of this section or so much of those provisions as are applicable, and any interest payable under those provisions shall be computed in the like manner.
(7) For the purposes of this section, "installation" means any mechanical apparatus set up or put in position for use or material set up in or on land or other equipment, but excludes any fixture in or on any building.

30. Where there arises any dispute as to the amount of compensation calculated in accordance with the provisions of section 29 of this Act, such dispute shall be referred to the appropriate Land Use and Allocation Committee.
31. The provisions of the Public Lands Acquisition (Miscellaneous Provisions) Act shall not apply in respect of any land vested in, or taken over by, the Governor or any Local Government pursuant to this Act or the right of occupancy to which is revoked under the provisions of this Act but shall continue to apply in respect of land compulsorily acquired before the commencement of this Act.

32. The revocation of a statutory right of occupancy shall not operate to extinguish any debt due to the Government under or in respect of such of occupancy.

33. (1) Where a right of occupancy in respect of any developed land on which a residential building has been erected is revoked under this Act, the Governor or the Local Government as the case may be, may in his or its discretion offer in lieu of compensation payable in accordance with the provisions of this Act, resettlement in any other place or area by way of a reasonable alternative accommodation (if appropriate in the circumstances).

(2) Where the value of any alternative accommodation as determined by the appropriate officer or the Land Use and Allocation Committee is higher than the compensation payable under this Act, the parties concerned may by agreement require that the excess in value in relation to the property concerned shall be treated as a loan which the person affected shall refund or repay to the government in the prescribed manner.

(3) Where a person accepts a resettlement pursuant to subsection (1) of this section, his right to compensation shall be deemed to have been duly satisfied and no further compensation shall be payable to such person.

PART VI – TRANSITIONAL AND OTHER RELATED PROVISIONS

34. (1) The following provisions of this section shall have effect in respect of land in an urban area vested in any person immediately before the commencement of this Act.

(2) Where the land is developed the land shall continue to be held by the person in whom it was vested immediately before the commencement of this Act as if the holder of the land was the holder of a statutory right of occupancy issued by the Governor under this Act.

(3) In respect of land to which, subsection (2) of this section applies there shall be issued by the Governor on application to him in the prescribed form a certificate of occupancy if the Governor is satisfied that the land was, immediately before the commencement of this Act, vested in that person.

(4) Where the land to which subsection (2) of this section applies was subject to any mortgage, legal or equitable, or any encumbrance or interest valid in law such land shall continue to be so subject and the certificate of occupancy issued, shall indicate that the land is so subject, unless the continued operation of the encumbrance or interest would in the opinion of the Governor be inconsistent with the provisions, or general intendment of this Act.

(5) Where on the commencement of this Act the land is undeveloped, then –

(a) one plot or portion of the land not exceeding half of one hectare in area shall subject to subsection (6) of this section, continue to be held by the person in whom the land was so vested as if the holder of the land was the holder of a statutory right of occupancy granted by the Governor in respect of the plot or portion as aforesaid under this Act; and

(b) all the rights formerly vested in the holder in respect of the excess of the land shall on the commencement of this Act be extinguished and the excess of the land shall be taken over by the Governor and administered as provided in this Act.

(6) Paragraph (a) of subsection (5) of this section shall not apply in the case of any person who was on the commencement of this Act also the holder of any undeveloped land elsewhere in any urban area in the state and in respect of such a person all his holdings of undeveloped land in any urban area in the state shall be considered together and out of the undeveloped land so considered together.
(a) one plot or portion not exceeding half of one hectare in area shall continue to be held by such a person as if a right of occupancy had been granted to him by the Governor in respect of that plot or portion; and
(b) the remainder of the land (so considered together) in excess of half of one hectare shall be taken over by the Governor and administered in accordance with this Act and the rights formerly vested in the holder in respect of such land shall be extinguished.
(7) No land to which subsection (5) (a) or (6) of this section applies held by any person shall be further subdivided or laid out in plots and no such land shall be transferred to any person except with the prior consent in writing of the Governor.
(8) Any instrument purporting to transfer any undeveloped land in contravention of subsection (7) of this section shall be void and of no effect whatsoever in law and any party to any such instrument shall be guilty of any offence and liable on conviction to imprisonment for one year of a fine ₦5,000.
(9) In relation to land to which subsection (5) (a) or (6) (a) of this section applies there shall be issued by the Governor on application therefore in the prescribed form a certificate of occupancy if the Governor is satisfied that the land was immediately before the commencement o this Act vested in that person.

35. (1) Section 34 of this Act shall have effect notwithstanding that the land in question was held under a leasehold, whether customary or otherwise, and formed part of an estate laid out by any person, group or family in whom the leasehold interest or reversion in respect of the land was vested immediately before the commencement of this Act, so however that if there has been an improvements on the land effected by the person, group or family in whom the leasehold interest or reversion was vested as aforesaid the Governor shall, in respect of the improvements, pay to that person, group or family, compensation computed as specified in section 29 of this Act.

(2) There shall be deducted from the compensation payable under subsection (1) of this section, any levy by way of development or similar charges paid in respect of the improvements on the land by the lessee to the person, group or family in whom the leasehold interest or reversion was vested and the amount to be deducted shall be determined by the Governor taking into consideration all the circumstance of the case.

36. (1) The following provisions of this section shall have effect in respect of land not in an urban area which was immediately before the commencement of this Act held or occupied by any person.

(2) Any occupier or holder of such land, whether under customary rights or otherwise howsoever, shall if that land was on the commencement of this Act being used for agricultural purposes, continue to be entitled to possession of the land for use for agricultural purposes as if a customary right of occupancy had been granted

to the occupier or holder thereof by the appropriate Local Government and the reference in this subsection to land being used for agricultural purposes included land which is, in accordance with the customary law of the locality concerned, allowed to lie fallow for purposes of recuperation of the soil.
(3) On the production to the Local Government by the occupier of such land, at his discretion, of a sketch or diagram or other sufficient description of the land in question and on application therefore in the prescribed form the Local Government shall, if satisfied that the occupier or holder was entitled to the possession of such land whether under customary rights of otherwise howsoever, and that the land was being used for agricultural purposes at the commencement of this Act, register the holder or occupier as one to whom a customary right of occupancy had been issued in respect of the land in question.
(4) Where the land is developed, the land shall continue to be held by the person in whom it was vested immediately before the commencement of this Act as if the holder of the land was the holder of a customary right of occupancy issued by the Local Government, and if the holder or occupier of such developed land, at his discretion, produces a sketch or diagram showing the area of the land so developed, the Local Government shall, if satisfied that that person immediately before the commencement of this Act has the land vested in him, register the holder or occupier as one in respect of whom a customary right of occupancy has been granted by the Local Government.
(5) No land to which this section applies shall be sub-divided or laid out in plots and no such land shall be transferred to any person by the person in whom the land was vested as aforesaid.
(6) Any instrument purporting to transfer any land to which this section relates shall be void and of no effect whatsoever in law and every party to any such instrument shall be guilty of an offence and liable on conviction to a fine of ₦5,000 or to imprisonment for 1 year.

37. If any person other than one in whom any land was lawfully vested immediately before the commencement of this Act enters any land in purported exercise of any right in relation to possession of the land or makes any false claim in respect of the land to the Governor or any Local Government for any purpose under this section he shall be guilty of an offence and liable on conviction to imprisonment for one year or to a fine of ₦5,000.

38. Nothing in this Part shall be construed as precluding the exercise by the Governor or as the case may be the Local Government concerned of the powers to revoke, in accordance with the applicable provisions of this Act, right of occupancy, whether statutory or customary, in respect to any land to which this Part of this Act relates. S

PART VII – JURISDICTION OF HIGH COURTS AND OTHER COURTS

39. (1) The High Court shall have exclusive original jurisdiction in respect of the following proceedings –
  (a) Proceedings in respect of any land the subject of statutory right of occupancy granted by the Governor or deemed to be granted by him under

this Act; and for the purposes of this paragraph, proceedings includes proceedings for a declaration of title to a statutory right of occupancy;

(b) Proceedings to determine any question as to the person entitled to compensation payable for improvements on land under this Act.

(2) All laws, including rules of court, regulating the practice and procedure of the High Court shall apply in respect of proceedings to which this section relates and the laws shall have effect with such modifications as would enable effect to be given to the provisions of this section.

40. Where on the commencement of this Act proceedings had been commenced or were pending in any court of tribunal (whether at first instance or on appeal) in respect of any question concerning or pertaining to title to any land or interest therein, such proceedings may be continue and be finally disposed of by the court concerned but any order or decision of the court shall only be as respects the entitlement of either of the parties to the proceedings to a right of occupancy, whether statutory or customary, in respect of such land as provided in this Act.

41. An area court or customary court or other court of equivalent jurisdiction in a state shall have jurisdiction in respect of proceedings in respect of a customary right of occupancy granted by a Local Government under this Act; and for the purposes of this paragraph proceedings includes proceedings for a declaration of title to a customary right of occupancy and all laws including rules of court regulating practice and procedure of such courts shall have effect with such modifications a would enable effect to be given to this section.

42. (1) Proceedings for the recovery of rent payable in respect of any certificate of occupancy may be taken before a Magistrate Court of competent jurisdiction by and in the name of the Chief Lands Officer or by and in the name of any officer appointed by the Governor in that behalf.

(2) Proceedings for the recovery of rent payable in respect of any customary right of occupancy may be taken by and in the name of the Local Government concerned in the area court of customary court or any court of equivalent jurisdiction.

PART VIII – SUPPLEMENTAL

43. (1) Save as permitted under section 34 of this Act, as from the commencement of this Act no person shall in an urban area –

(a) erect any building, wall, fence or other structure upon; or

(b) enclose, obstruct, cultivate or do any act on or in relation to, any land which is not the subject of a right of occupancy or licence lawfully held by him or in respect of which he has not received the permission of the Governor to enter and erect improvement prior to the grant to him of a right of occupancy.

(2) Any person who contravenes any of the provisions of subsection (1) of this section shall on being required by the Governor so to do and within the period of time fixed by the Governor, remove any building, wall, fence, obstruction, structure or thing which he may have caused to be placed on the land and he

shall put the land in the same condition as nearly as may be in which it was before such contravention.

(3) Any person who contravenes any of the provisions of subsection (1) of this section shall be guilty of an offence and liable on conviction to imprisonment for one year or to a fine of ₦5,000.

(4) Any person who fails or refuses to comply with a requirement made by the Governor under subsection (2) of this section shall be guilty of an offence and liable on conviction to a fine of ₦100 for each day during which he makes default in complying with the requirement of the Governor.

44. Any notice required by this Act to be served on any person shall be effectively served on him.

(a) by delivering it to the person on whom it is to be served, or
(b) by leaving it at the usual or last known place of abode of that person; or
(c) by sending it in a prepaid registered letter addressed to that person at his usual or last know place of abode, or
(d) in the case of an incorporated company or body, by delivering it to the secretary or clerk of the company or body at its registered or principal office or sending it in a prepaid registered letter addressed to the secretary or clerk of the company or body at that office; or
(e) if it is not practicable after reasonable inquiry to ascertain the name or address of a holder or occupier of land on whom it should be served, by addressing it to him by the description of "holder" or "occupier" of the premises (naming them) to which it relates, and by delivering it to some person on the premises or, if there is no person on the premises to whom it can be delivered, by affixing it, or a copy of it, to some conspicuous part of the premises.

45. (1) The Governor may delegate to the State Commissioner all or any of the powers conferred on the Governor by this Act, subject to such restrictions, conditions and qualifications, not being inconsistent with the provisions, or general intendment, of this Act as the Governor may specify.

(2) Where the power to grant certificates has been delegated to the State Commissioner, such certificates shall be expressed to be granted on behalf on the Governor.

46. (1) The National Council of States may make regulations for the purpose of carrying this Act into effect and particularly with regard to the following matters –

(a) the transfer by assignment or otherwise howsoever of any right of occupancy, whether statutory or customary, including the conditions applicable to the transfer of such rights to persons who are not Nigerians;
(b) the terms and conditions upon which special contracts may be made under section 8 of this Act;
(c) the grant of certificate of occupancy under section 9 of this Act;
(d) the grant of temporary right of occupancy;

(e) the method of assessment of compensation for the purposes of section 29 of this Act.

(2) The Governor may, subject to subsection (1) of this section make regulations with regard to the following matters –

(a) the method of application for any licence or permit and the terms and conditions under which licences may be granted;

(b) the procedure to be observed in revising rents;

(c) the fees to be paid for any matter or thing done under this Act;

(d) the forms to be used for any document or purposes.

47. (1) This Act shall have effect notwithstanding anything to the contrary in any law or rule of law including the Constitution of the Federal Republic of Nigeria and, without prejudice to the generality of the foregoing, no court shall have jurisdiction to inquire into –

(a) any question concerning or pertaining to the vesting of all land in the Governor in accordance with the provisions of this Act; or

(b) any question concerning or pertaining to the right of the Governor to grant a Statutory Right of Occupancy in accordance with the provisions of this Act; or

(c) any question concerning or pertaining to the right of a Local Government to grant a customary right of occupancy under this Act.

(2) No court shall have jurisdiction to inquire into any question concerning or pertaining to the amount or adequacy of any compensation paid or to be paid under this Act.

48. All existing laws relating to the registration of title to, or interest in, land or the transfer of title to or any interest in land shall have effect subject to such modifications (whether by way of addition, alteration or omission) as will bring those laws into conformity with this Act or its general intendment.

49. (1) Nothing in this Act shall affect any title to land whether developed or undeveloped held by the Federal Government or any agency of the Federal Government at the commencement of this Act and, accordingly, any such land shall continue to vest in the Federal Government or the agency concerned.

(2) In this section, "agency" includes any statutory corporation or any other statutory body (whether corporate or unincorporated) or any company wholly-owned by the Federal Government.

50. (1) Notwithstanding anything to the contrary in this Act or any other enactment, all laws and subsidiary legislation made at any time between the commencement of this Act and 30th September 1979 by an Administrator (or former Governor), the Executive Council, a Commissioner or any other authority or any public officer of a State shall be deemed to have been validly made and shall have effect as if they had been made under or pursuant to the Act and accordingly, shall hereafter continue to have effect according to their tenor and intendment as if they were regulations made under or pursuant to section 46 of this Act.

(2) For the purposes of subsection (1) of this section –

(a) all contracts and all executive and judicial act, including acts pertaining to the establishment, membership and functions of any Land Use and Allocation Committee or of any other authority or to the appointment of any person, shall be deemed to have been validly entered into or done and shall hereafter continue to have effect as provided in the said subsection; and

(b) any instrument or other evidence relating to the allocation of any land, whether or not expressed to have been made under this Act, shall be deemed to have been validly issued or given under or pursuant to this Act and shall continue to have effect according to its tenor and intendment accordingly.

51. (1) In this Act, unless the context otherwise requires –

"agricultural purposes" includes the planning of any crops of economic value;

"appropriate officer" means the Chief Lands Officer of a State and in the case of the Federal Capital Territory, Abuja, means the Chief Federal Lands Officer.

"customary right of occupancy" means the right of a person or community lawfully using or occupying land in accordance with customary law and includes a customary right of occupancy granted by a Local Government under this Act;

"developed land" means land where there exists any physical improvement in the nature of road development services, water, electricity, drainage, building, structure or such improvement that may enhance the value of the land for industrial, agricultural or residential purposes;

"easement" means a right annexed to land to utilize other land in different holding in a particular manner (not involving the taking of any part of the natural produce of that's land or of any part of its soil) or to prevent the holder of the other land from utilizing his land in a particular manner;

"Government" means the Government of the Federation or the Government of a State;

"Governor" means the Governor of the State concerned;

"grazing purposes" includes only such agricultural operation as are required for growing fodder for livestock on the grazing area;

"High Court" means the High Court of the State concerned;

"holder" in relation to a right of occupancy, means a person entitled to a right of occupancy and includes any person to whom a right of occupancy has been validly assigned or has validly passed on the death of a holder but does not include any person to whom a right of occupancy has been sold or transferred without a valid assignment, nor a mortgagee, sub-lessee or sub-underlessee;

"improvement" or "unexhausted improvement" means anything of any quality permanently attached to the land, directly resulting from the expenditure of capital of labour by an occupier or any person acting on his behalf, and increasing the productive capacity, the utility or the amenity thereof and includes buildings, plantations of long-lived crops or trees, fencing, wells, roads and irrigation or reclamation works, but does not include the result of ordinary cultivation other than growing produce;

"interest at the bank rate" means a simple interest payable at the rate per cent per annum at which the Central Bank of Nigeria will rediscount bills of exchange;

"Local Government" means the appropriate Local Government or any other body having or exercising the powers of a Local Government as provided by law in respect of the area where the land in question is situated;
"mortgage" includes a second and subsequent mortgage and equitable mortgage;
"occupier" means any person lawfully occupying land under customary law and a person using or occupying land in accordance with customary law and includes the sub-lessee or sub-underlessee of a holder;
"public purposes" include –
(a) for exclusive Government use or for general public use;
(b) for use by any body corporate directly established by law or by any body corporate registered under the Companies and Allied Mattes Act as respects which the Government owns shares, stocks or debentures;
(c) for or in connection with sanitary improvements of any kind;
(d) for obtaining control over land contiguous to any part or over land the value of which will be enhanced by the construction to be undertaken or provided by the Government.
(e) for obtaining control over land required for or in connection with development of telecommunications or provision of electricity;
(f) for obtaining control over land required for or in connection with mining purposes;
(g) for obtaining control over land required for or in connection with planned urban or rural development or settlement;
(h) for obtaining control over land required for or in connection with economic, industrial or agricultural development;
(i) for educational and other social services;
"statutory right of occupancy" means a right of occupancy granted by the Governor under this Act;
"sub-lease" includes a sub-underlease;
"urban area" means such area of the state as may be designated as such by the Governor pursuant to section 3 of this Act.
(2) The power of a Governor under this Act shall, in respect of land comprised in the Federal Capital Territory, Abuja, or any land held or vested in the Federal Government in any State, be exercisable by the President or any Minister designated by him in that behalf and references in this Act to Governor shall be construed accordingly.

52. This Act may be cited as the Land Use Act.

Bibliography

Abugu G., *Principles of the Land Use Act, 1978* (Kaduna:Badma Yole Publishers, 2008.

Alubo A.O., Contemporary Land Law in Nigeria(Jos: Abeson Press Ltd, 2006)

Bryan A.G., *Black's Law Dictionary*, 7th ed. (London: St. Paul Minn, 1999).

………… *Blacks Law Dictionary*, 9th .ed (London: St. Paul, Minn,2009)

Chappella D., *Land Law*, 6th ed. (London: Longman, 2004).

Newton, C.., *General Principles of Law*, 3rd ed. (London: Sweet and Maxwell, 1983).

Coker, *Family Property Among the Yoruba* (London: Sweet and Maxwell, 1966).

Dadem, Y,.D., *Property Law and Practice in Nigeria*(Jos: Jos University Press Ltd,2009)

Dias R.W.M. *Jurisprudence*

Elias T.O. *Nature of African Customary Law* (London: Manchester University Press, 1956).

Egute, M.A., *Essentials of Nigerian Land Law* (Makurdi: Onaivi Publishing Company, 2002).

Eguummuo, J.N., *Principles and Practice of Land Law* (Enugu: Onye Ventures, 2007).

Elias, T.O., *Nigerian Land Law and Constitution* (London: Routledge and Kegan Paul Ltd., 1962).

Gray, D. and Gray S.K., *Elements of Land Law* 3rd ed. (London: Butterworths, 2001).

Gray et al, *Land Law* 3rd ed. (UK: Lexis Nexis UN, 2003).

Idrisu, T., *Understanding Nigerian Land Law* 2nd ed (Zaria: Ahmadu Bello University Press Ltd., 2008).

Lugard, *The dual Mandate* (London: 1929)

Layi Afolabi, *Law and Practice of Banking* (Ibadan: Heinemann Education Books (Nig.) Plc)

Niki, Tobi, *Cases and Materials on Nigerian Land Law* (Lagos: Mabrochi Books, 1992)

Nwabueze B.O., *Nigerian Land Law* (Enugu: Nwaniye Publishers Ltd., 1972)

Olawoye, C.O., *Title to Land in Nigeria* (Ibadan: Evans Brothers Ltd., 1974)

Ollenu Customary *Land Law in Ghana*, (1962)

Olong M.A., Nigerian Legal System: An Introduction (Lagos: Malthouse Press Ltd., 2009)

Olong M,A., & Ogwo B., Land Law in Nigeria (Ilorin: Oluwole Press Ltd,2010)
Obilade, *The Nigerian Legal System* (Nig.: Spectrum Publishing Co., 1993)
Osamolu *et al* (eds) *Real Property Law & Conveyancing Practice in Nigeria* (Lagos: Law lords Publications, 2008)
Pottage, A., *The Measure of Land* (1994)
Smith I.O., *Practical Approach to Law of Real Property in Nigeria* (Lagos: ECWA Publishing Ltd., 1999)
-----------., *Land and Real Property Rights in Nigeria* (Lagos: University of Lagos, 2008)
Utuama A.A., *Nigerian law of Real Property* (Ibadan: Shaneson Co. Ltd., 1989)
Van Maanen and A.S. Van Der Walt (ed.) *Property Law in the Threshold of the 21st Century* (Mahlu:Antherp, 1996)

JOURNALS/ARTICLES

Acheneje, A.S. The Nigerian Land Use Act, 1978: A Critical Examination of some Eminent Contributions *Journal of Contemporary Legal Issues,* Idah Branch Nigerian Bar Association, 2009.
Agbana J.O., An Overview of the Position of Land Law and Century under the LUA, 1978, *Ikeja Bar Review,* Vol. 2, Pt. 2, Sept. 2007-March, 2008.
Ehi Oshio, "Customary Tenancy under the Land Use Act and Alternative Dispute Resolution of the Judicial Dilemma", *Nigerian Practice Journal of Finance and Investment Law* Vol. 2, Nos. 1-2, 2006.
Justice Nnamani A., "The Land Use Act 12 years After" *NIJ,* 1991.
Justice Nnamani, A., "The Land Use Act 11 years After" *2 GRBPL* No. 6, 1989.
Nelson D. "Real Property Management in Nigeria", *International Journal of Law and Contemporary Studies,* Vol. 2, Nos. 1 & 2, 2008
Oba, A.A., "The Land Use Act and Economic Development" *Modus International Law and Business Quarterl,y* December, 2001.
Obaloni, D.O., "Legal Mortgage: Problems and Controversies" *Modern Practice Journal of Finance and Investment Law,* 2006.
Olong, M.A., The Procedure for Recovery of Premises under the Recovery of Premises Law: An Appraisal, *Solicitors Law Journal,* Ministry of Justice, Ado-Ekiti, 2006.
Osimiri U.J., "Application for Contract of Occupancy in Practice and Procedure" 1991 *Justice* Vol. 2, No. 4.
Raimond A.L., The Land Use Act, 1978: A Blessing or Course, *Ikeja Bar Review,* 2007.
Shaakaah, S., An Appraisal of the Plateau State Rent Control and Recovery of Property Act, *Solicitors Law Journal,* Ministry of Justice, Ado-Ekiti, 2006.
Smith I.O., "The Land Use Act Twenty One years After" *Department of Public and Property Law, University of Lagos, Faculty of Law,* 2003.
Utuama "The Crocodile Tears in Savanah Bank v. Ajilo & Anor" *2 GRBPL* No. 7, 1989.

Index

www.ingramcontent.com/pod-product-compliance
Ingram Content Group UK Ltd.
Pitfield, Milton Keynes, MK11 3LW, UK
UKHW040233290926
15471UKWH00002B/161